About the Author

Jan Bondeson is a senior lecturer and consultant rheumatologist at Cardiff University. His many critically acclaimed books include *Animal Freaks, Freaks: The Pig-Faced Lady of Manchester Square & Other Medical Marvels, Cabinet of Medical Curiosities, The London Monster* and the best-selling *Buried Alive: The Terrifying History of Our Most Primal Fear*. He lives in Newport, South Wales.

PRAISE FOR JAN BONDESON

mazing Dogs
A thrilling read - alternately hilarious and harrowing...
Bondeson aims to explode canine myths, but his most
surprising findings tend to validate them'
FELIPE FERNÁNDEZ-ARMESTO, *THE*
'Charming... a great story' CESAR MILLAN *(THE
DOG WHISPERER), CESARWORLD.COM*
'A fascinating new book' *THE DAILY MAIL*

Queen Victoria's Stalker
'The amazing story of the first celebrity stalker'
THE SUN
'Victoria's secret' *THE TIMES*
'The lovesick stalker who stole Victoria's bloomers' *THE
DAILY MAIL*
'Intriguing' *THE DAILY TELEGRAPH*
'Bondeson tells a remarkable story... he also has a
Victorian journalist's eye for comedy'
KATE WILLIAMS, *BBC HISTORY MAGAZINE*
'Fascinating' *THE MAIL ON SUNDAY*

Buried Alive
'A little masterpiece of social history'
THE MAIL ON SUNDAY
'A wonderful book' *THE SUNDAY TELEGRAPH*

Animal Freaks
'Delightful' ALI SMITH
'Animal magic' *TLS*

Freaks
'Bizarre' *THE MAIL ON SUNDAY*
'Well written and superbly illustrated'
THE FINANCIAL TIMES

The London Monster
'Gripping... an 18th-century detective story of the most
piquant kind' *THE GUARDIAN*

Greyfriars Bobby
The Most Faithful Dog in the World

JAN BONDESON

AMBERLEY

This edition first published 2012

Amberley Publishing
The Hill, Stroud
Gloucestershire, GL5 4EP

www.amberley-books.com

British Library Cataloguing in Publication Data.
A catalogue record for this book is available from the British Library.

ISBN 978-1-4456-0762-7

Typesetting and Origination by Amberley Publishing.
Printed in Great Britain.

Contents

1

Introduction

A humble funeral! At the grave no loving mourners wept;
Only a dog, when all was o'er, a patient vigil kept.
Threats could not daunt his faithful heart, nor blows dislodge his form;
That was his chosen resting-place through sunshine and through storm.

The summer's heat, the winter's cold, still found him at his post,
Haunting the old kirkyard where lay his master, dear and lost,
Till men grew kind and reverenced that ministry of love,
And 'Grey Friars Bobby' won a name far higher names above.

> A poem by 'E.E.S.' from *Animal World* magazine
> of 1874, used for epigraphs for a number of chapters to come.

No visitor to Edinburgh will miss the monument to Scotland's most famous dog, the little Skye terrier Greyfriars Bobby. This amazing dog, the most faithful in the world, kept vigil at his master's grave at Greyfriars churchyard for fourteen long years, before expiring in 1872. Many children's books, and three successful films, have been inspired by the affecting story of this little dog, said to be the most inspiring tale of love and loyalty ever heard. Every summer, Bobby's statue is surrounded by tourists from all over the world, some of whom weep profusely when they hear the dog's pathetic story. Not less than 220,000 people visit Greyfriars Bobby's grave each year, as compared with 20,000 for Greyfriars church itself.

Although Greyfriars Bobby has been dead for nearly a century and a half, this dog of mystery has yet to find his biographer.[1] Much fiction has been based on the myth of the faithful Bobby, but no historian has taken care to investigate the authenticity of his story, and sift the facts from more than a century of exaggeration and legend.[2] Was Bobby really the canine paragon of virtue he has been presumed to be, or was he an unconscious impostor, taking advantage of the notions about extreme canine fidelity that were current at the time? In this book, the true story of Greyfriars Bobby will finally be told for the first time, using original sources.[3] Will it be possible, after nearly 140 years have passed, to solve the mystery of Greyfriars Bobby, Edinburgh's Dog in the Iron Mask?

"Greyfriars' Bobby," drawn by F. W. Keyl.

Right: 1. Greyfriars Bobby lying on his master's grave, a drawing by Friedrich Wilhelm Keyl from *Chatterbox* magazine, 22 June 1867.

Below: 2. Edinburgh Castle from Greyfriars, from the six-volume edition of James Grant's *Old and New Edinburgh*, volume 6.

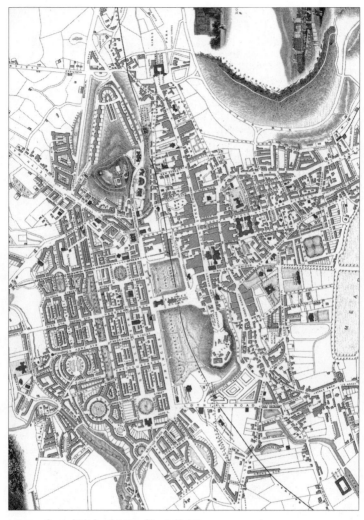

3. A map of central Edinburgh in Greyfriars Bobby's time.

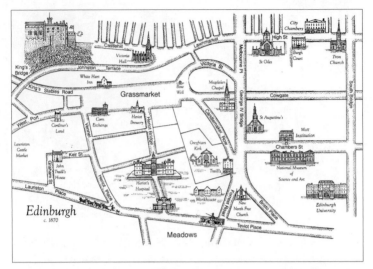

4. A simplified map of Greyfriars Bobby's Edinburgh, with various important sites highlighted, from George Robinson's *Greyfriars Bobby A–Z*, reproduced with permission.

2

Greyfriars Bobby Finds Himself Famous

> But ownerless no dog may rest, nor 'scape the social shame
> The outlawry which freedom brands on every canine name.
> So the Lord Provost's powerful hand the civic ægis spread
> Over the faithful one who lived to watch beside his dead.

Like Lord Byron, Greyfriars Bobby woke up one day, and found himself famous. Unlike the publicity-seeking poetical peer, the humble little Edinburgh dog had done nothing whatsoever to court newspaper attention, but there he was, fêted in dozens of newspapers all over Britain. Originating as a feature in the *Scotsman* newspaper of 13 April 1867,[1] the cult of Greyfriars Bobby spread to the *Caledonian Mercury* and the *Dundee Courier & Argus*, to provincial newspapers all over Britain, and to major London newspapers like the *Era*, *Standard* and *Daily News*.[2] With time, the extraordinary story of the most faithful dog in the world spread to Australia and New Zealand.[3]

STRANGE STORY OF A DOG – A very singular and interesting occurrence was yesterday brought to light in the Burgh Court, by the hearing of a summons in regard to dog-tax. Eight and a-half years ago, it seems, a man named Gray, of whom nothing now is known, except that he was poor and lived in a quiet way in some obscure part of town, was buried in Old Greyfriars' Churchyard. His grave, levelled by the hand of time, and unmarked by any stone, is now scarcely discernable; but though no human interest would seem to attach to it, the sacred spot has not been wholly disregarded and forgotten. During all these years, the dead man's faithful dog has kept constant watch and guard over the grave, and it was this animal for which the collectors sought to recover the tax.

James Brown, the old curator of the burial grounds, remembers Gray's funeral, and the dog, a Scotch terrier, was, he says, one of the most conspicuous of the mourners. The grave was closed in as usual, and next morning, 'Bobby', as the dog is called, was lying on the newly made mound. This was an innovation that old James could not permit, for there was an order at the gate stating, in the most intelligible characters, that dogs were not admitted. 'Bobby' was accordingly driven out; but next morning he was there again, and for the second time was discharged. The third morning was cold and wet, and when the old man saw the faithful animal, in spite

5. A newspaper drawing of Greyfriars Bobby, from life.

of all chastisement, still lying shivering on the grave, he took pity on him and gave him some food.

This recognition of his devotion gave 'Bobby' the right to make the churchyard his home; and from that time to the present he has never spent a night away from his master's grave. Often in bad weather attempts have been made to keep him within doors, but by dismal howls he has succeeded in making it known that this interference is not agreeable to him, and latterly he has always been allowed to have his way. At almost any time during the day he may be seen in or about the churchyard; and no matter how rough the night may be, nothing can induce him to forsake the hallowed spot, whose identity, despite the irresistible obliteration it has undergone, he has so faithfully preserved.

'Bobby' has many friends, and the tax-gatherers have by no means proved his enemies. A weekly treat of steaks was long allowed him by Serjeant Scott of the Engineers, but for more than six years he has been regularly fed by Mr John Trail, of the restaurant 6 Greyfriars' Place. He is constant and punctual in his calls, being guided in his mid-day visits by the sound of the time-gun. On the ground of 'harbouring' the dog in this way, proceedings were taken against Mr Trail for payment of the tax. The defendant expressed his willingness, could he claim the dog, to be responsible for the tax; but so long as the animal refused to attach himself to any one, it was impossible, he argued, to fix the ownership – and the Court, seeing the peculiar circumstances of the case, dismissed the summons. 'Bobby' has long been an object of curiosity to all who have become acquainted with his interesting history. His constant appearance in the graveyard has caused many inquiries to be made regarding him, and efforts out of number have been made from time to time to get possession of him. The old curator, of course, stands up as the next claimant to Mr Trail, and yesterday offered to pay the tax himself rather than to have 'Bobby' – 'Greyfriars' Bobby' to allow him his full name – put out of the way.

The story of this amazingly faithful dog and his long vigil at Greyfriars may well sound like fiction, but there is solid evidence that Bobby really existed, and that his friends and supporters were people of flesh and blood. In 1867, the Dog Duty Act was a novel concept in Edinburgh, aimed to regulate the canine population of the Scottish metropolis, and to provide the authorities with means to destroy stray, ownerless street dogs. Except for pups under the age of six months, dog owners had to pay for a licence costing seven shillings, with an annual renewal fee of five shillings. People harbouring unlicensed dogs were liable to a fine of five pounds.

In April 1867, the restaurant at No. 6 Greyfriars Place, just outside the churchyard, was kept by the former tailor John Traill, born in Dunfermline in 1834. To the dismay of any Scots who wanted a 'nip' with their luncheon or dinner, he had renamed it 'Traill's Temperance Coffee House' when he took it over in 1862. The restaurant appears to have done quite well under its new management. An unambitious eating-house, catering to local people of the lower and middle classes, it was open for breakfast, lunch and dinner every day except Sunday. Mr Traill and his wife Mary worked hard to keep the Coffee House going, assisted by two servant girls. Since the previous owner of the restaurant, James Currie, had kept the lease of Nos 5 and 6 Greyfriars Place, only subletting the restaurant premises themselves, the Traills had no on-site living accommodation. Instead, they lived in a flat in nearby Keir Street, with their children Alexander and Eliza, aged nine and seven respectively in 1867.[4]

Although John Traill appears to have been a kindly, hard-working and considerate man, he had at least one enemy in April 1867. This individual was malicious enough to report him to the police for harbouring the extraordinary dog Greyfriars Bobby, well known locally for having lived in Greyfriars churchyard for many years. Many people believed that Bobby was keeping vigil at the grave of his deceased master, as dogs were supposed sometimes to do. It was well known that for many years, Bobby had paid a daily visit to Traill's Temperance Coffee House, where he was given a meal. Sergeant Donald McNab Scott, a kind and dog-loving military man who lodged in a house nearby, had taught Bobby to go to dinner at the sound of the One o'Clock Gun, a time-gun fired at Edinburgh Castle every day at one o'clock. Mr Traill's enemy thought that since the restaurateur regularly fed and harboured Bobby in his eating-house, he should also be liable for the dog-tax. Accordingly, Mr Traill was summoned to attend the Burgh Court, the police court of the City and Royal Burgh of Edinburgh, situated on the second floor of the High Street police station.

On 11 April 1867, when John Traill was before the Burgh Court, Baillies Skinner, Handyside and Blackadder were on the Bench. Mr Robert Morham, the Deputy

Town Clerk, and city officer Alexander Macpherson were also in court. When asked to explain himself, Mr Traill said that Greyfriars Bobby enjoyed very considerable local fame for his fidelity, since this extraordinary dog had kept vigil on his master's tomb for many years. The master's name might well have been Gray, and he had lived in some obscure part of town. Mr Morham, the Deputy Town Clerk, said that he had seen Bobby in the churchyard many a Sunday, when on his way to worship at Greyfriars. The next witness, Greyfriars curator James Brown, said that he could remember the funeral with the little terrier present, and also that Bobby soon after began his long vigil in the cemetery. Although old and in poor circumstances, Brown offered to pay the dog-tax himself, rather than to have Bobby put out of the way, as he expressed it. The next witness was Mr Thomas Cowan, who kept the 'Hole in the Wa'' public house opposite. He stated that Bobby was a well-known animal locally, and that he himself had fed the little dog more than once. Probably affected by James Brown's generosity, Mr Traill once more stood up, to express his willingness to claim the dog and pay the tax. He still pleaded that this would be unfair, however, since as the animal would not attach itself to anyone, it was impossible to fix the ownership. The court agreed with him and the summons was dismissed.

Two of Bobby's other friends, the tailor Robert Ritchie and the upholsterer James Anderson, who both lived just by Greyfriars kirkyard, had been worried that the little dog would be destroyed as an unlicensed dog. Not trusting that Mr Traill and James Brown would manage to rescue Bobby, they clubbed together to pay the tax and called at the City Chambers, only to be informed that the summons against Mr Traill had been dismissed.[5]

If no journalist had been present at the Burgh Court, Mr Traill, James Brown and the other ordinary men would have returned to obscurity, and Greyfriars Bobby might well have remained just an ordinary dog. But the *Scotsman* newspaper had a reporter in court, and in early April 1867 there was a shortage of interesting news. As a result, the news of the amazing proceedings in the Burgh Court spread like wildfire, as outlined above, and Greyfriars Bobby's fame was established. People from all parts of Britain came to Greyfriars, neglecting its historic monuments to admire the world's most faithful dog.

Greyfriars, the Scottish Westminster Abbey, was the first church built in Edinburgh after the Reformation. In 1562, Mary Queen of Scots had allowed the Edinburgh town council to take over the grounds of a former Franciscan friary, for use as a cemetery. Half a century later, it was decided to build a church at this site, since the High Kirk at St Giles could no longer accommodate the growing population. In spite of its not inconsiderable size, Greyfriars was quite plain, with a very austere interior, devoid of chapels, statuary, and stained glass.

The first recorded use of Greyfriars was for the funeral service of William Couper, Bishop of Galloway, in 1619. This was a time full of religious strife in Scotland, with clashes between the old Episcopalism and the new Presbyterian

6. Greyfriars kirk, from the six-volume edition of James Grant's *Old and New Edinburgh*, volume 4.

structure led by the General Assembly. King Charles I's attempt to introduce a new liturgy in 1637 lit the fuse underneath this powder keg: the National Covenant was read out from the pulpit at Greyfriars on 28 February 1638, to be signed by the nobility, gentry, and burghers. Years of war and strife followed, and Greyfriars was actually used as a cavalry barracks by Oliver Cromwell's troops from 1650 until 1653. After the battle of Bothwell Bridge in 1679, 1,200 prisoners were taken to Edinburgh, and 400 of them were held in an open-air prison camp in a field at Greyfriars, on water and bread. Those who did not renege after five months in this dismal 'Covenanter's Prison' were executed or transported. In 1691, the infamous Lord Advocate Sir George Mackenzie, who had persecuted the Covenanters so very severely, was himself buried at Greyfriars; 'Bluidie Mackenzie' is said to have haunted the churchyard ever since.

In 1718, the tower of Greyfriars, which was used for storing gunpowder, blew up, laying the west end of the church in ruins. The east part was closed off, and a new church built, symmetrical with the surviving eastern part. Thus there were now two churches: Old and New Greyfriars, with their own parishes and ministries. After the Disruption of 1843, one belonged to the Church of Scotland, the other to the Free Church of Scotland. Old Greyfriars was rebuilt after a fire in 1845, and reopened in 1857.[6] Dr Robert Lee and Dr William Robertson, ministers of Old and New Greyfriars respectively, were kind and humanitarian clergymen who sought to improve the conditions for the poor people living in the slums nearby.

In Greyfriars Bobby's time, there was a contrast between the peaceful Greyfriars, with its historic churchyard and ancient monuments, and the cluttered and

TOMBS IN GREYFRIARS CHURCHYARD.

The Martyrs' Monument ; 2. Monument of Sir G. McKenzie, commonly called "Bluidy McKenzie," 1691; 3. William Carstares, Reformer, and Principal of the University of Edinburgh, 1715; 4. Entrance to the South Ground, known as the Covenanters' Prison ; 5. John Laying, Keeper of the Signet, 1614 ; 6. Chiesly of Dairy, 1635 ; 7. William Aiken, Architect, 1736, and William Robertson, D.D., 1757.

The Covenanters' Stone in Greyfriars Churchyard

Above left: 7. Tombs in Greyfriars kirkyard, from the six-volume edition of James Grant's *Old and New Edinburgh*, volume 4.

Above right: 8. The Covenanter's Stone in Greyfriars kirkyard, from Gordon Home's *Edinburgh*.

insalubrious surroundings. Just outside Greyfriars was Candlemaker Row, a long terrace of rubble-built Georgian houses leading to the Grassmarket. The street had been named from the candlemakers who were forced to leave Edinburgh's Old Town and settle here, since candle-making was such a fire hazard. The craft had fallen into a decline after the introduction of gas lighting, however, and very few candlemakers remained in Greyfriars Bobby's time. The houses were full of tenants and subtenants, some of whom did not even have a room to themselves. The houses in Greyfriars Place, on the other side of the main gates to the churchyard, were in a similar crowded condition.

One of the Edinburgh people who read about Greyfriars Bobby in the *Scotsman* was the Lord Provost himself, the successful printer and publisher William Chambers. Born in Peebles in 1800, he had moved to Edinburgh in 1814 to work in the bookselling trade. Together with his younger brother Robert, he soon branched out into printing and publishing. With considerable success, they published books and periodicals of Scottish interest, and from 1832 also their popular weekly halfpenny magazine *Chambers's Journal*, which achieved a circulation of 80,000. William Chambers was soon a wealthy man: he could purchase a grand manor house at Glenormiston near Peebles, which he set out to rebuild and improve. A popular and dynamic civic leader, he became Lord Provost of Edinburgh in 1865. He was in the process of

9. Edinburgh Castle from Greyfriars, from an old postcard.

10. Old houses in Candlemaker Row, from the six-volume edition of James Grant's *Old and New Edinburgh*, volume 4.

drawing up the City Improvement Act of 1867, an ambitious programme to improve the city's housing: the Old Town closes and tenements were to be demolished, and modern buildings erected in their place.[7] William Chambers was the director of the Scottish Society for the Prevention of Cruelty to Animals, and a firm lover of dogs. He had been very fond of his little spaniel Fiddy, after whose death in 1858 he had erected a memorial plaque at the Chambers Institute in Peebles.

THE LATE DR. WILLIAM CHAMBERS, OF EDINBURGH.

Above left: 11. William Chambers, the Lord Provost of Edinburgh, in his robes, from the six-volume edition of James Grant's *Old and New Edinburgh*, volume 1.

Above right: 12. Sir William Chambers, from *Illustrated London News*, 2 June 1883.

Lord Provost Chambers sent for city officer Alexander Macpherson and ordered him to inquire into the circumstances of Greyfriars Bobby and the Burgh Court proceedings. When it had been confirmed that what Mr Traill and James Brown had said was nothing but the truth, Chambers went to Greyfriars to see Bobby for himself. Since his wife Harriet also wanted to see the world's most faithful dog, Mr Macpherson and James Brown coaxed Bobby along to the Lord Provost's house at No. 13 Chester Street. Mr Macpherson took the little dog up to the drawing room, where Mrs Chambers, who shared her husband's fondness for animals, was delighted with the vigorous little Bobby. Such an extraordinary dog should not be wanting his dog tax, the Lord Provost reasoned, and Mr Macpherson received instructions to take Bobby to a saddler in George Street, to be given a collar with a brass plate, bearing the inscription 'Greyfriars Bobby, from the Lord Provost 1867. Licensed.'[8] A certain A. Fulton, 86 George Street, is listed as a saddler in the 1867 *Edinburgh & Leith Directory*; he may well have been the maker of Greyfriars Bobby's collar. According to William Chambers himself, 'Some of the magistrates hearing of the case, induced Brown to take care of Bobby, and give him shelter in his own house during the night.'[9]

Thus Greyfriars Bobby's fortune was made. Like some Dickensian character, he had been saved from the canine workhouse, to become a dog of great expectations, whose fame spread through the British Isles and beyond. Newspapers, magazines and books praised Edinburgh's canine wonder, the most faithful dog in the world. But fame and security breeds malice and envy: for decades, nay centuries, Greyfriars Bobby would also have his detractors. Was this dog of mystery, this canine Caspar Hauser, really what he purported to be, or was he an impostor?[10]

13. Greyfriars Bobby's collar, from the 1931 edition of Henry Hutton's *The True Story of Greyfriars Bobby*.

The very first newspaper reference to Greyfriars Bobby had occurred in the 'Edinburgh correspondence' column of the *Inverness Advertiser*, in May 1864. The journalist's mind had for some time been attracted to an instance of canine fidelity which, although it had not yet found its way into the Edinburgh newspapers, was well worth reporting. Five years earlier, the night after five burials had taken place at Greyfriars, 'a little terrier dog whined mournfully among the graves, and, under the shelter of an old pillared tombstone, that little dog has remained in the grave-yard almost ever since'. One day, 'Bob', as the dog was called, was run over by a passing cab when he went for a stroll outside Greyfriars, but he soon recovered and took up his old quarters in the cemetery.

Bob occasionally lodged with his friends living near Greyfriars, but he preferred to sleep outside:

> Indeed, on more than one occasion he became very violent when attempts were made to keep him in at night. Nobody knows whose death he mourns, or where he comes from, although the general belief is that he came from the country along with a funeral cortege. I saw the modest little animal to-day coming out of Greyfriars' gateway, but he is now looking old and grey, although he yet keeps his tail high, and trots cleverly across the street to get a little 'creature comfort' in the shape of a biscuit or a sandwich from the publican or baker.

Bob never left the vicinity of Greyfriars, the *Inverness Advertiser* article went on to claim. With his friend Sergeant Scott, of the Royal Engineers, he sometimes took a walk to the end of George IV Bridge, but he always trotted back to the churchyard and never went any further.

Unlike many of his species and his betters, Bob was never known to do a dishonest action, and it is believed that he would rather starve than steal. I make no excuse for giving you this interesting little history of certainly the most remarkable and faithful animal I ever knew.[11]

The next newspaper to notice Greyfriars Bobby was the equally provincial *Ayrshire Express* of 1865. Nearly six years earlier, this newspaper wrote, after a number of funerals from the country had taken place at Greyfriars, a terrier dog had been found underneath one of the horizontal gravestones in the cemetery. Little 'Bob' was coaxed out with some milk and other treats, but he resolutely refused to leave the churchyard. Nobody knew whom he was mourning. During the cold winter of 1863, Sergeant Scott had coaxed Bob into his house, but the dog returned to his lair underneath the table-stone. Knowing the Sergeant's habits, Bob would meet him at George IV Bridge at a certain hour each day, follow him home and share his midday meal. In the afternoon, when Sergeant Scott returned to office, the little dog would give him a 'scotch convoy' a short distance past Greyfriars, give a farewell wag or two with his tail, and trot back to the graveyard.[12]

Colour Sergeant Donald MacNab Scott, the friend of Greyfriars Bobby alluded to in these two newspaper articles, was born in Perth in August 1817. He was apprenticed to a blacksmith before joining the Royal Engineers as a sapper. Steady promotion through the ranks saw him posted to Edinburgh in the early 1860s, to assist with the Ordnance Survey of Scotland and the North of England. He is likely to have been attached to the Ordnance Survey Office in Melbourne Place, although this has not been confirmed. The reason that he did not live in the military barracks is likely to be that since he was married, he preferred to lodge in the house at the top of Candlemaker Row. This does not imply that Greyfriars Bobby's friend lived a life of luxury, however: according to the 1861 census, he had to share the crowded house with James Anderson and his family of six, Robert Ritchie and his daughter Maria, and four other lodgers. Colour Sergeant Scott was discharged from the army in 1866, with the Army Long Service and Good Conduct Medal and a pension of ten pounds a year. He thus left his lodgings at Candlemaker Row the year before the dog-tax debate, to become a brass founder and surveyor at Edinburgh Castle. He remained in Edinburgh, and resided at No. 8 Bristo Place, not far from Greyfriars at the time of the 1881 census. Colour Sergeant Scott died at the Royal Infirmary in June 1893. he was buried at Piershill Cemetery in Edinburgh, where a headstone to Greyfriars Bobby's friend was unveiled by the Royal Engineers Association and the One o'Clock Gun & Time Ball Association in August 2006.[13]

3

Greyfriars Bobby as an Edinburgh Celebrity

Thus, free among the graves, the dog his right to sojourn gained,
And, once dismissed with obloquy, an honoured guest remained.
There many a stranger heard his tale with softened heart and eye,
While to support his daily needs a constant friend was nigh.

The debate about Greyfriars Bobby's dog-tax, and the happy outcome thanks to the intervention of the Lord Provost, was reported in many newspapers. As a result, there was widespread curiosity about this amazing dog and his alleged nine-year vigil on his master's grave. According to a writer in the *Scotsman*, 'the animal has become an object of much interest, and many people have gone to see it in its home among the tombs'.[1] Remarking on the great interest in Greyfriars Bobby, also on the other side of the Tweed, a letter-writer to the *Scotsman* could record that the niece of a late celebrated English writer, residing in the neighbourhood of Leamington, had offered 'to subscribe for a kennel, to be placed over the grave so faithfully watched by the poor dog, to protect him from cold and rain'.[2]

After Greyfriars Bobby had become an Edinburgh celebrity, business picked up markedly for Mr Traill's eating-house. The restaurant was never short of customers, many of whom had come to see Bobby have his dinner just after the stroke of one. One of them, the old Edinburgh resident Andrew Hislop, described the scene many years later:

Towards one o'clock people would gather just outside the large entrance gates, forming a line on each side of the sloping causeway. So widespread was the interest that every class of society was represented, from the well-to-do and fashionably dressed to the artisan and humble message-boy. As the hour grew near there was a hush of expectation. Then bang went the gun in the castle, and every head turned to the gate, knowing that at the signal Bobby would break his lonely vigil and set off on the way out. Soon there was a hushed whisper, 'Here he comes!' and the grey, shaggy little figure appeared, pattering over the causeway between the two lines of people. Looking neither to one side nor the other, intent only on his own affairs, Bobby hurried round the corner to his right, up the street a few yards, and disappeared into Mr Traill's Dining Rooms for the meal he never failed to get for many years.[3]

14. The cabinet card of Greyfriars Bobby, from the photograph by W. G. Patterson in April 1867, reproduced by permission of the City of Edinburgh Council.

Greyfriars Bobby knew that Traill's restaurant was closed on Sundays, making no attempt to go there; instead, the little dog subsisted on various bones and scraps he had hidden at his den underneath one of the table-stones. The higher of these two table-stones near Bobby's lair has an inscription from Hebrews 13:16 to commemorate Jean Grant: 'With such sacrifices God is well pleased.' After Bobby had become famous, a shelter was built for him near the table-stones, for use in inclement weather.

Realising that paintings of Scotland's most famous dog would be sought after by the curious, many artists set course for Greyfriars to paint Bobby. The first to arrive was the celebrated Gourlay Steell (1819–1894), known as the Scottish Landseer for his particular talent in painting dogs and other animals. He had exhibited many paintings at the Royal Scottish Academy: his dramatic dog studies like *Llewellyn and Gelert* and *Dandie Dinmont and his Terriers* were much praised, as was *A Cottage Bedside at Osborne*, depicting Queen Victoria reading the Bible to an ailing fisherman.[4] Greyfriars Bobby had to return to Gourlay Steell's studio for three days in succession, for the official painting of the world's most faithful dog to be completed in style. On 18 April, when a *Scotsman* journalist went to see Steell, the painting was already well advanced, and a very impressive sight: 'Apart from the interest surrounding the dog, the picture is a very pleasing one, and worthy of the artist.'

One day, as Steell was painting away, the one o'clock gun sounded, and the little dog became quite excited. Bobby could only be pacified when supplied with a hearty meal.[5] James Brown was fearful that Bobby would be stolen, or that some

STRANGE STORY OF A DOG.—A very singular and interesting occurrence was yesterday brought to light in the Burgh Court, by the hearing of a summons in regard to a dog-tax. Eight and a half years ago, a man named Gray, of whom nothing now is known, except that he was poor, and lived in a quiet way in some obscure part of the town, died in Old Greyfriars' Churchyard. His grave, levelled by the hand of time, and unmarked by any stone, is now scarcely decernible; but although no human interest would seem to attach to it, the sacred spot has not been wholly disregarded and forgotten. During all these years the dead man's faithful dog has kept constant watch and guard over the grave,—and it was this animal for which the collectors sought to recover the tax. James Brown, the old curator of the burial ground, remembers Gray's funeral, and the dog, a Scotch terrier, was, he says, one of the most conspicuous of the mourners. The grave was closed in as usual, and next morning "Bobby," as the dog is called, was found lying on the new made mound. This was an innovation which old James could not permit, for there was an order at the gate, stating, in the most intelligible characters, that dogs were not admitted. "Bobby" was accordingly driven out; but next morning he was there again, and for the second time was discharged. The third morning was cold and wet, and when the old man saw the faithful animal, in spite of all chastisement, still lying shivering on the grave, he took pity on him, and gave him some food. This recognition of his devotion gave "Bobby" the right to make the Churchyard his home; and from that time to the present he has never spent a night away from his master's tomb. Often in bad weather attempts have been made to keep him within doors, but by dismal howls he has succeeded in making it known that this interference is not agreeable to him, and latterly he has always been allowed his own way. At almost any time during the day he may be seen in or about the churchyard; and no matter how rough the night may be, nothing can induce him to forsake the hallowed spot, whose identity, despite the irresistible obliteration, he has so faithfully preserved. "Bobby" has many friends, and the tax-gatherers have by no means proved his enemies. A weekly treat of steaks was long allowed him by Sergeant Scott of the Engineers, but for more than six years he has been regularly fed by Mr Traill of the Restaurant, 6 Greyfriars' Place. He is constant and punctual in his calls, being guided in his mid-day visits by the sound of the time-gun. On the ground of harbouring the dog, proceedings were taken against Mr Traill for payment of the tax. The defendant expressed his willingness, could he claim the dog, to be responsible for the tax; but so long as the dog refused to attach himself to any one, it was impossible to fix the ownership,—and the Court, seeing the peculiar circumstances of the case, dismissed the summons. "Bobby" has long been an object of curiosity to all who have become acquaint with his history. His constant appearance in the graveyard has caused many inquiries to be made regarding him, and efforts out of number have been made to get possession of him. The old curator, of course, stands up as the next claimant to Mr Traill, and yesterday offered to pay the tax himself, rather than have "Bobby"—"Greyfriars' Bobby," to allow him his full name—put out of the way.—*See "Scotsman," April 13, 1867.*

W. G. Patterson, 84 Frederick Street, Edinburgh.

Right: 15. The reverse of the Patterson cabinet card, quoting the original account of Greyfriars Bobby, from the *Scotsman* newspaper. Reproduced by permission of the City of Edinburgh Council.

Below: 16. An original drawing of Greyfriars Bobby, by Gourlay Steell, which he presented to Bobby's guardian John Traill. Reproduced by permission of the City of Edinburgh Council.

(From a Painting by Gourlay Steel, R.S.A.)

17. An engraving of Gourlay Steell's painting of Greyfriars Bobby, by Harrison Weir, from *Animal World*, May 1870.

mean-spirited person would take the opportunity to issue a pirated photograph of the famous dog, but to Brown's great relief, the little dog was duly returned to his friends at Greyfriars. Without any delay, the official photograph of Edinburgh's most famous dog was taken by Mr Walter Greenoak Patterson of No. 34 Frederick Street. This photograph was issued as a cabinet card, with the text from the famous *Scotsman* article about Greyfriars Bobby on the back. It was sold by Patterson in his book and print shop, and also enjoyed good sales to the many people who came to Greyfriars to see Bobby as a curiosity.[6] James Brown was always at hand to show them the little dog, for a tip, and to sell them a cabinet card or two. After four weeks, Traill is said to have added his own photograph, also taken by Patterson, to that of Bobby, with the caption 'John Traill – Bobby's benefactor'.

Gourlay Steell's painting was exhibited at Mr Clark's Art Gallery in Princes Street already in late April. It shows Greyfriars Bobby keeping vigil on his master's grave, lying down with his nose between his paws. Around the sad-looking little dog are the tombs and monuments in the churchyard, including the readily identified tombstone of James Chalmers. In the background, towering high above and beyond, is Edinburgh Castle itself. The time appears to be early morning, with the first glints of sunlight on the castle walls. Bobby looks as if he has just opened his eyes, but he seems reluctant to leave the grave of his beloved master.[7] It is curious

18. Another engraving of
Greyfriars Bobby, from the
painting by Gourlay Steell, from
Animal World, February 1874.

THE LIVING MONUMENT TO GRAY.

that this part of the churchyard is far from Jean Grant's table-stone, and the site
that is today pointed out as the tomb of 'the poor man Gray'. There is evidence
that Gourlay Steell painted at least three portraits of Greyfriars Bobby, with small
variations. The better-known variant (Figure 17) was engraved by Harrison Weir,
and used in F. O. Morris's *Dogs and their Doings*, *Animal World* magazine, and
other publications. A second variant, also used by *Animal World*, is similar, but the
alignment of the tombstones in the background shows that the composition of the
portrait is clearly different (Figure 18). Thirdly, a fine pencil sketch of Greyfriars
Bobby, again from a slightly different perspective, given to John Traill by Gourlay
Steel himself in 1868, is kept in the City of Edinburgh Museum (Figure 16).[8]

When Gourlay Steell exhibited his main portrait of Greyfriars Bobby at the
Royal Scottish Academy in March 1868, it was widely admired. A reviewer wrote
that '"Greyfriars Bobby" we previously noticed when exhibited in the Drill Hall
and the favourable opinion we then expressed we still hold.' Another reviewer was
even more enthusiastic: 'Gourlay Steell, the Scottish Landseer, is great in dogs, as
usual. A favourite with him, as with most people, is "Greyfriars' Bobby", whose
whole touching story he narrates …'[9] In 1889, one of the Gourlay Steell paintings
of Greyfriars Bobby was owned by the wealthy magistrate and antiquary Patrick
Dudgeon, at stately Cargen House near Dumfries.[10] After his death in 1895, Cargen
House and its contents were taken over by his son, Colonel R. F. Dudgeon, but evil
times overtook this fine old building; it was used as a military establishment during
the Second World War, and later pulled down altogether. No trace of the Gourlay

Left: 19. A 1918 etching of Greyfriars Bobby, from the painting by Robert Walker Macbeth.

Below: 20. The One o'Clock Gun is fired, from the 1931 edition of Henry Hutton's *The True Story of Greyfriars Bobby*.

Steell paintings of Greyfriars Bobby remains today, but at least the engravings show what they looked like.

Several other artists came to Greyfriars to paint Bobby. Gourlay Steel was closely followed by the obscure Dundee artist Cormack Brown, whose painting of *Faithful Bobby of Greyfriars* was exhibited in the window of Mrs Stevens's Shop, Reform Street, Dundee, on 29 April.[11] Then came Robert Walker Macbeth (1848–1910), the son of the well-known Edinburgh portrait painter Norman Macbeth, who became a painter himself at an early age, specialising in portraits and scenes of rural life.

21. A fine oil painting of Greyfriars Bobby, by the young Edinburgh artist Robert Sanderson. Privately owned, reproduced by permission of Mr George Austin.

In 1867 (or possibly 1868), at the age of just nineteen, he painted Greyfriars Bobby. In his painting, the gloomy, elderly-looking dog is sitting up, in a position similar to the Patterson photograph. It said to have been the property of a New Zealand lady in 1934, but has since been lost.[12] Fortunately, an etching from it was produced in 1918.

Another youthful Edinburgh artist, Robert Sanderson (1848–1908) painted Greyfriars Bobby later in 1867. The composition of Sanderson's small oil painting of Bobby is similar to those by Gourlay Steell in that Edinburgh Castle is in the background, although Bobby is now sitting up, keeping vigil on what again must be presumed to be his master's grave, and looking at the artist with mournful eyes. This painting was purchased at an Edinburgh auction around thirty-five years ago by Liz Austin, a well-known Skye terrier fancier, who with her husband George bred a string of champion dogs. Liz Austin found out about the auction from a fellow dog-breeder, and at once set out for Edinburgh without telling any other person, to make a successful bid for the painting. When she had the dirty old painting professionally cleaned, for the first time ever, Edinburgh Castle became visible in the background.[13] Sadly, Liz Austin has since died, but the Sanderson painting of Greyfriars Bobby is still kept by George Austin, who appreciates its historical value.

There were more portraits and drawings of Bobby than of some of the celebrated beauties of the time. No self-respecting illustrated magazine, in Scotland or England, could do without a drawing of Greyfriars Bobby, from life. Friedrich Wilhelm Keyl, a German animal-painter who had become a protégé of Sir Edwin Landseer and settled down in Victorian England, came to draw Greyfriars Bobby from life in June 1867. He was employed by the *Chatterbox*, a halfpenny illustrated weekly for children. Landseer scoffed at this kind of hackwork, but the impecunious Keyl needed it to be able to support his large family. In a letter to his daughter, Keyl wrote that 'There is a new Publication, the *Chatterbox* – I will send you some, – to which I contribute if I have Time, but unfortunately the Engravers can not cut as I and others draw and you get only the Skeleton instead of the Spirit of one's work.' Indeed, the *Chatterbox* engraving of Bobby from Keyl's drawing looks quite odd and truncated (Figure 1).[14]

John MacLeod, a Perthshire artist specialising in animals, painted Greyfriars Bobby more than once in 1867 and 1868. From his base in Edinburgh, he was often engaged by various Scottish country magnates, to paint their favourite dogs, horses, and other animals. His obituary says that 'he also painted several very good paintings of "Greyfriars' Bobby" of which, if we mistake not, one was exhibited'.[15] Indeed, one of MacLeod's paintings of Bobby, entitled *Greyfriars Bob* and the property of Mr Thos. Cowan, was exhibited at the Royal Scottish Academy in 1868; another (Figure 22) is today on exhibition at Greyfriars church. It depicts the mournful-looking Bobby lying inside what looks like a wooden dog-house, quite possibly the 'shelter' alluded to earlier. In 1927, this painting was hanging in the vestibule of the church; it was said to have been 'presented to the Kirk Session of Old Greyfriars'.[16] It has been claimed that the obscure artist John Charles Gunter (1824–1888), of Galashiels, also painted Greyfriars Bobby at some time, but very little is known about him and this purported portrait.[17]

Next to Greyfriars was (and still is) the impressive George Heriot's Hospital, established by bequest of the goldsmith George Heriot, known as Jinglin' Geordie for his great wealth. On his death in 1624, this philanthropic old Scot left £25,000 to found a 'hospital' (charitable school) to care for the 'puir, fatherless bairns' of Edinburgh. This very considerable sum of money was put to good use to erect a fine building, a masterpiece of Scottish Renaissance architecture. In Greyfriars Bobby's time, George Heriot's Hospital took in paying pupils in addition to the orphans for which it had been intended. The schoolboys were a rowdy lot, fond of all kinds of mischief. They once held a full-scale street fight against the boys of nearby Watson's Hospital, armed with catapults and cudgels. Although there was a private path from the school grounds to Greyfriars, it was out of bounds for the boys. This did not deter them from invading Greyfriars Bobby's territory, however. In a letter from a Heriot 'old boy', detailing various nocturnal escapades, he wrote that 'we used to climb over the wall of Greyfriars' Churchyard and skip across, but you did not go very far before Bobby was at your heels and a proper yelping he set up and he never stopped until we were over the Heriot's wall'.[18]

22. The 1867 painting of Greyfriars Bobby, by John MacLeod. Reproduced by permission of Greyfriars Tolbooth & Highland Kirk.

Greyfriars Bobby was more than once visited by journalists eager for copy. When some reporters from the *Aberdeen Journal* came to Greyfriars to see Bobby in July 1867, the little dog was nowhere to be found. Instead they met James Brown, whom they knew to be quite a knowledgeable, literary man, the author of both the *Deeside Guide* and a book on the Greyfriars monuments and literary remains. In addition, he was a skilled gardener who had, as they expressed it, transformed Greyfriars kirkyard from a wilderness of weeds into a picturesque garden. James Brown told them that Bobby was busy ratting inside the church. Indeed, this proved to be the case: the angry little dog stood snarling at a rat-hole. Brown told his visitors about Bobby's long residence in the churchyard, adding that in addition to his fidelity, the dog also possessed the virtue of orthodoxy: 'O, he hates to see a rottan in the kirk, but there's an thing he hates waur, and that's the whussles on Sunday.'[19] In January 1868, Greyfriars Bobby was featured in the *British Workman*, with an engraving from Gourlay Steell's portrait; in April 1871, the famous little dog had a page of his own in the American magazine *Harper's Weekly*.[20] 'Self Help' Samuel Smiles, author of many unctuous books promoting Protestant work ethics, used almost biblical language to describe Bobby and his vigil: 'His was a love utterly unselfish, faithful and self-sacrificing … What a lesson of gratitude and love for human beings!'[21]

Another article on Bobby, published as early as May 1867, is more than a little odd, however. Inquiring 'when wonders will cease', the journalist commented on 'the battle which took place in two Edinburgh newspapers over a poor little terrier, known in Edinburgh as "Greyfriars Bobby"'. One paper (the *Scotsman*) extolled Bobby's faithful vigil; the other (perhaps the obscure Edinburgh *Daily Review*) sneered at the story and called it mythical. One gentleman (Sergeant Scott?) had paid an eating-house keeper (Mr Traill) nearby to provide the little dog with his daily dinner. To a well-known painter (Gourlay Steell) he had been a sitter in many scenes.

> Odd little rough-coated Bobby, he has fallen on evil times since he became celebrated. He has not the old peace at the old grassy bed of his old master … And his big black eyes peer over his small black muzzle with a look half knowing, half melancholy, as if he wondered why everybody has begun of late to feel curious about him. Little, long-neglected mourner! it is a pity to disturb him. Even a dog's sorrow does not like to be vulgarised by public curiosity … The times were better, Bobby, when you were less famous, when you could mourn alone; and eat your dinner without being wondered at; and lay past the residue in the hole that served you for a pantry, by your old master's eight year old grave, either for yourself or him; and before newspapers fought over you, and Lord Provosts decorated you with a collar of honour.[22]

4

Greyfriars Bobby's Fairy Godmother

That was his home for twice seven years, that ancient hallowed spot
Where Scotland's Covenant was signed by heroes unforgot.
They witnessed for their fathers' Church with lofty loyalty
He for the only love of his life with meek fidelity.

Angela Burdett-Coutts was born in 1814, the daughter of the radical politician Sir
Francis Burdett, Baronet, and his wife Sophia Coutts, who was the daughter of the
very wealthy Scottish banker Thomas Coutts. In 1837, Miss Angela inherited the
Coutts fortune of nearly £3 million, and became the wealthiest woman in Britain.
Unsurprisingly, this prim-looking, intellectual young lady received many offers of
marriage, all of which she turned down. Her most persistent admirer was the Irish
barrister Richard Dunn, who stalked her relentlessly for many years, writing her
impertinent letters and accosting her in the street.[1] Herself, Angela Burdett-Coutts
fell in love with the elderly Duke of Wellington. In 1847, when she was thirty-
three years old and he seventy-eight, she asked him to marry her, but he tactfully
declined her offer.

Angela Burdett-Coutts instead settled down with her permanent female
companion, Mrs Hannah Brown. She entertained lavishly and became one of the
great hostesses of the Victorian era. She was a personal friend of Queen Victoria, an
intimate of leading politicians like Peel, Disraeli and Gladstone, a generous patron
of the arts, and a great philanthropist. Her friend and adviser Charles Dickens called
her 'The noblest spirit we can ever know'. Angela Burdett-Coutts devoted herself
and her immense wealth to a wide array of charitable duties, at home or abroad. She
endowed churches and bishoprics, supported missionary ventures, and interested
herself in the welfare of children and animals. A home for 'unfortunates', a ragged
school union, or a soup-kitchen in the slums, never saw its appeal to her for charity
turned down. When she was travelling around the country, the philanthropic lady
was sometimes greeted with the cry 'God save the Queen of the Poor!'

A great lover of animals, Angela Burdett-Coutts kept a number of parrots at
stately Holly Lodge, Highgate. Her particular favourite was the little dog 'Fan',
whose biography she wrote. Angela Burdett-Coutts was a leading member of
the ladies' section of the RSPCA, and spent much money on erecting drinking
fountains for dogs, horses and cattle around London and the Home Counties.

23. Greyfriars Bobby's fairy godmother, the Baroness Burdett-Coutts, from *Animal World*, February 1907.

Angela Burdett-Coutts paid regular visits to Edinburgh, where she took an interest in the plight of the horses pulling the trams, among other charitable concerns. In early November 1869, she and Hannah Brown visited Greyfriars Bobby, being greatly touched by the pathetic tale of the faithful little creature. Seeing that the grave of 'the poor man Gray' was unmarked, she wrote to the Plans and Works Committee of the Edinburgh Town Council, offering to erect a tombstone:

Balmoral Hotel, November 8, 1869

Sir,

A few days since, I visited the Churchyard of the Old Greyfriars with some friends and we saw the faithful little creature well known to all as 'Greyfriars Bobby' and we found, to our regret, that the spot where lay its poor master was wholly unmarked, so that in a very few years all record will be lost of this remarkable instance of canine attachment and intelligence. Might I be allowed to place in the Churchyard a memorial to Robert Gray the only records of whose humble life are so honourable to him for it seems he had served his Country as a soldier and the nature which could so impress the dog with such lasting affection must have been most kind, gentle and christian [*sic*]. I am informed that the ground belongs to the city and that applications should be made through you. May I therefore request you to bring the subject under the notice of the proper authorities and perhaps they will not feel indisposed to grant me this privilege which I feel the more encouraged to ask as a great niece of one of the Lord Provosts of the City of Edinburgh – the present or rather now the late Lord Provost having already taken the dog under his kindly protection.

I am, &c., Angela G. Burdett-Coutts

Unfortunately, Angela Burdett-Coutts did not mention who had provided her with the information that the master of Greyfriars Bobby had been an old soldier named Robert Gray. The minutes of the Town Council briefly and guardedly stated that the response to the request of Angela Burdett-Coutts was that if the name of the dog's owner could be ascertained, they would be willing to erect the gravestone. The Town Council felt 'bound to guard themselves against being considered as attesting the authenticity of the history of Robert Gray and his dog'.[2]

Some very interesting details from the debate can be gleaned from the newspaper reports of the transactions, however. After the Clerk had read the letter from Angela Burdett-Coutts, Mr William Law, the new Lord Provost, moved that it should be remitted to the Plans and Works Committee with powers to erect the tombstone. But then, a certain Baillie Miller stood up and called out, 'I have no objection to that, but the whole story about "Bobby" is a downright fabrication! [Laughter] I have the story from the old man, the grave-digger.' When Baillie Lewis asked Miller whether he was aware of the facts about Greyfriars Bobby as reported in the *Scotsman*, there was more laughter and the iconoclastic Baillie Miller retorted, 'I would not care supposing they had appeared in the *Reformer*! [Loud laughter]' 'What was narrated was believed at the time to be true,' Baillie Lewis replied, and there were cries of 'Agreed!' 'There are two sides to it,' objected the Lord Provost, probably meaning that it would be unwise to turn down the charitable offer from Angela Burdett-Coutts, but Baillie Miller was not to be stopped. 'I am not going to be snuffed out in that way. [Laughter] I am entitled to express my opinion upon the subject, and I am entitled to state the facts of the case.' Sensing trouble, the Lord Provost pointed out that the grave of 'the poor man Gray' was situated in 'a very bare part of the churchyard, and this monument will be a very great monument'.

When the stubborn Baillie Miller complained that 'It may be an ornament, but it will be putting up in this churchyard a statement that is not correct,' the Lord Provost retorted that 'There are a great many others of that kind there. [Laughter]' The obdurate Baillie Miller continued: 'I am entitled to be heard, and to receive some consideration at your hands. There may be stones not in accordance with fact, but that is no reason why the Council should give leave to put up another containing such a statement. [Hear! Hear!]' The Lord Provost emphasised that Angela Burdett-Coutts did not want to perpetuate the story of Greyfriars Bobby, but to put up a monument to 'the old man Gray'. It was only with difficulty that Lord Provost Law could rally his supporters to make sure that the proposal to erect a monument to Robert Gray was remitted to the Plans and Works Committee. The rabble-rousing Baillie Miller, who had been busy agitating among his colleagues, said that he did not object to this, since he had just taken the opportunity to put the Council right. When the Lord Provost said 'They will not believe you [Laughter]', Baillie Miller angrily retorted, 'I do not care whether they believe me or not!! [Renewed laughter].'[3]

A few weeks later, when the Plans and Works Committee reported back to the Town Council, there was another short and vigorous debate. When the inevitable Baillie Miller asked the Clerk whether it had been ascertained that Gray had actually been buried on the site where the Baroness wanted to erect his monument, the Clerk replied that the opinion expressed by Baillie Miller at the last meeting had been perfectly right, and a representation had been made to Miss Burdett-Coutts indicating this. 'It is a perfect myth altogether!' gloated Baillie Miller. Here the matter ended, and it was decided that the Town Council should taken no further action in the matter, meaning that 'the old man Gray' would have to wait many more years for his tombstone.[4]

In Greyfriars Bobby's time, the Royal Society for the Prevention of Cruelty to Animals (RSPCA) was a force to be reckoned in Victorian Britain. This valuable society did sterling work to outlaw animal baiting and suppress cruel blood sports, and tried its best to lobby Parliament to bring in sterner legislation against vivisection. In 1869, the RSPCA started its magazine *Animal World*, which would run for more than a century. It reported news from animal protection circles, and recent events within the RSPCA; newspapers from all over Britain were culled to find uplifting stories about animal devotion, loyalty and heroism. There was never any shortage of sentimental stories for children, like *Little Chirrup's Autobiography, or The Life and Adventures of a Robin Redbreast*, to teach the next generation about kindness to the brute creation. Angela Burdett-Coutts, Greyfriars Bobby's fairy godmother, was often praised in the pages of *Animal World* for her charity and dedication; in 1870, she presented the prizes at the RSPCA's annual meeting.[5]

The readership of *Animal World* varied from hearty, dog-loving country squires, who saw nothing wrong in shooting and fox-hunting, to mawkish sentimentalists, who wanted to protect even the most humble of creatures, as evidenced by this singular poem:

> I am only a Fly! So you think at your will
> You may frighten, and worry me, torture, and kill!
> Does it ever occur to your mind, that the Eye
> Of God watches over both you and the Fly?

Ladies wearing hats adorned with feathers were as bad as people swatting flies, according to the 'Ghost of the Humming-bird':

> Why do you trifle with my skin
>   To decorate your bonnet?
> Your friends would value you as much
>   Without myself upon it![6]

In the early volumes of *Animal World*, anthropomorphism was taken to its logical extremes, particularly regarding dogs. Among its cartoons was *The Lost Master*, depicting a doleful-looking sheepdog standing near a fallen shepherd's crook just by a high precipice. In *A Humane Dog teaching Man his Duty at Christmas time*, a well-nourished domestic dog allows a half-starved stray mongrel to eat some food from its bowl. *Their First Christmas Carol* features two jolly-looking young puppies sitting in a snow-surrounded kennel, devoutly listening to a robin singing on its roof. Many subscribers to this magazine wholeheartedly believed that dogs had near-human intellects, and that their affection for their masters reached the level of religious devotion. These sentimental Victorian dogs kept vigil on the grave, or even committed suicide, if their beloved masters were taken from them.

Already during his lifetime, Greyfriars Bobby was several times featured in *Animal World*. In 1869, it was reported that the last intelligence received from Greyfriars was that Bobby was still waiting and watching on the grave of his beloved master. Should any reader encounter cruelty to a dog, they should tell the touching story of Greyfriars Bobby, and even the most hardened heart would be unable to withstand its impact. A few months later, there was a long feature on Greyfriars Bobby in *Animal World*. Probably referring to Miss Burdett-Coutts' rebuff from the Edinburgh Town Council, it was remarked that

> It is said that Bobby's chroniclers imported into their narrative too much of Scotch poetry, and that the hero, after all, had not earned the praise which was given to him. Detractors are always to be found when applause are given to mortals; and Bobby must bear up like ourselves against the failings of a wicked generation.

But it remained a fact that Bobby was found resting on the grave of the poor man Gray, and that night after night, he made his pillow on the same spot. Bobby was a small, rough Scotch terrier, grizzled black, with tan nose and feet. After quoting the original story from the *Scotsman* newspaper, the *Animal World* columnist hoped that Miss Burdett-Coutts would have success in erecting a slab at the head of the poor man's grave, for the waiting dog and his departed master.

Many efforts had been made to entice Bobby away from Greyfriars, the *Animal World* columnist asserted, but he still clings to the consecrated spot, where he had remained since 1861.

> Upon his melancholy couch Bobby hears the church bells toll the approach of new inmates in the sepulchres around and about him; and as the procession solemnly passes, who shall say that the ceremony enacted over his dead master does not reappear before him. He sees the sobs and tears of the bereaved, and do those not remind him of the day when he stood with the other mourners over the coffin which contained everything he loved on earth.

Every new funeral brought fresh anguish to poor Bobby, the imaginative *Animal World* writer asserted, since the clergyman's slow and impressive tones reminded the poor mourning dog of the day he had lost his master. It was wrong to refer to 'the old man Gray' as 'poor', since would not the wealthiest of people have given a fortune to have placed upon their tombs a virtuous living monument like this amazing dog.

But here we have a monument that knows neither hypocrisy nor conventional respect, which appears to us not in marble (the work of men's hands), but in the flesh and blood of *a living creature that cannot be tempted to desert his trust* – in the devotion of a friend whose short wanderings to and fro prove how truly he gravitates to one yard of earth only – in the determination of a sentinel *who means to die on his post!*[7]

Wiping the slaver from his mouth, the prolix *Animal World* writer went on to tell the stories of 'Little Tiney, a Squirrel', 'The Singing Mice' and 'The Blind Man and his Dog Puss' for his juvenile readers. The canine news column had updates about the celebrated collecting dogs 'Help' and 'Brake', and their sagacious colleague 'Spot':

When he sees a stranger enter the house, Spot sits on his haunches, barks, sneezes, cries, and gets through a variety of other performances until he gets a piece of money. This he at once gives up, and receives half the value in biscuit, the remainder being saved for charity.

There was also a poem about the unfortunate draught dogs of Antwerp:

Hark! Ye merrie dogs of England, we send you greeting fair
We pray you lend a kindly ear to Antwerp dogs' despair.
For Flemish dogs, alas! must work, must toil the lifelong day.
While free and petted, soft and sleek, you English puppies play!
We all must wear a harness here, must draw a little cart,
Oh! surely such a tale of woe will touch each canine heart![8]

The reaction of Angela Burdett-Coutts when the ungrateful Scots turned down her charitable offer in 1869 has unfortunately not been recorded, even by *Animal World*, but she is unlikely to have been pleased with the 'faithful little creature' being called a fabrication by the iconoclastic Baillie Miller. She kept in touch with Bobby's benefactor Mr Traill, and maintained good relations with William Law the Lord Provost. Determined that Greyfriars Bobby should be honoured for his extraordinary fidelity, she made use of another strategy in 1871. By that time, Queen Victoria had made Angela Burdett-Coutts a Baroness in her own right, as the first woman ever: a suitable reward for her many good deeds. To avoid religious concerns entering the debate, the Baroness proposed that a monument for Greyfriars Bobby be erected just outside the gates of Greyfriars. It should be one of the drinking fountains, with an upper basin for humans and a low trough for animals, which had proved so very popular in London and its environs. The Baroness had always been a generous contributor to the Metropolitan Drinking Fountain and Cattle Trough Association, which had been widely praised for its practical humanitarianism to both men and beasts.[9]

In October 1871, the Baroness Burdett-Coutts was back in Edinburgh. It is very likely that she and Hannah Brown visited Mr Traill, and Bobby himself, before

24. Traill's Temperance Coffee House at No. 6 Greyfriars Place, photographed by John Dickson of Bristo Place. Reproduced by permission of the City of Edinburgh Council.

returning to the old Balmoral Hotel, in Princes Street, to meet a certain Mr Cousins, who had been employed to design the drinking fountain. Mr William Brodie, the celebrated sculptor, had been engaged to produce a bronze statue of Greyfriars Bobby, which was to sit on top of the monument. The son of a Banff shipmaster, Brodie had worked as a plumber in Aberdeen before moving to Edinburgh in 1847 to study sculpture at the Trustee's School of Design, and then in Rome under Laurence MacDonald. Returning to Edinburgh, he established a successful practice specialising in portrait busts, public monuments and architectural sculpture. His statue of Greyfriars Bobby, said by some to have been sculpted from life, is stated by a well-informed source to have been done from a photograph of the famous dog, by Edinburgh photographer Mr Burns.[10]

Feeling pleased with the drawings supplied by Cousins and Brodie, the Baroness went on to write to the Edinburgh Town Council. She referred to the conversation she had already had with the Lord Provost 'respecting a Drinking Fountain to record the curious and interesting facts connected with a Dog in the Greyfriars Church yard'. Enclosing the drawings of Cousins and Brodie, the Baroness hoped that this time, the offer of a valuable and artistic drinking fountain would not be turned down by the Town Council. The fountain would 'not simply serve to perpetuate a touching and remarkable instance of the power of affection and fidelity in the Dog', but also serve to create a sympathy with the animal creation generally, and 'foster those feelings of humane consideration of the creatures upon whom man is so dependent for the comforts and necessaries of life and whose claims are too often overlooked'.[11]

On its meeting on 31 October, the Edinburgh Town Council dealt with the two letters, with enclosures, from the Baroness. The design of the drinking fountain was approved of, and the site outside Greyfriars considered appropriate. Although Baillie Miller appears to have kept quiet this time, some of the other councillors could not resist having some 'fun' at Greyfriars Bobby's expense. When a certain Mr Temple said 'I would like to know if the story be correct?' ribald voices replied 'Quite true!' and 'Quite correct!' Mr Gordon spoke next: 'I move that the sanction of the Council be granted. I am sure of this, that it will serve "to point a moral or adorn a tale". [Great laughter]' Mr Wormald could not resist some further fun: 'Which is the moral and which is the tale? [Renewed laughter]'[12] But after these ribald and jocular exchanges, the Town Council unanimously passed a vote of thanks to the Baroness for her gift.

Both the Scottish and London newspapers praised the Baroness for her generosity, and the journalists found it very appropriate that something was done to perpetuate Greyfriars Bobby's memory. The *Graphic* referred to Bobby as 'that celebrated dog' and the *Star* called him a 'canine hero'. The *Pall Mall Gazette* stated that any person who did not know the story of Greyfriars Bobby ought to be ashamed of himself.[13] When a writer in the *Spectator* jocularly suggested that a suitable inscription on the proposed monument to Greyfriars Bobby would have been Cowper's lines on his dog Beau – 'My dog shall mortify the pride / of man's superior breed' – and presumed that Bobby would rejoin his master in a Better Place, the *Scotsman* thought such a notion rather hard on the many good dogs whose masters had been very bad to them.[14] A writer in the *Animal World* was jubilant that the Baroness had finally managed 'to erect a fountain in commemoration of the affecting story of Greyfriars Bobby, to be placed opposite the gate to the Grey Friars Churchyard, where the poor old faithful dog was still watching near the grave of his master'.[15]

There has been speculation that Queen Victoria herself visited Greyfriars Bobby. The arguments in favour of this are that she often went to Edinburgh, staying at Holyrood House, that she was interested in dogs and herself kept Skye terriers, and that she was a friend of the Baroness Burdett-Coutts. Would it not just be possible that the Baroness spoke to her about Bobby, and that the dog-loving Queen made an excursion to Greyfriars to see its canine wonder. An ill-researched book has boldly claimed as a fact that Queen Victoria personally suggested that Bobby should be buried at Greyfriars near his master.[16] For this there is no evidence whatsoever.

A very amusing drawing in one of the children's books about this famous dog depicts the portly Queen standing next to Bobby, and exclaiming, 'See Brown, he mourns his master as we mourn our Albert.' Her Scottish ghillie John Brown replies, 'Och, you're a foolish wumman!'[17] But there are no hard facts supporting any association between Queen Victoria and Greyfriars Bobby. Neither the Edinburgh newspaper press, nor any of the available biographical works on these two worthies, contain anything to suggest that their paths ever crossed. Queen Victoria kept Skye terriers long before Bobby was born, she was a haughty person who did not like to go 'slumming it', and her relationship with the Baroness was never particularly close. None of Queen Victoria's biographers have mentioned her ever having had any involvement with Greyfriars Bobby, nor do the Royal Archives at Windsor have any relevant information regarding this matter.[18]

Above left: 25. Mr Traill and his family with Greyfriars Bobby. Reproduced by permission of the City of Edinburgh Council.

Above right: 26. The Traill children with Greyfriars Bobby. Reproduced by permission of the City of Edinburgh Council.

But unbeknownst to the Baroness Burdett-Coutts and Greyfriars Bobby's other friends, an insidious attack was under way against the little dog and his proposed monument. A Scottish journalist resident in London, the Metropolitan correspondent for the *Glasgow Herald* and the *Leeds Mercury*, was quite incensed by all the praise for Greyfriars Bobby in the London press, after the story of the Baroness and her memorial fountain had become current. Taking particular umbrage at the *Pall Mall Gazette* journalist who had written that if some ignorant person might be disposed to ask 'Who is Greyfriars Bobby, and what has he done to deserve these honours?' he should be answered, 'Every person who does not know the history of Greyfriars Bobby ought to be ashamed of himself!' The London correspondent asked the same question, but gave it a very different answer. Many years earlier,

a poor mongrel of low degree, frowsy and half-starved in appearance, wandered by chance into historical Greyfriars churchyard at Edinburgh. The sexton, who was a kind man with a warm heart towards all brutes in distress, happened to be taking his dinner when the wretched dog entered. Seeing the pitiable plight of the beast, its rusty coat, lack-lustre eyes, and general forlornness, he threw it a portion of his meat, which was greedily devoured.

Bobby and the sexton (James Brown) soon became fast friends, and although 'ugly and unprepossessing in appearance, "Bobby's" mild behaviour and meek disposition pleaded eloquently in his favour, and the sexton not only tolerated him, but fed him with crumbs and bones of his table.' Bobby wandered among the antique tombs, and slept underneath one of the table-stones. The local people were soon talking about this extraordinary dog, and when the story came

> to the ears of an ingenious correspondent of a north country newspaper, he resolved to 'fit' the dog with an appropriate legend. He and one or two others accordingly concocted a story to the effect that 'Bobby' had followed his master's funeral from the country to Greyfriars, and was so smitten down with grief for his loss that he refused to leave the grave after the body was interred, but lay day and night, through summer and winter, over the remains of his deceased patron.

This tale had originally been intended as a joke, but it found its way back to Edinburgh, where people began to talk about this exceedingly faithful dog. In April 1867, at a time when there was little interesting news to report, the Edinburgh newsmen 'discovered' Greyfriars Bobby and praised him for his extraordinary fidelity:

> He lay all day upon the grave, refusing food, water, comfort, shivering under the unutterability of his feelings. So ran the tale in the daily prints until 'Bobby' became one of the lions of Edinburgh. He was petted and caressed, talked of and extolled, and the ladies and the weaker burghers clave to him as to an idol. Nothing was too good for him, nor could human speech sufficiently exalt his gentleness, his sagacity, his love for his dead master, and all the virtuous qualities which made him an exemplar among his race. Meanwhile those who had got up the hoax chuckled in secret, and marvelled much at the extent and fervour of the popular enthusiasm. They had digged a pit for themselves, and were afraid to reveal the real story, and so the fiction spread and became a city tradition.

Now the noble and illustrious Baroness Burdett-Coutts had been unwise enough to adopt Greyfriars Bobby, and sent money up north to immortalise the dog's memory. But, as the London correspondent expressed it, 'the sympathies of Baroness Burdett Coutts have been evoked to perpetuate an idle tale and bequeath a fountain, to extol faithfulness that never existed, and history whose entire foundation is fictitious'.

The full-length attack on Greyfriars Bobby was published in the *Leeds Mercury*, with a shorter version in the *Glasgow Herald*; these articles were reproduced in some other Northern English papers, but ignored in the Edinburgh press.[19] Greyfriars Bobby's friends at *Animal World* were particularly annoyed that the *Christian World* had reprinted this dastardly attack on their favourite dog. They promised to have more to say about the London correspondent's debunking of Greyfriars Bobby

27. An enlarged version of the
Patterson cabinet card of Greyfriars
Bobby, which he presented to Mr Traill
in late 1868. Reproduced by permission
of the City of Edinburgh Council.

on a future occasion, but this counterblow was never substantiated.[20] Nor was an
appeal, in the *Dundee Courier & Argus*, for the declaration of the *Glasgow Herald*'s
London correspondent that Greyfriars Bobby was an impostor to be contradicted
by people who knew the history of this famous dog.[21]

The London correspondent for the *Leeds Mercury* received support from a writer of a
review of 'The Dogs of the British Islands' in the anti-Bobby Edinburgh *Daily Review*:

We are soon to have a noble example in Edinburgh of a tribute of respect to a
dog. The Baroness Coutts has obtained permission to erect a monument to the
memory of an animal known as Greyfriars Bobby. A pity it is that the story which so
touched the heart of the benevolent lady is only a penny-a-liner's romance. 'Bobby'
was a decent dog, much too decent to have ever lent himself to an imposture, if
he could have helped it. Instead of being found disconsolate over a master's grave,
he was one of a tribe still too numerous, notwithstanding Mr Lowe's universal
five shilling tax. [This refers to Edinburgh's many stray dogs] At last he had the
sense to discover for himself a lair under a flat tombstone supported on pillars
in the Greyfriars Churchyard – a better shelter than our poor Covenanters had
in the same enclosure, with only the inclement sky for their canopy. The humane
proprietor of a neighbouring restaurant supplied Bobby with food, and so, having
no apprehension from the ghost of the 'bluidy Mackenzie' or any other inhabitant
below, he established himself in his singular quarters. If the good Baroness erects a
monument to all stray dogs who have wit enough to keep themselves out of the wet,
and to wait upon benevolent dispensers of scraps, even her wealth would hardly
suffice to immortalize them all.[22]

5

Greyfriars Bobby's Monument

His fame will live, for one there is who will not let it die,
Who bids a graceful fount arise to enshrine his memory.
Even she, whose deeds of charity are blessed throughout the land,
The lady of the tender heart, the open, generous hand.

For telling men and suffering beasts alike those waters flow,
Just as her gifts, her sympathies, nor stint nor limit know,
While Bobby's image, crowning all, pleads for each subject race
of creatures, asking in their name for gentleness and grace.

As the years went by, Greyfriars Bobby remained an Edinburgh celebrity. Bobby kept patronising Mr Traill's restaurant, but he also paid visits to some other public houses nearby. William Albert Cunningham, a Heriot's schoolboy, could well remember seeing Greyfriars Bobby come into Traill's dining room looking for a bite to eat.[1] The neighbour, A. Watson, made it a habit to look out of his attic window each day, just after the one o'clock gun had been fired, to see Bobby go to dinner. Mrs I. M. Martin could remember seeing Bobby coming out of Mr Traill's restaurant, returning to Greyfriars via the main gates. Some people watching told her the little dog's story. William Watson, a young man working for a business nearby, frequently had his meals at Mr Traill's, where he saw Bobby many times, having his dinner at one o'clock, before returning to the kirkyard.[2] Bobby was popular locally and had many friends who fed him. A certain Mrs Denholm later recalled that when she had worked in a butcher's shop near Greyfriars as a young girl, Bobby had often been brought into the shop for a scrap of food. She had used to feed him some meat, and given him milk to drink.[3] Lockie's *Edinburgh Guide* of 1899 said that 'Bobby was a great favourite with the shop keepers around who fed him daily. He would often trot as far as the High Street where a kind-hearted shop woman gave him food.'

William Dow, the joiner and cabinet-maker at George Heriot's Hospital, taught woodwork to the rowdy pupils there. They called him 'Muscle' Dow and sometimes played some wicked pranks on him, like climbing onto the roof of his workshop and pouring handfuls of gravel down the chimney into his glue-pot. Mr Dow knew Greyfriars Bobby from quite an early time. One day, perhaps in 1862 or 1863, when he went along the private path from Heriot's to Greyfriars to visit his friend Mr Traill, Bobby ran up to him at the gate and accompanied him, at the sound of the one o'clock gun, to the restaurant, where the little dog was given a meal. After that time, Bobby was often waiting for Mr Dow at the gate, to escort him to Traill's restaurant; if the joiner did not arrive, Bobby went there on his own at the sound of the gun. William Dow's little daughter Helen sometimes went with him to Mr Traill's temperance coffee house, where she often stroked Bobby and held him in her arms. Mr Dow and his daughter were both very fond of Bobby, and more than once tried to coax him to follow them to their house, but Bobby did not go with them.[4]

In 1871, when the young Edinburgh lad Wilson MacLaren went into Mr Traill's coffee house in Greyfriars Place, he saw a Skye terrier chewing a bone, and gave the little dog half a buttered 'bap'. Mr Traill said, 'That doggie has a bit of a history. His name is Bobby, and his master, a Midlothian farmer, named Grey, died in 1858, almost thirteen years ago. He aye came for his dinner here on market days, and Bobby was always wi' him.' When Grey died, Bobby followed his coffin to Greyfriars, although the little dog remained a customer at Mr Traill's restaurant at the sound of the time-gun. In his memoirs, MacLaren gave a slightly different account of his encounters with Greyfriars Bobby, inexplicably reducing the time of Bobby's vigil to nine years.[5]

Later, in 1871, Greyfriars Bobby was permanently adopted by John Traill and his family, and kept indoors most of the time. Atoning for his lack of generosity back in 1867, the restaurateur took good care of Bobby, keeping him warm and well fed. His family were now living at No. 5 Greyfriars Place, the house behind the restaurant, having taken over the lease of both No. 5 and No. 6 from Mr Currie when it expired in May 1870. Showing praiseworthy concern to document the famous dog for posterity, Traill had Bobby photographed by Walter Greenoak Patterson, the same photographer responsible for the original 1867 cabinet card. One of the photographs shows Bobby with Mr Traill and his entire family; in the second, the little dog is with the two Traill children.[6] Traill's daughter Eliza, eleven years old at the time, later recalled that taking Bobby for walks was no sinecure, since he was extremely pugnacious and wanted to attack all other male dogs in Bristo and the district, irrespective of their size.[7]

When Greyfriars Bobby fell ill with a swelling of the jaw, Professors William Williams and Thomas Walley, from the Edinburgh Veterinary College, were consulted, but the diagnosis was untreatable cancer of the lower jaw.[8] Bobby was nursed by young Eliza Traill, in the living room in the house behind the restaurant. On 14 January 1872, Bobby fell asleep in front of the fire, never to awake again.[9] As the generous and poetical 'E. E. S.' expressed it,

> Then came the end, and Bobby sleeps a flowery grave beneath,
> Where the warm heart, the active limbs, lie cold and still in death.
> Only a dog! Long may the light of his mild virtues shine!
> Was not the spark within his breast lit by a Hand Divine?

Bobby's obituary was in the *Scotsman* of 17 January:

> Many will be sorry to hear that the poor but interesting dog, 'Greyfriars Bobby,' died
> on Sunday evening. Every kind attention praised was paid to him in his last days by
> his guardian, Mr. Traill, who has had him buried in a flower-plot near Greyfriars
> Church. His collar, a gift from lord provost Chambers, has been deposited in
> the office at the church gate. Mr. Brodie has successfully modelled the figure of
> Greyfriars Bobby, which is to surmount the very handsome memorial to be erected
> by the munificence of the Baroness Burdett Coutts.[10]

Bobby's collar would remain in the little office or 'bothy' by the churchyard gates
for many years to come.

John Traill and his friends buried Bobby in a triangular patch of ground facing
the entrance to the cemetery itself. A rose-bush was later planted on the grave. A
small tombstone, marked only with the roughly chiselled words 'Greyfriars Bobby'
was put on the spot, and a photograph was taken by a friend of Traill's. However,
this stone was either stolen by some mean-spirited individual, or taken away by the
curator of the burial grounds.[11]

Mr Traill made sure that Bobby was examined after death, by a competent
veterinarian, as judged from the following letter:

> Edinburgh Veterinary College, March 1872
> To those who may feel interested in the history of the late Greyfriars Bobby, I may
> state that he suffered from disease of a cancerous nature affecting the whole of the
> lower jaw.
>
> Thomas Walley, Professor of Animal Pathology.[12]

In the meantime, the Baroness Burdett-Coutts was busy supervising the erection
of Greyfriars Bobby's monument. There was a debate about what inscription it
should have. Sir Alexander Grant, Principal of Edinburgh University, provided a
Latin poem:

> *Me quondam fidus domini super ossa sepulti*
> *Stratum inter tumulos usque tenebat amor.*
> *Huic liquido fonti sedeo nunc, cernite cives,*
> *Æneus invigilans: Angela sic voluit.*

This inscription was eloquently translated into:

> Me faithful love, among the grass-grown heaps,
> Kept watchful where my buried master sleeps.
> Now – Angela so willing it – this well
> I guard, in living bronze its sentinel.[13]

28. A very early print of the monument
to Greyfriars Bobby.

Still it was not used on the fountain. The distinguished Edinburgh scholar John Stuart Blackie wrote an equally eloquent Greek poem for the drinking fountain, which was not used either, although it is rescued from undeserved obscurity in this book (Figure 31). In plain and simple English, the Greyfriars Bobby drinking fountain instead has the following inscription:

> A tribute to the affectionate fidelity of Greyfriars' Bobby. In 1858 this faithful dog followed the remains of his master to Greyfriars' Churchyard and lingered near the spot until his death in 1872. With permission, erected by Baroness Burdett-Coutts.

The Greyfriars Bobby drinking fountain was unveiled without ceremony on 14 November 1873. Supervised by Mr Brodie and Mr Cousins, a party of workmen erected the structure on the inner edge of the foot pavement at the corner of George IV Bridge and Candlemaker Row, and connected its water pipes. When completed, the beautiful Westmoreland granite drinking fountain stood 7 feet in height. The base was in the form of an octagonal trough in axed granite, raised only a few inches above the ground, and intended to be a perfect drinking place for dogs. From the centre of this trough rose a cylindrical column of polished granite, 3 feet high and 20 inches in diameter, finished at the top with a moulding, on which rested a vase-shaped drinking basin for humans, 3 feet in diameter. Another column, 12 inches in diameter and 18 inches high, rose from the centre of the basin. On each side, it had a large bronze plaque, one with the arms of

GREYFRIARS BOBBY'S MEMORIAL, EDINBURGH

THE GRANITE MONUMENT TO " BOBBY."

PROFESSOR BLACKIE'S GREEK INSCRIPTION.

ORIGINAL.	TRANSLATION.
	This monument was erected
Ἱερύθη τοῦτο τὸ μνημεῖον	By a noble lady,
ἐαπάναισ τῆς εὐγενοῦς γυναικὸς	THE BARONESS BURDETT-COUTTS,
τῆς Βαρωνίσσης Βουρδέττίας Κούτσης	To the memory of
τῇ Ῥοβερτιδίῃ,	"GREY FRIARS' BOBBY,"
τῷ τῶν Λευκαφρίων Μονάχων,	A faithful and affectionate
πιστῷ μάλα καὶ φιλανθρώπῳ	Little dog,
Κυνιδίῳ,	Who followed the remains of his beloved master
ὃ δὴ ἔτει φωνῇ, μετασχὸν	To the churchyard
τῆς τοῦ ἀγαπητοῦ δεσπότου ἐκφορᾶς,	In the year 1858,
ἐπικαρτέρει φαιτῶν	And became a constant visitor to the grave,
εἰς τὸ κοιμητήριον,	Refusing to be separated from the spot,
καὶ οὐκ ἤθελεν ἀποσπῆσθαι,	Until he died
μέχρις οὗ ἀπέθανεν ἔτει φωόβ.	In the year 1872.

Above left: 29. An 1873 newspaper engraving of the monument to Greyfriars Bobby, probably from The Illustrated London News.

Above right: 30. The monument to Greyfriars Bobby, from Animal World of 1874. In the background can be seen David Ritchie's blacksmith's shop at Candlemaker Row.

Left: 31. The suggested Greek inscription for Greyfriars Bobby's monument, by Professor Blackie, from Animal World of 1874.

32. The distinguished Edinburgh scholar John Stuart Blackie, author of the Greek poem in honour of Greyfriars Bobby, from the six-volume edition of James Grant's *Old and New Edinburgh*, volume 1.

the Baroness Burdett-Coutts, the other with those of the City of Edinburgh. Two bronze drinking cups were attached to these plaques with chains. A couple of ornate water spouts made sure both trough and basin were well filled with water. This second column supported the bronze statue of Bobby. According to the *Scotsman*, 'The shaggy little terrier has been modelled with Mr Brodie's wonted skill, and the artist's design has received ample justice in a casting of remarkable excellence.'[14] Greyfriars Bobby's statue had the inscription 'Grey Friars' Bobby, from the life just before his death. W. H. Brodie Sc. R.S.A., 1872'. Brodie's original plaster statue of Bobby, from which the bronze casting was performed, is still kept at the City of Edinburgh Museum, Huntly House.

The erection of Greyfriars Bobby's monument was described in newspapers all over Britain. Bobby's old friends at *Animal World* were particularly enthusiastic, devoting two full spreads to the Edinburgh dog saint and his drinking fountain.[15] It was illustrated with engravings of *The Living Monument to Gray* (Gourlay Steell's painting) and *The Granite Monument to Bobby*. Everyone had heard the heart-warming story of Greyfriars Bobby, the *Animal World* columnist wrote, and although some might scoff at it as a poetical myth, it was denied by no person who had taken care to investigate it. Here, *Animal World* conveniently ignored Baillie Miller, the sneering London correspondent to the *Glasgow Herald*, and his colleague at the Edinburgh *Daily Review*. Bobby deserved his drinking fountain, so that 'unreflecting people may be taught by the monument that dogs sometimes exhibit the highest moral qualities'.

MONUMENT TO GREYFRIARS BOBBY.

33. The monument to Greyfriars Bobby, from *The Child's Companion*, 1 June 1880.

Alongside tales of brave, lifesaving St Bernard and Newfoundland dogs, the story of Greyfriars Bobby had, by this time, become a cornerstone in the RSPCA's educational work on animal welfare. If a dog could act altruistically and save people's lives, displaying extraordinary courage and intelligence, or alternatively become so attached to its master as to keep vigil on his grave for fourteen long years, was it not a crime that cried out to heaven for vengeance for any person to mistreat one of these canine paragons of virtue, or to reward them with torture and an ignominious death in a research laboratory? None of the slide shows for children arranged by the RSPCA or the Band of Mercy was complete without a heroic Newfoundland dog leaping into the water to save a struggling swimmer, Barry the brave St Bernard giving a child a ride on his back, and faithful little Greyfriars Bobby keeping vigil on his master's grave. *Animal World* proposed to issue the illustrated four-page feature on Greyfriars Bobby as a tract for use in Sunday schools.[16]

Even the French, with their habitual tendency to sneer at any news emanating from the British Isles, were impressed with the 'Mausolée d'un Chien Fidèle' in Edinburgh. In 1873, the *Musée Universel* had a feature on Greyfriars Bobby, with a translation of the inscription on the drinking fountain:

Ceci est un tribut offert à l'affecteuse fidélité de 'Greyfriars Bobby'.
En 1858, ce chien fidèle suivit la dépouille de son maître jusqu'au cimetière de Greyfriars et resta près de la tombe jusqu'à sa mort, en 1872.

The year after, the *Rappel* of the *Petit Moniteur* had an account of Bobby's fourteen years on his master's tomb, and of the Edinburgh monument. M. Cheval, the secretary general of the Société Protectrice des Animaux, gave a lecture '*d'une charmante histoire relative à Bobby, chien d'Edimbourg, qui à donné des preuves d'un fidélité inexprimable …*'[17]

But in spite of all the newspaper compliments to Mr Brodie, it soon became apparent that the Greyfriars Bobby drinking fountain had some serious design flaws. Unhygienic people felt free to spit tobacco into the drinking basin, and to deposit rubbish there. The canine partakers of water from the drinking fountain were facing worse hazards, since the dogs sometimes felt the urge to relieve themselves, cocking their legs at the drinking trough. Since the dogs did not share the human option to fill their drinking cups from the water spout, they were left with the polluted water in the lower trough, as pointed out in an amusing letter from 'An Old Edinburgh Dog':

> Sir – Having heard from a friend of mine in Rutland Street that Lady Burdett Coutts had erected a fountain for our especial benefit, and also to commemorate the fidelity of my old and esteemed companion Bobby, I made it a point to stray in that direction. I at once recognized the figure of my old friend, but alas! was sadly disappointed with the arrangements made for our comfort. The days especially named after our race are gradually approaching, and her Ladyship's gift would then indeed be a great boon to all of us, but if the trough placed at our disposal is not kept clean, and attended to in a manner that would satisfy our most charitable benefactor, I doubt if there is a dog in town who could with any safety to himself, attempt to reap the benefit of her kindness. I growl this to you, knowing your feelings regarding humanity.
>
> I am, &c.   An Old Edinburgh Dog.[18]

Another interesting matter is the Edinburgh tradition that the Greyfriars Bobby monument had originally been set up to have Bobby's statue looking towards Greyfriars and the grave of his master. Then, one of the landlords of Greyfriars Bobby's Bar had turned the statue around at some stage, so that the pub would be seen in the background of all the photographs and picture postcards of the drinking fountain. It would appear that there was a small licensed house at the ground floor of the house at the top of Candlemaker Row already during Greyfriars Bobby's lifetime. The present-day pub dates back to 1893, but it did not get its present name until later. But there is solid evidence, from the early engravings of Greyfriars Bobby's monument, that the dog statue was looking away from the Greyfriars gates from the beginning, and that it has never been turned around.

William Gordon Stables qualified as a doctor in 1862 and became a naval surgeon. In 1871, he contracted severe rheumatic and jungle fever in Africa, and was invalided home. He became a general practitioner, but many years of cruising

MR. GORDON STABLES, M.D., B.N.

34. Dr William Gordon Stables, from *Penny
Illustrated Paper*, 19 March 1892.

abroad and examining sailors for venereal disease had not done his general medical
knowledge any good: he was quite a dangerous doctor, particularly after becoming
addicted to alcohol and chloral hydrate. After nearly killing a child with a carelessly
written prescription, he gave up medical practice, for good. After weaning himself
off the chloral hydrate, Dr Stables settled down in Twyford with his family, in a
house called the Jungle, to become an author of juvenile literature. Unaffected by
the miserable end to his medical career, he was quite a jolly, eccentric character,
with a great fondness for animals. He rose at 4.30 each morning, had a cold bath,
looked after his various pets, had breakfast, and retired to a small garden bungalow
called the Wigwam, to settle down with pen and paper to write all day. In the
coming twenty years, he would write at least a hundred books, and countless
articles for *The Boy's Own Paper* and other juvenile periodicals.[19]

Dr Stables was very fond of his two Newfoundland dogs, the champion
Theodore Nero and his 'wife' Aileen Aroon. Aileen was a simple, honest dog, but
Theodore was clever and enterprising: a great fighter, and the hero of the dog-show
and the water-trial. Dr Stables was fond of teaching his dogs various silly tricks, like
imitating a circus elephant, or carrying a large sheep's head through the streets, with
a placard saying 'I am starving!' He thought it great fun to teach Theodore to grab
people's sticks, but this sentiment was probably not reciprocated by an old Irish
sailor with a wooden leg, who was toppled over by the great dog. When Theodore
grabbed an admiral's bamboo cane, Dr Stables was severely reprimanded. It would
also be quite hilarious, the doctor thought, to teach Theodore to take people's hats
off, but this time the fun was ended when the massive Newfoundland wrestled a
police constable to the ground, and tried his best to wrench the constable's helmet
off his head.

Although a somewhat irresponsible dog owner, who allowed his unruly beasts to
do all kinds of mischief, Dr Stables was genuinely fond of his two Newfoundlands.
When Aileen died, he decided to write her biography. Since she had not done
much that was interesting in her life, the book was bolstered with various tales

35. An old picture postcard of the monument to Greyfriars Bobby, postally unused. Note Ritchie's blacksmith's shop in the background, and also the lamp post erected next to the drinking fountain.

of Theodore amusing himself and his master through doing various pranks. The great dog did not lie down on his 'wife's' grave, but the astute doctor noticed that he visited it regularly. Once, when Dr Stables went to dig a hole to plant a rose-bush on Aileen's grave, the overjoyed Theodore thought that he was about to dig her up, to bring her back to life and him, or so at least the doctor claimed.

Having read about Greyfriars Bobby in *Animal World* magazine, to which he of course was a subscriber, Dr Stables dedicated a chapter of Aileen's biography to this Edinburgh paragon of canine virtue. Deploring that so little was known about Bobby's antecedents, and the private history of the poor man Gray, he had made various inquiries in Edinburgh, but 'even an advertisement in a local paper failed to elicit the information I so much desired'. Dr Stables found it odd that 'a stranger arrived in Edinburgh bringing with him a little rough-haired dog, that slept in the same room with him, and followed him in his walks, but no one knew who the stranger was, or whence he came'. To try to solve the problem, he wrote to Bobby's guardian Mr John Traill, who was still running the restaurant in Greyfriars Place. Mr Traill sent him Bobby's brief obituary from the *Scotsman* newspaper, and also a copy of the valuable letter from Professor Walley, who had examined Bobby's body after death. The fanciful Dr Stables thought that Bobby's cancer of the jaw must have been the result of his constant resting of his chin on the cold earth of the grave of his master.[20]

In his letter to Dr Stables, John Traill also wrote:

> In 1858, this faithful dog followed the remains of his master to Greyfriars churchyard, and lingered near the spot until his death in 1872. Old James Brown died in the autumn of 1868. There is no tombstone on the grave of Bobby's master. Greyfriars Bobby was buried in the flower plot near the stained-glass window of the church, and opposite the gate.

Dr Stables found it likely that Bobby was happy now, in a Better World, although it was troubling that his nameless master still lacked a gravestone: 'surely there must have been good in the breast of that man whom a dog loved so dearly, and to whose memory he was faithful to the end.'

The erection of the Greyfriars Bobby drinking fountain was just one of the many good deeds in Angela Burdett-Coutts' long and charitable life. In July 1872, the City of London made her its first woman Freeman, and in January 1874, Edinburgh gave her the same honour, in a grand ceremony in the Music Hall. The Baroness thanked the Town Council in an eloquent speech, paying a tribute to her Scottish grandfather Thomas Coutts, who had also been a Freeman of Edinburgh.[21] William and Harriet Chambers were both present during the ceremony. If Baillie Miller and his fellow scoffers had managed to gatecrash the party, they kept their mouths firmly shut, making no further ribald comments about the dog monument in Candlemaker Row.

The Baroness kept in touch with John Traill over the years to come. In 1873, when her little dog Fan died, she wrote the dog's biography, published it privately, and sent a copy to Mr Traill, along with a letter:

> Fan's mistresses feel sure that Greyfriars Bobby's kind friend will like to read this account of their dear faithful wee doggie. The gentle creature died May 3 pm at S Molton St London. Loving and intelligent, it recognised back to the last minute of its life.

When Mr Traill wrote back to her through William Chambers, enclosing an enlarged photograph of Greyfriars Bobby, the haughty Baroness returned the compliment:

> The Baroness Burdett-Coutts begs to thank Mr Traill for the pretty remembrance of grand old Greyfriars Bobby, which he sent her through Mr Chambers. The Baroness values it very much and is pleased that Mr Traill likes the fountain she has executed to recall the touching story with which Mr Traill's name in connection with it is significantly linked.[22]

In the iconography of wealthy and influential Victorian ladies, there is sometimes a marked contrast between the idealised paintings and the brutally honest

36. The monument to Greyfriars Bobby, from a postcard stamped and posted in 1914. In the background is the spirit shop kept by Alexander Dow at No. 34 Candlemaker Row.

Monument to Greyfriars Bobby, Edinburgh

photographs. For example, the paintings of the young Queen Victoria all show her as a beauty, although she was really quite plain.[23] The same is true for Angela Burdett-Coutts: although the paintings of her as a young woman depict her as quite attractive, she was never much to look at in real life – a thin, frumpish woman with a gloomy expression and demeanour. When the uncouth Shah of Persia was introduced to her in 1873, he exclaimed '*Quelle horreur!*' when he saw her face.[24] Still, after Hannah Brown had died in 1878, the 64-year-old Baroness contemplated marriage. In February 1881, she married her 29-year-old secretary William Ashmead Bartlett. Queen Victoria was not amused, since she felt it was undignified for a woman of that age to marry, but the wealthy Baroness did not care.[25] One of the newspaper reports of her marriage mentions that 'In Edinburgh, at the corner of George IV Bridge and Candlemakers' Row, the baroness erected a fountain in memory of "Greyfriars' Bobby", a faithful and affectionate dog, who from 1858 to 1872 visited his former master's grave daily. This is perhaps one of the noblest mementoes extant towards the brute creation.'[26] The Baroness would live on for many years, in comfort and security. In contrast, her gift to Edinburgh, the Candlemaker Row dog monument, would be facing some very troubled times.

6

Attack on Greyfriars Bobby

With eye upraised, his master's looks to scan,
The joy, the solace, and the aid of man;
The rich man's guardian, and the poor man's friend
The only creature faithful to the end.

George Crabbe, 'On the Dog'

During the decade after Greyfriars Bobby's death and beatification, the little dog's memory was treated with respect and decorum. The attacks from that miserable politician, Baillie Miller, and that dastardly scribbler, the London correspondent of the *Glasgow Herald*, were soon forgotten about. The cult of Bobby the Greyfriars anchorite continued unimpeded, particularly in *Animal World* and in various religious and children's magazines.

In 1876, the *Children's Treasury* had an illustrated account of 'Greyfriars Bob', as they called him. Poor Bob had been lying shivering on his master's grave, half starved and growing weaker every day, until finally he crept out one final day, lay down and died: 'Look at his picture, dear children, and may it make you at all times kind and thoughtful in the treatment of your dumb favourites!' Bobby's pathetic story was also unctuously retold in *Little Folks* magazine, and in the *Child's Companion*.[1] The moral of the tale is the same: Bobby's long vigil on his master's tomb should make the children reflect on canine virtues, and induce them to treat animals with kindness and consideration.

But in the 1880s, Bobby and his amazing story would come under repeated attack from the rationalists. The first, ominous sign came in a short review of Samuel Smiles' *Duty*, in which he had praised the virtues of Greyfriars Bobby: a newspaper writer curtly wrote that 'Now, if Mr Smiles does not know, he ought to be informed, that the story of the dog, "Greyfriars Bobby," is a hoax that was perpetrated by an Edinburgh press man.'[2]

The one to cast the first stone at the Candlemaker Row dog monument was the eccentric newspaper man Thomas Wilson Reid, who was born in Ayr in 1834. As a young journalist, he moved to Edinburgh to join the *North British Agriculturalist* newspaper. He is likely to have worked for this newspaper, and possibly for the Edinburgh *Daily Review*, in the mid-1860s.[3] He married his wife Mary when he

37. A drawing of Greyfriars Bobby, from *Little Folks* magazine of 1876, based on the W. G. Patterson photograph of Bobby during life.

was quite young, and they had many children. Reid later moved from Edinburgh to London, where he worked as a hack journalist. In the early 1870s, his name sometimes crops up in the London correspondent's column of the *Glasgow Herald* and the *Leeds Mercury*, suggesting that Reid might well have been the hidden hand behind the venomous stab in the back of Greyfriars Bobby in 1871, and possibly the attack in the Edinburgh *Daily Review* as well.[4]

The adventurous Thomas Wilson Reid moved to Boulogne for a while, bringing his large family with him, before returning to London. In 1879, he published his first literary work, an obscure schoolbook entitled *The Newspaper Reader*, which was swiftly forgotten. The 1881 census finds him living in Lambeth with his wife and ten children. The year after, he compiled the *Traits and Stories of Ye Olde Cheshire Cheese*, a collection of anecdotes about one of the few survivors of London's old hostelries. This book was published in several editions and became Reid's main claim to fame, although his name was removed from some of the future reissues, since they were edited by other people. In 1882, he also published the novel *Gabrielle Stuart*, an insipid Scottish adventure that found few readers, in spite of being serialised in the *Glasgow Weekly Herald* in May 1881.[5]

Thomas Wilson Reid had his own way of writing novels, peppering the plot with lengthy digressions about Scottish historical subjects of little interest to the reader, and autobiographical anecdotes from his own career. In Chapter 20 of *Gabrielle Stuart*, musing that history is sometimes strangely compiled, he notes that:

The story of 'Greyfriars' Bobby', now recorded in the archives of Edinburgh. Bobby, according to the legend, was a dog that followed its master's remains to Greyfriars' Kirkyard, and lay until the day of its death on his grave, only going outside occasionally to obtain food.

Now I well know that this tale concerning 'Greyfriars' Bobby' is utterly untrue, notwithstanding that a certain dog was given a gold chain by the Lord Provost of Edinburgh, and that the Baroness Burdett-Coutts raised a monument in the form of a fountain to a certain dog's memory.

After promising to expose Greyfriars Bobby's infamy further in a later chapter of his novel, Reid abruptly changes the subject to the history of Paisley under James IV.

Chapter 24 of *Gabrielle Stuart* has the title 'A Couple of Scotch Hoaxes', and quotes the lines by Crabbe used as an epigraph to this chapter. It was indeed remarkable, Reid mused, how a silly hoax could be twisted into a solemnly believed reality. An example was the tale of an ugly, dark-yellow mongrel dog which, around twenty years before, had been a familiar sight around the south end of George IV Bridge in Edinburgh. One day, that half-starved street dog had been run over by a passing vehicle near Greyfriars churchyard, Fortunately, the accident had been witnessed by the kind, dog-loving gravedigger, who took care of the mongrel. He put it underneath one of the table-stones and fed it well. When the dog had recovered, it remained at Greyfriars, where it had been so very well treated.

The mongrel was also befriended by a neighbouring publican and a close-by restaurateur, who named him 'Bobby'. A well known Sergeant of the Engineers, who saw that Bobby was old and not very strong, tried to entice the dog to stay indoors, but Bobby preferred to remain in the churchyard. Here he would have ended his days in a quiet, respectable manner, had not two jolly young journalists come past Greyfriars one evening. One of them, the Edinburgh correspondent of the *Inverness Advertiser*, had difficulties to find anything interesting to write about that particular week. The other journalist (probably Reid himself) pointed out the little dog in the cemetery, and said that here was a story, right in front of him; surely, this faithful dog was keeping vigil on its master's grave!

The journalist went to work, inventing the story of the faithful dog following a funeral cortege from the countryside, and resting on its master's grave for many months, only leaving the kirkyard to beg some food at the nearby eating-house.[6] This surely was one of the most interesting instances of canine affection, he exclaimed, and it was a great pity that the name of the dog's owner could not be found out, although the journalist claimed to have made every inquiry. This tale duly appeared in the *Inverness Advertiser*, and was copied in some other Scottish provincial papers, but did not reach Edinburgh, perhaps because the journalists there thought that the yarn that the identity of the dog's master could not be discovered was rather drawing on public credulity. After all, dead people were not usually consigned to the earth, particularly in a crowded graveyard like Greyfriars, without something being known about them when alive.

As several years went by, the yarn of the dog in Greyfriars kirkyard once or twice cropped up in the newspapers, but still, few knew of its existence. Then all of a sudden, in April 1867, the dog reappeared in a blaze of publicity, with the newspapers gushing columns about the faithful dog, and the sentimental Lord Provost publicly investing Bobby with a collar and chain. Enigmatically, Reid wrote that the old mongrel dog was soon 'honoured to death', but he was instead 'transformed into the similitude of a pure Skye terrier'. Thanks to the generosity of the Baroness Burdett-Coutts, this celebrated dog got his drinking fountain, where the bronze Bobby could still be seen, 'presiding over the public participation of the cup that neither cheers nor inebriates'. The English were wrong to claim that the Scotchman was a hard-headed, incredulous being, Reid exclaimed: here we have a yarn of canine fidelity that entirely lacked substance, being magnified into a city monument, and a famous story to be told to generations yet unborn!

Thomas Wilson Reid would not have long to rejoice that he had settled his old score with Greyfriars Bobby. He died in September 1884, aged just fifty-one, leaving his large family in straitened circumstances. If they had to subsist on the sales of Reid's books, they would face hard times indeed: apart from *Ye Olde Cheshire Cheese*, the books barely sold at all, and *Gabrielle Stuart* is today very scarce indeed.

The second missile to strike Greyfriars Bobby's statue was hurled by John Colquhoun, a well-known writer on Scottish field sports. Colquhoun had started out as an officer, before becoming a lawyer; his great passion was hunting and fishing, however, and he wrote several books on these topics. The son of a baronet, he was a member of the Clan Colquhoun, and his collection of stuffed birds is still kept at Rossdhu House, the home of the chiefs of that clan.

In a chapter on the instincts of dogs in his 1884 book *The Moor and the Loch*, John Colquhoun attacked the tale of Greyfriars Bobby.[7] The moment he had read the story of this faithful dog in a daily paper back in 1867, he had exclaimed, 'This is too richly spiced!' Annoyed that letter after letter was published in the Edinburgh newspapers, each more touching and pathetic than its predecessor, and that no person was willing to investigate this remarkable dog 'so endowed with human intelligence and feeling', Colquhoun went to Greyfriars to see Bobby for himself.

Colquhoun searched the cemetery but found no dog keeping vigil at its master's tomb. When he questioned James Brown, the latter said that Bobby was often at Greyfriars, but that this particular day, the little dog seemed to have business elsewhere. When asked about the newspaper stories about Bobby, James Brown said there was no truth in the statement that Bobby was some pitiful waif of a dog; he was well fed at an eating-house nearby, and quite a local celebrity. Bobby was fat and happy when making his rounds of the neighbourhood, and certainly no object of pity. On his way back home, Colquhoun called at the *Scotsman* office to complain about the paper's patronisation of the sentimental story of Greyfriars Bobby, but although he was convinced he had been able to kill off the story, the Edinburgh journalists would keep milking it for many decades to come.

John Colquhoun ended his demolition of the Greyfriars Bobby legend by recounting a more recent visit to Greyfriars. When he met the sexton Mr Thomson, James Brown's successor, Colquhoun asked him, 'Do you remember Greyfriars Bobby?' The dour Scot answered him curtly, 'It was a black lee [lie], frae end to end!'

In 1885, a reader of *Animal World* magazine went to Edinburgh to see the monument to Greyfriars Bobby. He also tried to find the grave of 'the poor man' and Bobby's own final resting place, but could find no trace of either of them.[8] He called on the care-keeper of the graveyard, who told him that although a sum of money had been subscribed to in London, to mark the spot of the poor man and his most noble dog's last resting places, the money had never been sent. The visitor wrote a letter to the editor of *Animal World*, urging him to investigate this matter, since 'there certainly ought to be a stone to mark the place for such noble constancy'. The editor contacted Mr Andrew Cuthbert, an inspector of the Scottish SPCA, who visited Mr Traill at Greyfriars Place. Traill advised him to call on Mr Thomson the Greyfriars sexton, who told him that he knew that something was being done in London, and that he would be pleased to prepare the stone. He knew of no collection in Edinburgh. The editor of *Animal World* urged his readers to support this subscription, since it was desirable to mark the resting place of both dog and master.

This subscription to erect a monument to Greyfriars Bobby and his nameless master was superintended by Mr and Mrs Slatter, of Tunbridge Wells.[9] For several years, the Slatters had kept collecting pennies from the local children in order to perpetuate the memory of the most faithful dog of the world. Each year, many hundreds of children subscribed their pennies, and soon there was enough money to erect a fine grave monument to Greyfriars Bobby, in Sicilian marble, with the inscription:

A CHILDREN'S MEMORIAL TO GREYFRIARS BOBBY
In memory of Greyfriars Bobby,
Who for fourteen years would have no home
But on the grave of his beloved master
Until Death relieved the faithful sentinel
On January 4th, 1872.

There was need to obtain a formal permission from Edinburgh Town Council before the second monument to Greyfriars Bobby could be erected. Mr Archibald Langwill, C.A., the secretary and treasurer to the Scottish SPCA, wrote to the Town Council, and this letter was read at the meeting of 5 February 1889. Councillor James B. Gillies stood up, saying that he hoped this proposal would not go before the committee without some statement. Councillor Gillies knew for a fact that the story of Greyfriars Bobby was nothing but a penny-a-liner's romance. There was no truth in the story, and Bobby had no 'beloved master' at all. Greyfriars Bobby had been a very respectable dog, but he was just a stray mongrel of the High Street

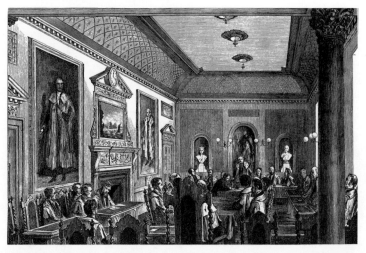

38. Edinburgh Town Council Chamber; from the six-volume edition of James Grant's *Old and New Edinburgh*, volume 2.

breed, who had just enough sense to take cover against the elements under one of the great table-stones at Greyfriars. A neighbouring restaurateur had kept Bobby well with scraps, and the little dog was kept in tolerably good quarters. It was not the fault of the dog, but of various busybodies and credulous fools, that the story of Bobby's alleged faithful mourning had been blown out of all proportion.

There had been enough fuss about this dog, Councillor Gillies continued. There was already one monument to Greyfriars Bobby, just outside the churchyard, and if people did not think that enough to hand down the myth, they could put up another one elsewhere. They should not be allowed to erect a monument in Greyfriars churchyard, however. A historic churchyard, with its famous Martyrs Monument and Covenanter's Prison, was no place for a monument to a dog, and he urged the council to give no countenance to such a proposal. The other councillors present agreed, one of them suggesting that it should be pointed out to the Slatters that they ought to spend the money, collected in such an arduous manner, on some more laudable object. Accordingly, the following decision was entered into the Town Council minutes:

> There was presented:–
> Letter from Mr Archibald Langwill, C.A., asking permission to erect a monument to 'Greyfriars' Bobby' in Greyfriars Burying Ground.
> The Magistrates and Council declined to grant the permission asked.[10]

The attacks on Greyfriars Bobby from Reid and Colquhoun had occurred in quite obscure publications, but Councillor Gillies' assault on Edinburgh's dog saint was reviewed, with surprise and outrage, in the leading Scottish and London newspapers.[11] The Edinburgh friends of Greyfriars Bobby of course closed ranks to defend the Candlemaker Row dog monument. Retaining its pro-Bobby attitude from 1867, the *Scotsman* newspaper was first to counter-attack. Armed with a copy of Councillor Gillies' speech, one of its journalists went round to visit various people who were likely to have personal knowledge of Bobby's life and career.

The *Scotsman* journalist visited Mr Traill and Gourlay Steell, who both verified the original story from 1867. Mr Traill could well recall the Burgh Court proceedings, saying that since he had only fed Bobby through his back window, the case against him had been dismissed. When interviewed, Alexander Macpherson, now chief city officer, remembered conveying Bobby to the house of the Lord Provost, for Mrs Chambers to see the little dog. Mr Hay, of the National Security Savings bank, remembered visiting Bobby on the grave, with Angela Burdett-Coutts. Many people who had met Greyfriars Bobby could attest that he had been nothing like a 'mongrel of the High Street breed', but a handsome Scotch terrier.[12] The very same day, Robert Scott Riddell, the Greyfriars organist, independently wrote to the *Scotsman* to point out that he had many times seen and spoken to Greyfriars Bobby: 'The story is no myth, the dog was no mongrel, being a fair specimen of the Scotch terrier, and the monument at the end of George IV Bridge is a very fair likeness.'[13]

The unrepentant Councillor Gillies also wrote to the *Scotsman*, to point out that the evidence collected by the paper's journalist did not provide any authentication for the story of Greyfriars Bobby. There was no question that the dog had existed, and that it had resided at Greyfriars for some considerable period of time, but no evidence had been presented to prove that Bobby had followed the remains of his master to the grave, or indeed that the dog had had a master at all. Surely, if 'poor old Gray' had been Bobby's master, some person would have known about him. Indeed,

> no relative or acquaintance of Gray or of anyone else buried in Greyfriars' churchyard was ever found to say that he knew anything of the dog or its ownership, and the story in this essential part rests, therefore, upon the fact that 'Bobby', having no home so far as was known, selected quarters in the churchyard, where he had both shelter and food, and was better off than many others of his brethren in the same humble ranks of canine life.

Councillor Gillies had received several letters from various anti-Bobby campaigners, he claimed, one of which was printed in full by the *Scotsman*:

> James B. Gillies, Esq.
> Dear Sir, – I read with satisfaction your speech about Greyfriars' Bobby. It is neatly and truly described, and I at once adopted every word of it. At that time I was a member of Greyfriars, and saw Bobby often, and when the story appeared I investigated it and found it altogether a sensation myth. – Yours truly, James Stillie.[14]

At the *Edinburgh Evening Dispatch*, another pro-Bobby newspaper, swords also flew from their scabbards in the dog saint's defence. Their journalists went one better and actually found the Burgh Court records from 1867, as quoted earlier in this book, with the evidence from Mr Traill, James Brown and others. It was considered particularly blameworthy that Baillie William Skinner, who had been at the Bench of the Burgh Court back in 1867, had also been present at Councillor Gillies' speech, holding the position of Town Clerk; yet he had not uttered a single word in Bobby's defence! It was shameful indeed, the *Edinburgh Evening Dispatch* journalist continued, that not a single councillor present had had 'patriotic sentiment or spirit enough to raise a word of protest: they were all like dumb dogs!' It would not surprise him in the slightest if, at the next town council meeting, an attempt would be made to prove that Wallace and Bruce were mythical personalities. But the romance of Greyfriars Bobby was no myth! Wilson MacLaren, the aforementioned friend of Greyfriars Bobby, who had fed the little dog as a schoolboy back in 1871, appended a suitable poem:

> Whaur is the dowg that bears a name,
> That winna hing his head wi' shame?
> Since that bauld billie in the Chaumer –
> Wi'meikle o' an auld wife's yammer,
> Has ta'en the task upon himsel'
> To break the sweet romantic spell;
> To delve in history o' the past,
> And now proclaim to east and wast,
> To north and south, that Greyfriars' Bobby
> Is just a myth – a hearsay hobby;
> In fact to give a dowg a bad name
> Wha only what is truthful wad claim.[15]

Interestingly, the *Edinburgh Evening Dispatch* journalist pointed out that back in 1867, Councillor Gillies had been a journalist at the now defunct Edinburgh *Daily Review*, a newspaper that was always very critical of its more successful rival the *Scotsman*. When the virtues of Greyfriars Bobby were extolled in the *Scotsman*, the *Daily Review* of course had to go the other way. At the 'Hole in the Wa'' tavern, three *Daily Review* journalists met to concoct a scoffing newspaper story on Bobby: a Mr Manson, a Mr (Thomas Wilson) Reid, and a third, unnamed member of the *Daily Review* staff (Councillor Gillies?).[16]

The *Weekly Scotsman* newspaper tried a more conciliatory approach. Whereas the newspaper accepted the *Edinburgh Evening Dispatch* journalist's version of events that Greyfriars Bobby was no myth, it still found it unsuitable, for religious reasons, that the sacred memories of Greyfriars were defiled by a monument to a mere dog.[17] Greyfriars Bobby's friends at the *Animal World* were of course outraged at Councillor Gillies' attack on their favourite dog:

An unworthy, and we may say a dastardly, attempt has recently been made to play havoc with the pathetic story of a dog – a story, now classical, which has engendered sweet sympathy towards the canine race in the breasts of thousands of young people during the last thirty years. As a poem merely, the story of Grey Friars Bobby was a gem worth preserving for 'a thing of beauty is a joy for ever', and even if it be thought legendary, as contended, we are astonished that an Edinburgh Town Councillor could be iconoclast enough in this era of religious humanity to make a malicious, ruthless onslaught on it.[18]

The story of Greyfriars Bobby was not legendary, the *Animal World* exclaimed, and good evidence had been presented by the *Edinburgh Evening Dispatch* to prove the contrary. Councillor Gillies would have to find solid evidence to contradict James Brown's words before the Burgh Court, that Bobby had been present at the funeral of 'poor old Gray'. Bobby had not been buried in consecrated ground, but in the flower-plot by the great window of Greyfriars church. Still, the people of Edinburgh should ignore Councillor Gillies and feel proud of their canine saint:

Here is a tomb that contains the bodies of martyrs faithful to their convictions. Under this monument lie covenanters who fought and bled for the liberty of conscience. Here is buried a poor dog who kept vigil on his master's tomb for fourteen long years. Each loved a master, and each remained faithful to him even unto death!

The Greyfriars Bobby monument, which was called 'Bobby's Well' by the locals, was very popular indeed, and served to quench the thirst of both men and beasts. Still, it was a shame that Bobby's grave would have no marker, thanks to that miserable scoffer Councillor Gillies:

The Corporation of Edinburgh might refuse to grant the application of several hundred children giving their penny offerings for a stone for the grave of this noble dog in Greyfriars Churchyard, but what amount of scoffing can obliterate Bobby's life and efface the beauty of his story? They are already written in the hearts of thousands of admirers, and recorded in the history of Greyfriars Churchyard.

Indeed, Bobby 'raises Scotch dogs in particular to a higher place in the esteem of reflecting persons, and bequeaths to future generations of mankind a touching moral lesson. Why does Councillor Gillies call him a mongrel? Is not virtue more virtuous when found in a peasant than in a duke? Fie! Councillor Gillies!'

Councillor Gillies did not ignore this angry tirade against him. In fact, he and his henchmen had quietly been gathering evidence, to strike the Candlemaker Row dog monument a glancing counterblow in the anti-Bobby *Edinburgh Evening News*. Although there was no doubt that Greyfriars Bobby had really existed, and that he had been a well-known dog in the district of Greyfriars, Councillor Gillies had

39. George Heriot's Hospital, from the south-west; was this impressive-looking old school the *alma mater* of Greyfriars Bobby? From the six-volume edition of James Grant's *Old and New Edinburgh*, volume 4.

found several witnesses whose testimony suggested that the tale of Bobby's faithful mourning on the grave was pure fabrication.[19]

The first witness was Peter Brown, for many years gardener at Heriot's Hospital. This grizzled veteran could well remember that many years ago, a mangy little stray dog had been in the habit of taking refuge in the hospital grounds. Brown more than once put the dog out through the wicket gate leading to the Vennel, a steep lane leading from the West Port to Lauriston Place, but since many people were using this gate, the dog always returned to Heriot's. In the end, the old gardener became exasperated with this canine invader of his grounds. He carried the dog across the grounds and put it into Greyfriars churchyard, thinking that his namesake and opposite number there might deal with it. Since the wicket gate between Greyfriars and Heriot's was seldom opened, the dog could not get back into the hospital grounds.

At Greyfriars, the ailing little dog was befriended by 'a gentleman' living at the head of Candlemaker Row (Robert Ritchie). He fed the dog and allowed it to sleep in his house at night. Bobby, as the dog was called, used to call at the house in the evening to gain entry, whereupon he was fed and allowed to sleep in the gentleman's bed. James Brown did not like Bobby much, and the headstrong little dog returned these sentiments in full. In fact, Peter Brown remarked that Bobby never seemed to like a working man, preferring people in 'gentle' clothing, something that of course spoke against him ever being a poor man's dog. For many years, Bobby slept in the gentleman's house at the head of Candlemaker Row, until his protector died. It was not until after the prosecution in the Burgh Court that James Brown began to care for the little dog, and to have him photographed. Peter Brown suspected that James Brown's story of Bobby following a funeral procession was intended to prove that he was 'no man's dog' so that Bobby would evade the dog-tax. James Brown received a very good income from selling his pocket photographs of Bobby to the throng of visitors, many of whom also tipped him a sixpence to purchase food for the little dog. It was known to many people living near Greyfriars that there was no truth in the story of Bobby's faithful mourning, but since so many people had been gulled into believing this very fine story, it was in their own interest not to divulge the truth.

Councillor Gillies' second witness was a certain Mrs Watson, who had lived in the house at the head of Candlemaker Row for about fifty years. She agreed with Peter Brown that Bobby often visited their tenement, and that he slept there at night. Her husband liked Bobby, and the little dog was often in his workshop in Bristo. The story of Bobby keeping vigil at a certain grave was completely untrue: the little dog went all over the district, as it pleased him. She had more than once told James Brown that he was an old rascal for keeping the story going, and earning money from the dog although he knew the story about his devotion was a falsehood. In the end, Bobby got cancer of the jaw, and since the Watsons were fearful their own dog would be affected (the old wife's tale of cancer being transmitted by contagion was still current at this time), they kept Bobby out of the house. Not long after, a girl serving nearby (with Mr Traill) told Mrs Watson that Bobby had died in her master's premises.

The third witness was a lady who had lived for thirteen years in the same stairs as Mrs Watson, but who did not want her name to become known. She said that her father (the same 'gentleman' mentioned by Peter Brown, thus Robert Ritchie, whose daughter Maria also lived at No. 28 Candlemaker Row) had been the first to take notice of Bobby, and that he had taken care of the little dog for many years. The dog's back had been sore when he came, and her father had done what he could to cure it. A lodger in their house (Sergeant Scott) had also taken an interest in Bobby, although he no longer lived nearby. After he had become famous, Bobby was taken away to an artist's (Gourlay Steell) house. James Brown had been 'in a state' about him, and as soon he was returned, the little dog was photographed for the cabinet cards that Brown used to sell. Maria Ritchie had left Candlemaker Row before Bobby died.

The fourth witness, Mr A. J. Baillie of No. 11 Hanover Street, thought Greyfriars Bobby a very crafty dog, who knew where to get a good dinner, and exactly what time to go for it. Since Bobby had been the only Edinburgh dog to legally avoid the dog-tax, he was not unworthy of his monument. Unlike the previous witnesses, Mr Baillie thought Bobby a bad-tempered, snappish little dog, and hardly a friend of humankind. He had once heard Peter Brown tell the story of how Bobby first got into Greyfriars, in exactly the same manner as quoted above from Brown's own testimony.

Above: 40. George Heriot's Hospital from the castle, from the six-volume edition of James Grant's *Old and New Edinburgh*, volume 4.

Left: 41. Some further interiors from George Heriot's Hospital, from the six-volume edition of James Grant's *Old and New Edinburgh*, volume 4.

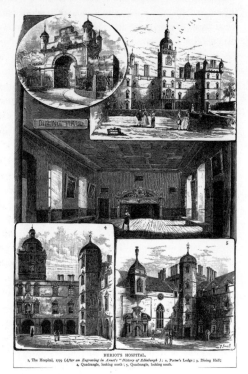

HERIOT'S HOSPITAL.
1, The Hospital, 1779 (*After an Engraving in Arnot's " History of Edinburgh "*); 2, Porter's Lodge; 3, Dining Hall; 4, Quadrangle, looking north ; 5, Quadrangle, looking south.

Finally, the *Edinburgh Evening News* journalist quoted John Colquhoun's *The Moor and the Loch*, and also the conclusions of an anti-Bobby correspondent to the *Ayrshire Post*:

> It is a pathetic little tale – the dead man, the affectionate dog stretched upon the grave, the futile attempts to coax it away, and all the rest of it. The only unfortunate thing about it is that the story is untrue. It was the device of a journalist, fond of a joke, who clothed a mangey cur that was wont to sleep in Greyfriars' Churchyard, in romance, and who, till the day of his death, never ceased to chuckle over the success of his invention. We have heard him tell the story many a time. In the circumstances the Town Council did wisely when they declined the offer of the monument.[20]

A letter to the *Scotsman* also quoted this article, adding that William Robertson, the editor of the *Post*, had been connected with the Edinburgh press at the relevant time to be 'in the know' about the mystery surrounding Greyfriars Bobby.[21]

Peter Brown's version that Greyfriars Bobby had his origins at Heriot's Hospital receives unexpected support from a quaint Scottish book discovered by George Robinson: Jamieson Baillie's *Walter Crighton, or Reminiscences of George Heriot's Hospital*. Walter and Ross, two naughty Heriot's schoolboys, make plan for an expedition to steal pears from an old woman's garden, when they hear a yelping and barking outside:

> 'What's that?' asked Ross; 'it's like a dug.'
>
> Going over to the pend gate, which was shut and locked, they listened.
>
> 'A ken what it is,' said Walter, 'it's a wee terrier that I've seen auld Peter, the gardener, chasing about fur this day or twa; whenever it's put out aye wants in again. He put it into the Vennel twice yesterday, but as soon as the wicket's opened, it just bolts in again. It's an ill-natured little beggar. I was gaun to clap it the ither day when it turned around and showed its teeth – just like yin o' yon monkeys in the menagerie, when we gien them the nit-shells fu' o' soap and cayenne pepper.'
>
> They chuckled quietly to themselves at the reminiscence, and made their way up to the ward.

Later, when Walter and Ross take a walk in the Hospital grounds, they meet Peter Brown. He is walking towards the gate to Greyfriars kirkyard, with the angry little terrier under his arm. When they ask him what he is about, he answers: 'I've tried ower and ower again to put it out by the Vennel door, but it'll no gang, so I'm just gaun to try it at the ither side, and see if that'll dae ony guid.' The boys walk along with him to the strong iron wicket, which Peter opened, pitching the little dog into the kirkyard. Here, the terrier took up his abode, and apparently 'took a notion to auld Brown the sexton for a maister, and no being extra partickler for a draft o' wind as long as it was sheltered frae the wet, lay under yin o' the table tombstanes'. Through time it found its way into Traill's coffee house, where the workmen used to feed it with scraps, and strange to say it soon learned to know the one o'clock gun. 'Walter was not sure, but he thought old Brown called it "Bobby". However, it's dead now, and has a monument.'[22]

In 1891, the barrage against Greyfriars Bobby continued, this time from a traitor within the ranks of the animal protection movement. When a certain B. Douglas wrote an article about 'Intuition and Instinct' for *The Animal's Guardian*, the monthly record of the London Anti-Vivisection Society, he discussed, in a sneering and sceptical manner, the tendency to anthropomorphise the actions of pet animals. He quoted the story of Greyfriars Bobby, supposed to be the real-life version of Landseer's *The Old Shepherd's Chief Mourner*, but did not believe in it at all.[23]

During Greyfriars Bobby's lifetime, a gentleman of Mr Douglas' acquaintance, who was a great lover of animals, had gone to Edinburgh to see this canine prodigy for himself. He had been much disappointed when no Bobby was to be found, on the grave or in the Greyfriars grounds. The sexton (Mr Thomson, James Brown's successor) had told him that the whole affair was 'a gooseberry story'. The dog was indeed often about the burial ground, but it came and went as it wanted to. Bobby had grown fat and sleek on the choice bits he had been fed at the eating-house opposite, and the sexton presumed that this reliable supply of good food was the main reason Bobby had remained at Greyfriars.

When Bobby eventually appeared, the dog-loving gentleman could see that 'he was in good case, quite cheery in going his rounds, and not in any sense an object for pity'. The sceptical Mr Douglas found Bobby's pathetic story of interest not as an example of canine fidelity, but as yet another remainder that 'the credulous public will gulp down any exaggeration by the mongers of the marvellous'.

7

Eleanor Atkinson's Novel about Greyfriars Bobby

I hear they say 'tis very lang,
  That years hae come and gane,
Sin' first they put my maister here,
  An' grate an' left him lane.

I could na, an' I did na gang,
  For a' they vexed me sair,
An' said sae bauld that they nor I
  Should ever see him mair.

Thus speaks Greyfriars Bobby himself, suitably in the Scots dialect, in a long poem written by a certain Mrs Boardman, and published in *Animal World*.[1] That valuable magazine remained a Victorian bulwark of wholesome Christianity and kindness to all creatures great and small, and a faithful supporter of Greyfriars Bobby. It must have pleased its editorial staff that the dog monument in Candlemaker Row withstood the attacks from Councillor Gillies and his cohorts without even being dented.

Wherever Scots emigrated, they brought the story of Greyfriars Bobby with them. In 1900, there was an approving feature on Bobby in *Chambers's Journal*, which was reprinted in many foreign newspapers, including the *New York Times*.[2] The same year, the Edinburgh dog saint was praised in *Our Animal's Friends*, the magazine of the American SPCA; this feature was also used in several American newspapers.[3] The Australians and New Zealanders were also fond of Greyfriars Bobby, and featured him in their newspapers more than once.[4] Two years later, a brief pamphlet on Greyfriars Bobby was written by a certain Henry Hutton, and published in Edinburgh for use as a guidebook for visitors to the dog monument, which is featured on the cover. Picture postcards of the Candlemaker Row dog monument were already published by the turn of the century; they made Greyfriars Bobby into one of the symbols of Edinburgh.[5] After the death of the Baroness Burdett-Coutts in December 1906, she was remembered by many Edinburgh friends, one of whom ordered a wreath to be put on the Greyfriars Bobby monument.[6]

In 1911, the little dog was featured in *TP's Magazine*, and later in the *London Chronicle*.[7] Councillor Gillies and the remainder of his fellow rationalists must have ground their teeth when they perceived that their efforts to end Greyfriars Bobby's career had failed dismally. And in 1912, things would get much worse for the remainder of those Caledonian iconoclasts.

> I ken he's near me a' the while,
>   An' I will see him yet;
> For a' my life he tended me,
>   An' noo he'll not forget.

> Some blithsome day I'll hear his step,
>   There'll me nae kindred near;
> For a' they grat that gaed awa', –
>   But he shall find *me* here.

Eleanor Stackhouse was born in 1863, in Rensselaer, north-western Indiana. Her family was middle-class: her father a Philadelphia Quaker and her mother a Connecticut 'colonial'. The mother in particular had a positive influence on young Eleanor, reading Tennyson and Burns to her, and inspiring an enduring fondness of poetry and literature. Eleanor soon became a voracious reader of both fiction and non-fiction. After studies at the Indianapolis Normal School, she became a schoolmistress. Being a somewhat adventurous young woman, she soon tired of this occupation, and decided to seek pastures new, becoming a journalist at the *Chicago Tribune* in 1888.[8]

Using the pen name Nora Marks, Eleanor became an investigative reporter. She took various undercover jobs to see how the poor people of Chicago fared, posing as a dining-room waitress, a workwoman in the stockyards, and even a beggar woman seeking refuge in a hostel. In the first of these roles, she was pleased that her fears of being roughly treated by the rowdy male clientele did not materialise; in the second, she rightly predicted that such monotonous, low-paid jobs would soon be taken over by machinery; in the third, she gave a graphic description of the cockroaches infesting the hostel bathroom.

A talented writer, 'Nora' described her adventures with gusto. Her column appears to have been a popular one, and she would remain with the *Chicago Tribune* for several years to come. During this period, her undercover stunts became increasingly risqué: she infiltrated the Salvation Army, investigated baby-farming scams, and visited a 'divorce shark' to seek a divorce from a non-existent husband. She even investigated a Chicago 'white slavery' scare, without ending up in a box addressed to 'Sheik Adbul, The Harem, Araby'; the white slavers, if there were any to start with, behaved themselves with decorum and did not even make 'Nora' any indecent suggestions.

The adventurous journalistic career of Eleanor Stackhouse ended in 1891 when she married the Chicago editor and educationalist Francis Blake Atkinson. Together, they published *The Little Chronicle*, a weekly newspaper for children, to which Eleanor supplied serial stories. The paper may well have run into financial dire straits, and it was eventually sold. The Atkinsons were instead employed by a company issuing juvenile encyclopaedias. In 1903, Eleanor Atkinson published her first novel, *Mamzelle Fifine*, about the Martinique youth of the future Empress Josephine of France. All her other novels would be structured in the same manner: she would find some appealing historical incident, and present it in a manner appealing to juvenile readers. Issued by small-time American publishers, Eleanor Atkinson's early novels are (often deservedly) quite scarce today.

> Is time sae lang? – I dinna mind;
>   It's cauld? – I canna feel;
> He's near me, and he'll come to me,
>   And sae 'tis very weel.
>
> I thank ye a' that are sae kind,
>   An feed an' mak me braw;
> Ye're unco gude but ye're no *him* –
>   Ye'll no wile me awa.

When interviewed much later in life, Eleanor Atkinson would say that although she had written many novels, the only two that had been premeditated and properly prepared had been *Greyfriars Bobby* and *Johnny Appleseed*. The latter book, an insipid account of the eccentric Ohio nurseryman John Chapman, known for his great fondness for growing apples, need not concern us further, but the classic *Greyfriars Bobby* remains Eleanor Atkinson's only literary claim to fame.

With *Greyfriars Bobby*, Eleanor Atkinson was able to leave behind the small-time firms that had published some of her early works; the book was accepted by prestigious Harper & Brothers, of New York. On 13 February 1912, they published a relatively large first edition, bound in blue cloth. There appear to be two different versions of the first edition, without either having an indication which is the first printing. One of them features Bobby's head on the front board, with what looks very much like a golden halo behind his head, and the title in gold; the other has no image on the front board, but instead a frontispiece depicting Bobby and a couple of rustic-looking Scots by the fireside, and the text: 'Gie 'im a penny plate o' the gude broo.' With true Yankee ingenuity, Harper & Brothers thought of a clever publicity stunt to increase the book's circulation. Each copy of the first edition included a postcard with a photograph of a shaggy little Skye terrier, and a red one-cent McKinley stamp, to be sent to a friend of the reader, touting the book. 'Did you like Bobby? If so, maybe you would care to sign and send the attached postal card to one of your friends who also loves "wee bit doggies?"'

Eleanor Atkinson's *Greyfriars Bobby* begins at Cauldbrae Farm in 1858. Although nominally the pet dog of the farmer's daughter Elsie, the little Skye terrier Bobby considers rustic farm labourer Auld Jock his proper master. Jock is a pathetic figure:

42. 'Gie 'im a penny plate o' the gude broo' – the frontispiece of the 1912 first edition of Eleanor Atkinson's *Greyfriars Bobby*.

a grizzled, gnarled little man possessing neither wit of mind not skill of hand, and worn out by fifty winters of herding sheep on the bleak hills of Midlothian. It is in the Atkinson novel that 'the poor man Gray' finally gets a first name: John or 'Jock'; it is likely to be derived from her imagination rather than genealogical research. Still, he is the only person that Bobby cares for, and after the old man loses his job at the farm and goes to Edinburgh, the little dog leaps out of the kitchen window and runs after the carriage. When Bobby reaches Edinburgh, he goes into Mr Traill's restaurant, Ye Olde Greyfriars Dining-rooms, at the sound of the one o'clock gun, just like Jock had taught him to do, and he is later reunited with his master. When Mr Traill sees that Jock is very unwell, feverish and shaking so much he can hardly hold his spoon, he kindly offers to call a doctor, but the rustic and superstitious old shepherd refuses. When the ailing Auld Jock wants to get a room at his usual lodging-house, he hides Bobby in a bag since no dogs are allowed.

The following morning, the landlady finds Auld Jock's dead body, and he is buried at Greyfriars. Bobby follows the funeral procession, and later keeps vigil on the grave. James Brown is in a bother to keep Bobby out of Greyfriars, but the little dog is equally determined to keep vigil on Jock's tomb. Greyfriars Bobby is supported by the stalwart Mr Traill, who feeds the little dog every day, after the one o'clock gun has been fired. But when the farmer from Cauldbrae comes to see Mr

43. Greyfriars Bobby gives
Auld Jock a hand with the
sheepherding – an illustration
by Marguerite Kirmse to
the 1929 edition of Eleanor
Atkinson's *Greyfriars Bobby*.

Traill, he takes Bobby with him to the farm. The little dog digs his way out of the Cauldbrae stables, however, and runs back to Edinburgh, arriving at Auld Jock's grave very tired and footsore.

The next day, James Brown is very much perturbed when he sees Greyfriars Bobby ratting in the churchyard, since Traill had promised him the dog would be sent away. But Mrs Brown likes Bobby and gives the little dog a bath, persuading her dour husband to let him stay. Dr Lee, minister of Old Greyfriars, allows Bobby to stay in the kirkyard unrestricted, even on the Sabbath. When Sergeant Scott comes to dine at Ye Olde Greyfriars Dining-rooms, he wants to purchase Bobby and take him to Edinburgh Castle, but Mr Traill refuses to sell the little dog. The local children become very fond of Bobby, and play with him in the cemetery.

When Mr Traill is prosecuted for harbouring an unlicensed dog, the Edinburgh slum children start collecting pennies in the neighbourhood. After the children come into the Burgh Court with their pennies, the Lord Provost gives Bobby his collar, and the Freedom of the City. Angela Burdett-Coutts, referred to as 'The Grand Leddy', comes to Edinburgh to see Greyfriars Bobby, and to provide him with his monument. Although Bobby is now an old dog, he is still healthy and vigorous. When the Grand Leddy suggests that he should come with her to Holyrood House to see the Queen, the little dog seems quite enthusiastic. The book ends with all the children wishing Bobby a good night.

44. Bobby on his way back to Greyfriars, an illustration by Marguerite Kirmse to the 1929 edition of Eleanor Atkinson's *Greyfriars Bobby*.

I'll bide an' hope! Do ye the same;
 For ance I heard that ye
Had aye a Master that ye loo'd
 An' yet ye might na' see.

A Master, too, that car'd for ye
 (O, sure ye winna flee!)
That's wearying to see ye noo –
 Ye'll no be waur than me?

The Harper & Brothers first edition of Eleanor Atkinson's *Greyfriars Bobby* sold quite well; it can still be purchased, from antiquarian booksellers, for a reasonable price. Unlike Eleanor Atkinson's previous books, it was widely and enthusiastically reviewed. The *New York Times* reviewer liked its quaint humour, and thought it told its simple story with consummate skill, including the sentimental ending. Almost prophetically, the review ended with the words, 'Whether it is going to be a classic or a near-classic does not concern us. It is enough to know that the book is good, very good, and that its readers will appreciate it.'[9]

There were respectful reviews also in the *Boston Daily Globe*, the *Baltimore Sun* and the *New York Sun*.[10] The reviewer in the *Bulletin* of the American SPCA exclaimed that 'Except *Rab and His Friends* and *Black Beauty*, I know of no story of dog or horse comparable to *Greyfriars Bobby!*' This endorsement was used by Harper & Brothers in their advertisements for the book. In another newspaper advertisement, *Greyfriars Bobby* took precedence over all other Harper & Brothers books, including Theodore Dreiser's *Sister Carrie*.[11] According to a newspaper article, Eleanor Atkinson, the famous author of *Greyfriars Bobby*, had received letters from almost every state offering to sell her Skye terriers of every shape and shade. In spite of her deep affection for the memory of the original Bobby, she felt disinclined to establish a large kennel of 'wee bit doggies' in his honour, however.[12] When, in 1913, she took a well-deserved holiday, this was reported in the press: 'Eleanor Atkinson, whose story of the wee Scotch doggie, Greyfriars Bobby, is being endorsed by numerous humanitarian societies, is spending her summer on the shores of Grand Traverse Bay, Michigan.'[13]

With such excellent publicity, and the support of many charities, humanitarian leagues and Sunday schools, Eleanor Atkinson's *Greyfriars Bobby* could not fail to sell. Later in 1912, a cheaper edition was issued by A. L. Burt & Co., of New York, using lower-quality paper and dispensing with the frontispiece. The A. L. Burt dust jacket had the text, 'The story of Greyfriars Bobby—so beloved that the tenement dwellers kept their windows washed that they might see his frolics!' After being out of print for some years after the First World War, *Greyfriars Bobby* was reissued by Harper & Brothers in 1929. This was quite a handsome edition, with four full-page plates, and numerous vignettes in the text, by the artist Marguerite Kirmse.[14]

Eleanor Atkinson's *Greyfriars Bobby* was reissued by Harper & Row in 1940, with the Candlemaker Row dog monument featured on the dust jacket, and a cheaper edition, by Grosset & Dunlap, followed the same year. Neither of these used the Kirmse illustrations. Harper & Row printed yet another edition in 1947. In 1949, the first British edition of Eleanor Atkinson's *Greyfriars Bobby* was published, by Hamish Hamilton. In 1962, Penguin acquired the American rights to the book, and they have kept it in print ever since, with numerous reprintings, as a Puffin children's book. In addition, hardback editions of *Greyfriars Bobby* have been issued in 1991, by Buccaneer Books, and in 1996, as a Penguin Classic.

There have been several translations of Eleanor Atkinson's *Greyfriars Bobby*. Already in 1930, it was translated into Polish, as *Bobik od franziszkanów*. In 1980, a Danish translation was published as *Bobby*, and in 2001 and 2006, the Chinese got the opportunity to read it in two different versions. It is strange that there are no French, German or Spanish translations of this popular book.

It has been debated whether Eleanor Atkinson visited Edinburgh prior to writing *Greyfriars Bobby*. Reading the book, it is hard not to be impressed with her knowledge of the city, and the accuracy of her descriptions of the topography of various streets. In an autobiographical sketch published in *Twentieth Century Authors*, Eleanor Atkinson claimed that as a youngster, she

Above left: 45. Bobby sits on a cannon at Edinburgh Castle, an illustration by Marguerite Kirmse to the 1929 edition of Eleanor Atkinson's *Greyfriars Bobby*.

Above right: 46. Bobby chases a cemetery cat, an illustration by Marguerite Kirmse to the 1929 edition of Eleanor Atkinson's *Greyfriars Bobby*.

was exploring our own and other people's bookshelves, and finding whatever was there for me. And I was scribbling industriously on any topic that kindled the imagination. With that good start I should have gone faster and farther, and might reasonably have been expected to find literary material in my own experience. Instead, I went as far afield as Edinburgh, French Flanders, the Island of Martinique, and the Ohio wilderness of a century before.

This obtuse paragraph has been interpreted as indicating that Eleanor Atkinson had travelled far and wide to research her books.[15] Either she had been touring Scotland looking for inspiration, finding it at Edinburgh and Greyfriars, or she had purposely gone there after finding out about Greyfriars Bobby from some other source. Once, when asked by readers as to her source for the story of Bobby, she confidently pointed out the account in the *Scotsman* for 13 April 1867, adding that Bobby's collar was still to be seen at the caretaker's lodge at Greyfriars.[16]

The somewhat cryptic statement in *Twentieth Century Authors* may just as well be interpreted to mean that Eleanor Atkinson's *imagination* had travelled far and wide, however. After all, she contrasted her alleged 'travels' with 'her own experience', and to visit the Ohio of Johnny Appleseed's time would have required time-travelling abilities. Edinburgh local historian George Robinson suspects that the knowledge of Edinburgh history and topography demonstrated in Eleanor Atkinson's *Greyfriars Bobby* is the result of literary research rather than her own experiences. For example, her description of the Grassmarket belongs neither to her own time, nor that of Greyfriars Bobby, but to the eighteenth century. During Bobby's life it was a modern commercial centre with two banks and a brewery. Eleanor Atkinson puts the Book Hunter's Stall, a well-known Edinburgh second-hand bookshop, next to Mr Traill's restaurant, when it in fact was at the corner of Candlemaker Row and George IV Bridge. And if Eleanor Atkinson had seen the set-up for the one o'clock gun with her own eyes, she surely would have expanded on it. Mr Robinson finds it likely that Eleanor Atkinson had access to James Grant's *Old and New Edinburgh*, among other standard works on Edinburgh history, and that she made good use of these sources when writing her novel.

If it is assumed that Eleanor Atkinson made it to Edinburgh after all, her key written source on Greyfriars Bobby must surely have been Henry Hutton's short pamphlet, previously alluded to. If we go with the more likely version that this obscure and impecunious American literary lady, bogged down with literary and pedagogical hackwork, never had an opportunity to cross the Atlantic, then the question arises how she found out about Greyfriars Bobby in the first place? As we know, there were features on Edinburgh's dog saint in many American newspapers, from 1900 until 1911. It may well be that Eleanor Atkinson had read about Greyfriars Bobby in the *New York Times* or *Our Animal Friends* already in 1900, and that as a part-time author, she had taken quite a few years to research her novel. Her reference to the dog-collar in the caretaker's lodge at Greyfriars may well have derived from one of these newspaper accounts, or from the Hutton pamphlet; she did not say that she had seen it there herself.

After the great success with *Greyfriars Bobby*, one would have expected that Eleanor Atkinson would have gone on to even greater things; after all, she possessed both talent and energy. But all her later novels were potboilers, and reviewers more than once contrasted their confused narratives to that of the bestselling *Greyfriars Bobby*. One of them bluntly pointed out that *Johnny Appleseed* 'was not nearly so good, however, as *Greyfriars Bobby*'.[17] Her later novels *Hearts Undaunted* and *Poilu, Dog of Roubaix* were hardly reviewed at all, in spite of the latter returning to the sentimental dog story theme that Eleanor Atkinson had shown she could master.

Probably annoyed at her career declining so dismally, Eleanor Atkinson put down her pen in 1918, for good. In 1924, her husband Francis Blake Atkinson, to whom she had once dedicated *Greyfriars Bobby*, was granted a divorce, claiming that she had become impossible to live with, due to her severe deafness and very short temper.[18] When the aforementioned reporter from *Twentieth Century Authors* visited Eleanor Atkinson in the late 1930s, the latter was living in comfortable retirement at Manhasset, Long Island. He wrote that although she had published nothing for more than two decades, she remained an intelligent, humanitarian woman in her late seventies. Eleanor Atkinson expired at Rockland State Hospital, Orangetown NY, in 1942.

8

Rebecca West v. Greyfriars Bobby

Of all the speechless friends of man
The faithful dog I deem
Deserving from the human clan
The tenderest esteem:

This feeling creature form'd to love
To watch, and to defend,
Was given to man by powers above,
A guardian, and a friend!

William Hayley's *Ballads,*
founded on Anecdotes relating to Animals (London 1805)

When Eleanor Atkinson's *Greyfriars Bobby* was briefly noticed in the *Scotsman* newspaper, it received short shrift from the local patriotic reviewer: it was just a semi-mythical story dressed out in detail and circumstance, and surely the American touches must grate on Scottish readers.[1] This criticism of their countrywoman did not deter a wealthy American couple, Mr and Mrs Howell Reed, of Boston, from visiting Edinburgh in 1914, after reading the *Greyfriars Bobby* novel. They saw Greyfriars and the drinking fountain, but were disappointed that Auld Jock had no headstone. They offered to erect one at their own expense, and this time the proposal was more congenially received by the town council.[2] Although Mr Reed died during the winter, his widow went through with the deal, and after another decade, a red granite gravestone was duly erected at Greyfriars in 1925, with the inscription:

John Gray,
Died 1858.
'Auld Jock,'
Master of
'Greyfriars Bobby.'
'And even in his ashes
most beloved.'
Erected by
American lovers of 'Bobby.'

47. John Gray's headstone, from the 1931 edition of
Henry Hutton's *The True Story of Greyfriars Bobby*.

The 1920s came and went, with the bronze Greyfriars Bobby looking enigmatically
at his friends from the Candlemaker Row dog monument. He was one of the
sights of Edinburgh, and the considerable sales of Eleanor Atkinson's novel meant
that there was a steady influx of American tourists keen to see him. The quaint
postcards depicting the Greyfriars Bobby monument enjoyed steady sales. In 1926,
a bold Edinburgh lady lecturing on 'Animals and a Future Life' proposed Greyfriars
Bobby as an example of a dog refusing to take any food after the death of its master.
Later the same year, a poetical newspaper writer extolling the historical memorials
of Greyfriars included a vision of a fierce little terrier dashing past him from under
a table-stone, chasing a cat – it was the ghost of Greyfriars Bobby![3]

In 1930, a journalist writing on the restoration scheme for Greyfriars mentioned
Bobby's long vigil on Auld Jock's tomb, presuming that the old shepherd's
conceptions of the next world may well have been as humble as Pope's 'Poor
Indian':

> He asks no angel's wing, no seraph's fire;
> But thinks, admitted to that equal sky,
> His faithful dog shall bear him company.[4]

The same year, Bobby was again featured in the *New York Times*, by a careless
woman who had probably never been near Edinburgh, since she alleged that
Bobby's statue 'in worn gray stone' was situated in the Grassmarket![5] In 1931, the

Above left: 48. The monument to Greyfriars Bobby, from a postcard marked '1925'. The lamp post is no longer there. Note the signs for the Book Hunter's Stall and John Grant's bookshop in the background.

Above right: 49. A postcard from the 1920s depicting the monument to Greyfriars Bobby, and the dog's collar.

Henry Hutton pamphlet was reissued in a new and improved edition, with several photographs. But later the same year, the Candlemaker Row dog monument would once more come under attack, from an unexpected assailant.

Cicely Isabel Fairfield was (and still is) much better known by her pen name Rebecca West. A prolific author who wrote in many genres, with considerable critical and commercial success, she was committed to feminist and liberal principles. Her books include *Black Lamb and Grey Falcon*, on the history and culture of Yugoslavia; *A Train of Powder*, her coverage of the Nuremberg trials; *The Meaning of Treason*, a study of the Second World War and Communist traitors; and *The Return of the Soldier*, a modernist First World War novel. Throughout her long and distinguished career, Rebecca West also maintained a considerable output of journalism and criticism. It was in her column in *Nash's Pall Mall Magazine* that her path would cross that of Edinburgh's canine saint, in November 1931.[6]

   Although not by any means a close student of dogs and their doings, Rebecca West decided to achieve what Thomas Wilson Reid, Councillor Gillies and their henchmen had failed to do forty years earlier: to finally crush the myth of Greyfriars

50. The monument to Greyfriars Bobby, from the
1931 edition of Henry Hutton's *The True Story of
Greyfriars Bobby*.

Bobby. In her article, she described how she had recently met an old Scottish
gentleman. Although well stricken in years and seemingly mild in temperament,
he gnashed his teeth with fury when she said that she had bought a book about
Greyfriars Bobby (the Atkinson novel, or perhaps the 1931 reissue of the Hutton
pamphlet?) 'Greyfriars Bobby! Greyfriars Bobby! I will tell you the truth about
Greyfriars Bobby!' the fierce old Scot exclaimed. He went on to tell Rebecca West
that back in 1876, when he had been a railway clerk in Edinburgh, he had known a
fellow clerk named Walter who was called 'Lying Wattie' for his untruthful ways.

One day, Wattie was employed to become the travel guide of a very wealthy lady
and her companion who were visiting Edinburgh. When Wattie returned from this
expedition, he had exclaimed, 'Och, it wasna ony fun. The women were fools.' He
went on to explain how they had taken little notice of the Castle, or Holyrood, only
to be fascinated with

an awful lie I told them about a dog that wouldn't leave its master's grave in
Greyfriars Churchyard, and lay there till it died. They were near crying over it. Did
you ever hear such nonsense? Even if a dog saw its master put in a coffin, which isn't
likely to happen, it would never be allowed to go to the funeral, so it would never
know which was its master's grave. I tell you the women were fools.

But two weeks later, the Edinburgh newspapers were full of the Baroness Burdett-
Coutts erecting a memorial to Greyfriars Bobby. A few people wrote to the papers

51. A picture postcard of the Greyfriars Bobby monument, by the celebrated North Berwick artist Reginald Phillimore.

to ask why they had never heard about this famous dog, but it was nobody's business to bother about it. Then some Americans put up another monument to Greyfriars Bobby not far away: 'Such a waste of good money! Two monuments that are just to our Lying Wattie!' Rebecca West ended her article with the resounding words, 'Thus is history made, and thus is the dog made a ham actor. You cannot blame it. It has no more chance of austere sincerity than, say, a little girl reared to be a child evangelist.'

The number of Edinburgh subscribers to *Nash's Pall Mall Magazine* is difficult to estimate, but there was at least one of them. Aghast at Rebecca West's attack on Edinburgh's dog saint, a certain 'G.C.' contacted the 'Weekly Club' of the *Weekly Scotsman*, asking for evidence for and against the existence of Greyfriars Bobby to be produced by the readers of this newspaper.[7] All over Scotland, and beyond, swords again flew from their scabbards in Bobby's defence. One letter-writer, who had lived in Edinburgh in 1872, could well remember all the fuss about this celebrated dog and his monument. Mrs Mary Dickson, Mr Traill's granddaughter, also wrote to support Greyfriars Bobby. Twenty years earlier, her grandmother Mrs Traill had given her a pewter bowl engraved with the words 'Greyfriars Bobby's Dinner Dish' and she had faithfully preserved this sacred relic of Edinburgh's dog saint ever since. Three other eyewitnesses of Greyfriars Bobby, Mr William Watson, now living in Co. Down, A. Watson, who had lived in Edinburgh as a young man, and the 80-year-old Mrs I. M. Martin, whose testimony has been quoted earlier

GREYFRIARS BOBBY, EDINBURGH
THE DOG WHICH WOULD NOT LEAVE HIS MASTER'S GRAVE
STATUE ERECTED BY THE BARONESS BURDETT COUTTS
SUTHERLAND

52. The monument to Greyfriars Bobby, a postcard showing the decline down Candlemaker Row.

in this book, could also vouch for the traditional story of Greyfriars Bobby being nothing but the truth.[8]

The pro-Bobby campaigners were answered by the instigator of the whole affair, an individual calling himself 'Miss Rebecca West's Informant'.[9] He boldly claimed that Mr Traill, the Edinburgh restaurateur who often gave scraps to hungry dogs, had always been of the opinion that the story of Greyfriars Bobby, which had duped the credulous Baroness Burdett-Coutts, and through her millions all over the world, was 'pure myth'. The instigator of the Greyfriars Bobby hoax, whose identity the Informant claimed to know, but did not divulge, had been dead for a third of a century. This hoaxer had instigated several other myths, 'some of which resulted in painful experiences to himself, and details of which fill columns of your paper'.

The Informant was answered by none less than John Traill Leitch, Mr Traill's grandson, who coolly pointed out that Greyfriars Bobby had certainly existed. The opinion proposed by another correspondent to the *Weekly Scotsman*, that Bobby had died on the grave, was wrong, since the dog had in fact died at the Traill house in Keir Street, nursed by John Traill Leitch's mother. John Traill Leitch had seen Rebecca West's original magazine article, but had paid no attention to it, 'as it seems quite a common thing for popular authors to pose as authorities on subjects of which they know very little'.[10]

Although nothing further was heard from Rebecca West herself in the Greyfriars Bobby debate, the bold Informant refused to give up. He wrote back to the *Weekly*

53. A postcard of the Greyfriars Bobby drinking fountain, from the 1940s. The Book Hunter's Stall is still in the background.

Scotsman, still professing his total disbelief in the mythical Greyfriars Bobby, although he conceded that Mr Traill might of course have befriended some stray masterless dog, which had been allowed to live in Greyfriars churchyard. If Greyfriars Bobby had been able to form such a strong affection for his master, he must have been at least four years old when he began his fourteen-year vigil in 1858; in spite of enduring hunger, cold and privations, he had thus lived to become 18 years old, a much more advanced age than the average dog could aspire to. 'Marvellous!' exclaimed the Informant, before appealing for 'photos, pedigrees and documents' to prove the existence of the mythical 1858 dog.[11] But either the readers of the *Weekly Scotsman* did not possess such material, or they were unwilling to share it with the obnoxious Informant; at any rate, the Greyfriars Bobby debate came to a temporary halt.

Probably aware of what a can of worms she and the Informant had opened through their unwise meddling in the Greyfriars Bobby affair, Rebecca West would stay well clear of Edinburgh's dog saint for the remainder of her long and productive literary career. But since many Edinburgh people were curious about the real or mythical Greyfriars Bobby, the debate refused to die.

In 1934, a London correspondent wrote to the *Scotsman*, asking whether Greyfriars Bobby belonged to myth or history. The writer had been

told – so many years ago that I have forgotten who was my informant – that the story was the work of a brilliant journalist who, having spent a convivial afternoon

54. Another postcard of the monument to
Greyfriars Bobby, from the 1940s or 1950s; note
that the drinking fountain is still operational.

and being called upon to justify his absence from duty produced the moving tale,
based merely on his having seen a small dog wandering in Greyfriars' Churchyard.

As a result of this appeal, many eyewitnesses wrote to the *Scotsman* to report their
meetings with Edinburgh's most famous dog. Among them were William Albert
Cunningham, Mrs Denholm, Andrew Hislop and Councillor Wilson McLaren,
as quoted earlier in this book. McLaren was particularly knowledgeable about
Greyfriars Bobby, whom he had often met and fed at Mr Traill's restaurant. He also
described Councillor Gillies' attack on Bobby back in 1889, and how he and other
Edinburgh Evening News journalists had come to the dog saint's relief.[12]

Another old Edinburgh resident, Mr R. T. Skinner, wrote to point out that thirty
years earlier, a friend of his, the Sessions' Clerk at one of the Greyfriars churches,
pointed at the centre of the triangular flower-plot between the Greyfriars gates and
the older church, and said that Greyfriars Bobby had been buried there.[13]

Thus, the outcome of the 1931–34 debate was, in the end, a positive one: Rebecca
West and her Informant were rebutted, and a wealth of eyewitness testimony on
Greyfriars Bobby collected for posterity. In 1936, Miss Mabel Gosling, of Beaumont
Paget, Bermuda, received permission from the Edinburgh Town Council to erect
a memorial to Auld Jock's dog Greyfriars Bobby on Jock's grave in Greyfriars
churchyard. No memorial was erected, however, possibly due to the outbreak of
the Second World War.[14]

9

Two Films about Greyfriars Bobby

Mid the rugged Scottish mountains
Lived a shepherd long ago
Tending sheep whate'er the weather
Whether wind, or rain, or snow.
He was tired, but never lonely
Though he roamed both far and wide,
For his doggie, faithful Bobby,
Never left the shepherd's side.

But the shepherd, growing older,
Suffered great infirmity;
All alone he fled to Edinburgh,
There to die in poverty.
But the faithful Bobby followed,
Only instinct was his guide
Till he found his ailing master;
Then he never left his side.

From the song 'Greyfriars Bobby'
by the Alexander Brothers, quoted by permission.

The earliest appearance of Greyfriars Bobby on the silver screen is a far from prepossessing one. In the 1940s, the American producer Val Lewton wanted to make a horror film based on Robert Louis Stevenson's short story *The Body Snatcher*. The 1945 film with the same title, directed by Robert Wise and starring none less than Boris Karloff as the grave-robbing murderer John Gray, is set in Edinburgh in 1831, three years after the Burke and Hare murders. The plot is that a student named Fettes is employed as the assistant of the surgeon MacFarlane, who has his own medical school, for which he needs a steady supply of fresh corpses. The bodies are supplied by the sinister Gray, but Fettes soon suspects that some of them are the remains of people whom the body-snatcher has murdered himself.

In one of the early scenes, Fettes sees a woman feeding a small terrier dog, sitting on the Jean Grant table-stone in Greyfriars churchyard. She tells him that the dog is named Bobby and that he is guarding her recently buried son's grave. In the night,

55. Stamps issued by the Scottish Philatelic Secretariat in January 1972 to commemorate the 100th anniversary of the death of Greyfriars Bobby. This is an uncommon stamp; see the article in *Greyfriars Bobby Magazine*, June–August 2006, 15.

John Gray enters Greyfriars and steals the young man's body. When Bobby tries to stop him, the grave-robber strikes the little dog with his shovel, killing him. The next morning, Fettes sees the woman running past him, holding the dead Bobby, and crying out that the body-snatcher has taken her son. The reader will be pleased to learn that John Gray does not have long to rejoice after this deplorable canicide. After he has added to his tally by killing MacFarlane's servant, he is himself murdered by the infuriated surgeon.

It is obvious that in his researches into Edinburgh history for *The Body Snatcher*, Val Lewton had come across the Greyfriars Bobby story, and decided to use it in his film, although it takes place many years before Bobby was even born. Nor can it be a coincidence that the film's villain shares his name with the purported master of the faithful dog.[1]

Greyfriars Bobby exacts his revenge for being flattened by Boris Karloff's heavy shovel in John Landis' 2010 comedy *Burke & Hare*. This rather forgettable film is notable only for its cheerful unconcern for historical fact and chronology. Burke and Hare, two sinister scoundrels if there ever were any, are depicted as wisecracking buffoons, and the film features a hodgepodge of Victorian characters, selected entirely without concern for their age at the time of the Burke and Hare outrages in 1831. When the two villains go body-snatching at Greyfriars, they are attacked by a time-travelling Greyfriars Bobby, keeping vigil at the grave of his master, and one of them falls into a newly dug grave.

In 1943, the sentimental story 'Lassie Come Home', about a faithful collie making a long and heroic journey to rejoin her young master after his family is forced to sell her for money, was made into a major film by Metro-Goldwyn-Mayer. Starring Roddy McDowall and Elizabeth Taylor, the film was a huge hit. It also launched the career of the handsome collie Pal, handled by the Americans Frank and Rudd Weatherwax. Pal starred in seven films and two TV shows between 1943 and 1954. Like all other collies to play Lassie over the years, Pal was a male; not only are male collies larger than the females, they also retain a thicker summer coat which looks better on film.

Although Lassie was a male in drag, her onscreen adventures were often quite sentimental. The theme from the original film was resorted to more than once, with weeping children mourning their departed Lassie, and the resourceful dog escaping from heartless new owners, or even dognappers, to rejoin them. In the films, Lassie had an impressive homing instinct, and she sometimes boarded trains or stagecoaches when she felt the need for faster transportation. With her superior intelligence, Lassie was very adept at looking after foolish and imprudent children getting into trouble. If they fell into the water, she dragged them ashore; if they got struck by an avalanche, she dug them out; if they got caught by Red Indians, she braved arrows and tomahawks to liberate them. If there was a landfall across the railway line, Lassie understood the danger, grabbed a red flag and stopped the train.[2]

In 1948, during the height of the 'Lassie' craze, Metro-Goldwyn-Mayer bought the rights to Eleanor Atkinson's *Greyfriars Bobby* and substituted Lassie for the humble little Scottish terrier. At first, the titles *Greyfriars Bobby* and *Greyfriars Lassie* were considered by the canny film moguls, but neither found favour: instead, the film was provisionally named *Highland Lassie*. The MGM directors must have exclaimed a collective 'Goddamit!' when some geographically minded person informed them that Edinburgh was certainly not part of the Scottish Highlands! Eschewing the logical alternative *Greyfriars Lassie*, they went for *Challenge to Lassie* instead, and this time the name stuck.[3] The film was directed by the experienced Richard Thorpe, and released on 31 October 1949. *Challenge to Lassie* was the fifth Lassie film and the fourth that would star the popular veteran actor Donald Crisp, who claimed to be of Scottish descent, although it was later discovered he was actually a London Cockney.

MGM's *Challenge to Lassie* follows the Atkinson novel relatively closely. It is set in Edinburgh in 1860, with Lassie (or rather *Pal*, as we know) turning in an excellent performance, with her (or rather *his*) son Yip-Yip acting the part of Lassie the puppy in the early scenes. Looking every part of a rustic old Scottish shepherd, Donald Crisp was also praised for his acting in the part of Auld Jock. During filming, there had been some difficulty in the early scenes, where Lassie was supposed to be herding sheep; this was something the celebrated dog had never done before. The experienced border collie 'Ross' was recruited to teach Lassie the rudiments of sheepherding, and after a few lessons, the clever acting dog had grasped what was expected of him.

Challenge to Lassie improves on the Atkinson novel in that it introduces a dramatic scene where Lassie and Auld Jock are attacked by robbers. To protect

Jock, the brave dog attacks and bites both miscreants, but Lassie fails to rescue the feeble old man, who later dies of his wounds at a lodging-house. Lassie follows the coffin when he is buried at Greyfriars. She is barred from the churchyard by the stern James Brown, but sneaks in when the gates are opened, to keep vigil on Auld Jock's grave. Lassie is supported by the kind Mr Traill, who keeps her well fed. Traill's son, a law student who is also the boyfriend of James Brown's daughter, also becomes fond of Lassie. The two Traills find out where Jock had been working, and restore Lassie to the farm, but the stubborn dog returns to Greyfriars, to keep vigil on the old shepherd's grave.

In *Challenge to Lassie*, nobody in Edinburgh seems to have any more pressing matters to attend to than to debate the future of Lassie the cemetery dog: the Traills, the Browns, the vicar, and the police. In particular, a mean-spirited police sergeant objects to Lassie's presence in the cemetery. With the help of a colleague, he kidnaps her using a net, and prosecutes Traill for keeping an unlicensed dog, but the kind Lord Provost saves the day. Outside Greyfriars, the wicked policeman has his truncheon taken away by Lassie, and is much laughed at as a result. He is further punished by having to act as a guide outside the churchyard gates, telling and retelling the story of Greyfriars Lassie to all comers. *Challenge to Lassie* appears to have been quite a successful film, with excellent reviews, although not as financially lucrative as some of the other instalments in the *Lassie* series. It was followed by the official *Challenge to Lassie* book, illustrated with stills from the film.[4]

In 1961, Eleanor Atkinson's book was adapted into the full-length film *Greyfriars Bobby: The True Story of a Dog* by Walt Disney Productions. Walt Disney visited Edinburgh in person, giving directions for some scenes to be shot on location, in Edinburgh or at an East Lothian farmhouse, whereas the majority were filmed at Shepperton Studios in West London. After holding auditions for acting Skye terriers, Disney found his shaggy star, a Skye terrier from Stornoway, who was suitably renamed Bobby. Managed by the Hungarian dog trainer John Darlys, Bobby was insured for £20,000 and installed in his own mobile caravan. He had a stand-in named Jerry, but Bobby was quite co-operative and managed to act in the great majority of scenes himself.[5]

Walt Disney's *Greyfriars Bobby* begins at Cauldbrae Farm in 1865, where the jolly-looking little Bobby improbably helps the rustic farm labourer Auld Jock to tend the sheep. When Auld Jock goes to Edinburgh after losing his job at the farm, he leaves Bobby behind with the farmer's young daughter Elsie, but the little dog leaps out of the kitchen window and runs after the carriage. When Bobby reaches Edinburgh, he goes into Mr Traill's restaurant at the sound of the one o'clock gun, and is later reunited with Auld Jock. Mr Traill sees that Jock is far from well, and offers to call a doctor, but the rustic old shepherd refuses. When Auld Jock wants to get a room at his usual lodging-house, he hides Bobby in a bag since there is a 'no dogs' policy. In a pathetic scene, the dying old man plays with Bobby, and has the little dog smell some heather he has planted in a pot. Although Jock cannot read, he has his Bible with him, and enough money to pay for his funeral.

The following morning, the landlady finds Auld Jock's dead body. He is identified from the name in his Bible, and his money is made use of to pay for a decent burial in 'the kirkyard that is nearest'. When Bobby follows the coffin to Greyfriars, the dog-trainer had to be hidden inside Auld Jock's coffin to direct his charge walking mournfully after it. James Brown, played by the aforementioned Donald Crisp, is in a bother to keep Bobby out of Greyfriars, but the little dog is equally determined to keep vigil on Jock's tomb. Greyfriars Bobby is supported by the stalwart Mr Traill, who has a low opinion of his neighbour James Brown; he feeds the little dog every day, after the one o'clock gun has been fired. But when the farmer from Cauldbrae comes to see Mr Traill, he takes Bobby with him to the farm. The little dog digs his way out of the stables, however, and returns to Edinburgh, arriving at Auld Jock's grave very weary from his travels.

The next day, when James Brown sees Greyfriars Bobby ratting in the churchyard, he exclaims 'Mr Traill has said a wicked lie!' since he had expected that the dog would have been sent away. But Mrs Brown likes Bobby and gives the little dog a bath, persuading her dour husband to let him stay. Mr Traill has employed some poor children from the local tenements, among them the crippled boy Tammy and the little girl Ailie, to return Bobby to him. As a reward after the little dog has been recovered, the kind restaurateur provides the half-starved urchins with a hearty meal. When Bobby returns to Auld Jock's grave, James Brown is waiting to take Bobby into his house, but Bobby snarls at him, refusing to give up his vigil on the tomb.

One day, a mean-spirited police sergeant named McLain sees Greyfriars Bobby playing with the children. He decides to prosecute Mr Traill for harbouring an unlicensed dog. As usual, Traill and James Brown are unable to see eye to eye, squabbling over who ought to take responsibility for the dog. In the meantime, the Edinburgh slum children hear of the Burgh Court proceedings. Hearing that seven shillings are needed for Bobby's dog-tax, they start collecting pennies in the local neighbourhood. In the end, both Traill and James Brown offer to pay for the tax. But after the children come into the Burgh Court with their pennies, the jovial Lord Provost declares that Greyfriars Bobby belongs to all the children of Greyfriars. He gives Bobby his collar, and the Freedom of the City. In the final scene, Greyfriars Bobby follows a band of pipers in the esplanade in front of Edinburgh Castle, running between their legs. He then comes into Mr Traill's restaurant at one o'clock, before returning to keep vigil at Auld Jock's tomb. Mr Traill and James Brown become friends at last: they share a dram of whisky, and all the children wish Bobby a good night.

There were murmurations from the direction of Edinburgh at Disney's various uncalled-for improvements of the story, but the producers retorted that they should be grateful that the film had not been recorded in some American film studio, as may well have been the original plan. The 'blurb' for the film was:

The story of the wee Skye terrier
with the great big heart.
It actually happened!
It was photographed where it happened!
You'll have to see it to believe it!

The grand World Premiere of Walt Disney's *Greyfriars Bobby*, held at the Caley Picture House in Lothian Road on 17 July 1961, was attended by the Lord Provosts of Edinburgh, Perth, Glasgow, Dundee and Aberdeen, by the Dukes of Buccleugh, Roxburghe and Queensberry, and by many others of high rank and accomplishments. Bobby the acting dog paid a visit to Greyfriars Bobby's Bar, a public house situated just by the Candlemaker Row dog monument, to have a drink and get a good photo opportunity, before the little dog travelled on to attend the premiere. The official brochure claimed that

> True to the Walt Disney tradition, the story of Greyfriars Bobby has been translated to the screen with the highest regard for authenticity of fact, characterization and period atmosphere of the Scotland of one hundred years ago; a fact which must bring pleasure and satisfaction both to her present inhabitants and the legion of Scots-blooded folk scattered all over the globe.[6]

Albeit no blockbuster like some of the other Disney films, *Greyfriars Bobby* enjoyed very respectable takings throughout the world. There was considerable newspaper publicity: some reviews were favourable, but others complained about the maudlin sentimentality of the story, and the indifferent acting by the saucer-eyed children in their over-large caps.[7] Nevertheless, the Disney film cemented the influence of Eleanor Atkinson's novel upon the legend of Greyfriars Bobby, and catapulted Bobby into becoming one of the world's most famous dogs. It was followed up by the tasteless official 'Walt Disney's *Greyfriars Bobby*' comic book, with the human characters speaking ludicrous pseudo-Scots and the dog barking 'Yark! Yark!' Understandably, this comic book was released in the United States only. When Eleanor Atkinson's novel was reissued, and illustrated with stills from the film, it enjoyed unprecedented sales, and has never been out of print since. When the filming was completed, Bobby the acting dog was given to Chief Constable William Merrilees of the Lothian & Peebles Constabulary, on the condition that the dog should not make any public appearances except for charity.

In December 1954, the Greyfriars Bobby monument was cleaned and repaired after suffering the effects of a traffic accident. When back in place in March 1955, the dog statue had been given a good polish: it shone like burnished gold. But just a few months later, the drinking fountain was crashed into by another motorist, a youth who was arrested for suspected malicious mischief. For the second time within months, Greyfriars Bobby's statue was catapulted off its pedestal, landing in the road. The base of the drinking fountain was completely wrecked. There was a debate whether the monument should be moved further down Candlemaker Row, to avoid these traffic perils, and also whether it was advisable to keep its water supply connected. Piety towards Greyfriars Bobby prevailed over these practical concerns, however, and after the monument had been restored in August 1955, with a strong metal rod to stabilise the statue, it was reassembled in its original position. The water supply was turned off in 1957, and two years later, a plaque was added to the column, between the two coats of arms, to state this fact.[8] In 1960, a newspaper writer found the drinking fountain an unprepossessing sight: it was very dirty, and the nozzle of the water spout was gone.[9] In January 1963, three jolly Edinburgh University students unscrewed the dog statue from the drinking fountain and took it away. Although they claimed to have been caught on the way back to restore the statue, they were fined £5 each for their prank, and Greyfriars Bobby was once more restored to his position.[10]

Greyfriars Bobby was safe until 1971, when a butcher's van hit the drinking fountain with considerable force, toppling the dog statue and wrecking the column of the monument. Seventeen days later, the drinking fountain had been repaired, and Bobby restored to his position. By this time, both the trough and the drinking basin had been filled to prevent littering.[11] In 1972, the Edinburgh Town Council and the Scottish SPCA planned a memorial service for Greyfriars Bobby, on the 100th anniversary of his death. Making use of some very dubious clerical logic, the kirk's minister pointed out that 'in this age of easy abortion and ecological disaster, Bobby's regard for life has a message for us all'![12]

In 1979, when a bucket of paint was emptied over the dog statue by some mindless vandal, there was outrage in Edinburgh. The Lord Provost promised a swift restoration of the monument, and retribution against the vandal. The Revd Stuart Louden, for thirty years minister of Greyfriars kirk, said that due to repeated accidents and vandalism, the best thing might well be to move Greyfriars Bobby's monument inside the kirkyard, which was kept locked at night.[13] In 1986, it was the old story again: a careless out-of-towner drove into the drinking fountain, and received a proper thumping from some angry locals as a result. The plinth of the drinking fountain was cracked, and Greyfriars Bobby knocked off the plinth for the fourth time. Again it was debated whether the drinking fountain should be moved; again, it was left in its original position.[14]

10

Forbes Macgregor's Investigation

> Nae cobra, adder, rattlesnake
> Could stushie or canally make
> Nor Nessie risin oot her lake
> Inspire sae terror
> As oot the Greyfriars mools ye brake
> A nine-inch horror.
>
> The fare-ye-well ye crawlin ferlie
> Long may ye haunt, baith late and early
> Greyfriars Yard in hurly-burly
> Like Greyfriars Bobby
> Long may ye crawl, baith straicht and curly
> Your earthy lobby.
>
> Forbes Macgregor, 'A Greyfriars Serpent'

Forbes Macgregor was born in Edinburgh in 1904. He was educated in the city and gained an Honours BA in geography at London University by private study in 1937. In 1924, he started a teaching career that ended in 1965 when he retired as headmaster of South Morningside Primary School. Alongside his schoolteaching day job, Forbes Macgregor flourished as a poet, novelist and author on Scottish ethnology and literary history. His amusing anecdotes and felicitous poems struck a chord with his countrymen, and books like *Scots Proverbs and Rhymes*, *Macgregor's Mixture* and *More Macgregor's Mixture* were published in several editions that were never short of readers.

In the early summer of 1979, when the 75-year-old Forbes Macgregor visited the Ampersand remainder bookshop, situated just by the Greyfriars Bobby monument, he was approached by Mr Gordon Grant, the shop's owner.[1] Both tourists and Edinburgh people kept pressing him for books about Greyfriars Bobby, Grant explained, and he was heartily tired of telling them that nothing was available apart from Henry Hutton's short pamphlet and Eleanor Atkinson's novel. Surely, there should be a proper account of Greyfriars Bobby, Scotland's most famous dog, and surely the distinguished Edinburgh scholar Forbes Macgregor was the right person to write it. After due consideration, Macgregor accepted the commission to become Greyfriars Bobby's biographer.

It would appear as if, throughout his long life, Forbes Macgregor had regarded Greyfriars Bobby as something of an Edinburgh institution. Although a prolific writer of both prose and poetry, and a frequent visitor to Greyfriars, he had never written anything about Bobby, except a brief mention of the famous dog in a poem, quoted as an epigraph to this chapter, about a particularly long earthworm he had once encountered at Greyfriars.[2] When he reacquainted himself with the relevant source material, he was unimpressed with Henry Hutton's outdated pamphlet on Greyfriars Bobby, and very suspicious of Eleanor Atkinson's novel about the famous dog. Knowing his way around the various Edinburgh repositories, the veteran researcher went to see the collection of press cuttings and other material on Greyfriars Bobby in the Edinburgh Room of the Central Library. He also consulted the old files of the *Scotsman* and other Edinburgh newspapers, and went to the Edinburgh City Archives in a vain search for the destroyed Burgh Court archives from 1867.

Looking through the files of the *Scotsman* of 1934, to follow the Greyfriars Bobby debate of that year, Forbes Macgregor found the letter from Councillor Wilson MacLaren, a mine of information about old Edinburgh, saying that when he had fed Greyfriars Bobby in 1871, Mr Traill had told him that

> That dog has a history: his name is Bobby, and his master a Midlothian farmer named Gray, died in 1858. He aye came for his dinner here on market day. Suddenly Gray died. Three days later at the usual hour I was surprised to see Bobby come into the shop …

This certainly spoke in favour of Eleanor Atkinson's version of the story, and for some reason, Macgregor also took on board that the first name of the elusive Gray (or Grey) had been John. But in the *Scotsman* files, Forbes Macgregor found a letter from the old Edinburgh resident Andrew Hislop, claiming that the only John Gray (or Grey) listed in the 1858 Register of Burials in Greyfriars churchyard was a 45-year-old policeman by that name.[3]

To determine whether Bobby's master had been a farmer or a policeman, Forbes Macgregor consulted the relevant archives. He could soon prove that there was no farm called Cauldbrae, and that no John Gray residing in Midlothian or Edinburghshire did expire from early 1858 until 1860. Importantly, Forbes Macgregor also found solid evidence that John Traill had not had any connection with the restaurant in Greyfriars Place prior to May 1862. Not entirely unreasonably, he lambasted Traill as a humbug, who had monopolised Greyfriars Bobby and served himself heir to the dog's fame and fidelity. Nor did the veteran scholar have any kind words to spare for the hapless Eleanor Atkinson, whose story of Bobby he had effectively demolished. He sneeringly described her book as

> a pleasant romance with pseudo-Scots dialogue here and there, but, for example, to have the one o'clock gun fire in 1858 when it did not fire until June 7, 1861; and to have John Traill feed Bobby in 1858, when, in fact, he did not take over the restaurant

until May 1862, are 'facts' that can easily be shown false. In many lands, no doubt, the story and films based upon it, go down well, but it is specious in Scotland, to anyone who knows the country and the period.[4]

In an unpublished manuscript, the sarcastic old Scot was even more outspoken. The characters in Eleanor Atkinson's novel were about as credible as Cinderella and Santa Claus, although the mawkish Americans, with their Sunday schools and humanitarian leagues, had made the book 'almost required reading in every state in the Union, along with the Good Book and other *absolutely true* stories'.[5]

To determine whether the elusive 'John Gray' had really been a policeman, Forbes Macgregor returned to the Edinburgh City Archives. Disappointingly, he found that there was no policeman named John Grey in the 1858 Greyfriars burial records. But when the veteran scholar inspected the Burial Charges volume for February 1858, he found the following entry:

> John Grey, Hall's Court, 45 years, decline. Registration 3/-, Turf 4/-, Grave digging 3/-, Certificate 1/-, Mortcloth 5/-, Total 16/-'.

Clearly, Gray had been omitted from the Greyfriars burial records by mistake! Contacting the Register House, Forbes Macgregor found John Gray's death certificate, saying that John Gray, Police Constable, had died on 8 February 1858, at Hall's Court, Cowgate, at 8.45 p.m. He died of phthisis (pulmonary tuberculosis), after three months illness, as certified by Dr Henry D. Littlejohn, who last saw him on 7 February. The informant was his son, also named John Gray. The policeman had been laid to rest at Greyfriars churchyard on 10 February, as certified by John Raeburn, undertaker. Waving this certificate about, the delighted Forbes Macgregor exclaimed 'Do you know the significance of this?' to the archives assistant, but her blank stare told him that he had in fact been the first person to find out the truth about Greyfriars Bobby's master, or so at least he believed.[6]

Later research has considerably improved our knowledge of John Gray the Edinburgh policeman.[7] Born in Forfar in 1814, he had served his apprenticeship as a wright, before becoming a country gardener. As a young man, he moved to Dundee, where he married Jess Petrie in June 1838; their son John was born in April 1840. Since work as a gardener was hard to find, John Gray migrated to Edinburgh in search of employment. In 1853, he managed to get a job as a police constable, an unattractive and badly paid position for which there were few able-bodied applicants. Gray lived in a hovel called Hall's Court, situated off the Cowgate, with his wife and son. Importantly, Forbes Macgregor found out that John Gray was actually the local policeman: he was assigned to cover the St Cuthbert/Tron parish beat, which included Greyfriars, Candlemaker Row and the Cowgate. He may well have held the keys to the front gates of Greyfriars churchyard, and patrolled it at night. In late 1857, John Gray fell dangerously ill with tuberculosis; he died at Hall's Court in February 1858, after three months of illness, and was buried at Greyfriars churchyard.

Above left: 57. Old houses in the Cowgate, not far from where John Gray the policeman lived.

Above right: 56. The spurious image of Bobby watching the time-gun, alleged by Forbes Macgregor to emanate from *Good Words* magazine of 1861.

On old maps, Forbes Macgregor was able to track down Hall's Court, also known as Hell's Kitchen since it had been such an insalubrious, rat-infested slum. It was entered from the Cowgate by an archway, and had gone under different names over the years: Cessford's Close, Dobie's Close and Leichman's Close. Both Hall and Cessford had stabled horses in it. This notorious Edinburgh slum had survived the rebuilding plans made by William Chambers and others; it had remained until 1922, and Forbes Macgregor could well remember avoiding it when he went along the Cowgate as a young man.[8]

Moving along to the canine hero of the story, Forbes Macgregor believed that the appositely named Bobby must have been John Gray's watch-dog, rather than a simple family pet. He had seen a reference to watch-dogs being employed by the police guarding the Edinburgh cattle market – namely that in 1856, a constable named Farquhar had been allowed compensation by the Town Council for the loss of his watch-dog. From this slender evidence, he concluded that other constables must also have used canine companions on their beats. With his poetic imagination, Forbes Macgregor could see John Gray, Police Constable No. 90, trudging along one of the paths of Greyfriars churchyard, dressed in his old-fashioned uniform, with the faithful Bobby on a lead. After Constable Gray's death, his wife and seventeen-year-old son may well have wanted to take care of Bobby, but the mourning dog must have preferred to keep vigil at his master's grave, and it must have been impossible to keep him indoors.

In the Edinburgh Room ledger on Greyfriars Bobby, Forbes Macgregor found a newspaper clipping from the *Kilmarnock Standard*, saying that *Good Words*, a magazine edited by Dr Norman Macleod, had an article about Greyfriars Bobby.[9] Forbes Macgregor searched the relevant volumes of this magazine without finding anything relevant to Bobby, however. The *Kilmarnock Standard* journalist had probably mixed it up with *Kind Words*, another mawkish Sunday magazine, which really did have an article about Greyfriars Bobby.[10] But in another volume of *Good Words*, Forbes Macgregor found something else that interested him: an article describing the Edinburgh time-gun, with an illustration depicting a warrant officer, a sergeant and a gunner watching the gun being fired. In a corner of the illustration stands a jolly-looking little terrier! Surely, Forbes Macgregor thought, this must have been Greyfriars Bobby paying a visit to Edinburgh Castle, with his friend Sergeant Scott![11]

When Forbes Macgregor went to Ritchie's, clockmakers, at No. 54 Broughton Street, to inquire about the mechanism of the Edinburgh time-gun, he made yet another serendipitous discovery. The clockmakers showed him a copy of a message found in an old longcase clock, sent for repair from Glasgow twenty years earlier, with the following wording:

Greyfriars Bobby

My great-grandfather Robert Ritchie lived with his daughter, my grandmother, at the house above the licensed house at the top of the Candlemaker Row.

As my grandmother was born in 1834 I think was about 20 years old at the time it must be about 1854. Mr Ritchie and Mr Anderson who lived in the house at the back went up to the Sheriff Court to get a free license for Bobby.

Bobby took refuge at night either with Mr Anderson or with my grandmother. Every day when the 1 o'clock gun went off Bobby went into Traill the Piebakers shop for his pie. Mr Ritchie was a brother of the founder of the firm Jas. Ritchie & Son, Clockmakers.

Alice M. Clark, 1032 Pollockshaws Road, Glasgow.

Forbes Macgregor was highly encouraged by this obscure communication. From the Edinburgh Valuation Rolls, he found out that James Anderson had been the tenant and occupier of the back house of No. 28 Candlemaker Row before and during John Gray's funeral in February 1858, and for some years after. The Ritchies had come to Candlemaker Row in 1858, occupying the front house at No. 28 until 1868.[12]

Forbes Macgregor was a clever and experienced researcher. Having made note of James Brown's statement that he remembered Gray's funeral with Bobby as a mourner – and that on the third morning after the funeral, he had fed the little dog since the weather was cold and wet – Macgregor got the excellent idea to look up old weather reports from the *Edinburgh Courant* newspaper. If Saturday 13 February 1858, the third day after the funeral of John Gray the policeman, had indeed been very cold and wet, his theory about the policeman as Bobby's master would achieve considerable bolstering. But it turned out that Edinburgh had enjoyed a continuous spell of fine weather from 5 to 20 February, and that the only morning there might have been a shower was 11 February, the day after Gray the policeman's funeral. But since Forbes Macgregor had made up his mind about what to believe, he merely concluded that James Brown's memory must have been at fault.[13]

From the *Kilmarnock Standard* clipping referred to earlier, Forbes Macgregor had been made aware of the scoffer Thomas Wilson Reid, and his attack on Greyfriars Bobby. Although unable to track down the obscure novel *Gabrielle Stuart*, the veteran scholar valiantly sought to rebut the iconoclastic journalist's assault on Edinburgh's dog saint. Firstly, Forbes Macgregor presumed that the message from Alice M. Clark found inside the clock proved that Anderson and Ritchie had begun taking care of Bobby soon after Gray's funeral in 1858, a somewhat adventurous conclusion. Secondly, he fastened on a detail in the *Kilmarnock Standard* account, namely that in the evening, Reid and his fellow journalist had seen a dog run out through the Greyfriars gates. When Forbes Macgregor made inquiries, he found out that the gates had been dog-proof, and always kept locked; no dog, except a spectral one, could have run out that way![14] Thus the scoffer's lie had been exposed, and Greyfriars Bobby vindicated, Forbes Macgregor concluded. Unfortunately for him, the tale of the dog running out through the gates was merely a figment of the *Kilmarnock Standard* journalist's imagination; it does not occur in Reid's original version.

When Forbes Macgregor delivered his manuscript to George Grant the remainder bookseller, the latter declined to include the veteran scholar's lengthy research notes in the 51-page pamphlet *The Story of Greyfriars Bobby*, published and sold from the Ampersand. Macgregor published his valuable notes himself as *Authentic Facts relating to Greyfriars Bobby*. For a decade, these two humble pamphlets enjoyed slow but steady sales from the Ampersand and other local outlets. The more commercially viable *The Story of Greyfriars Bobby* was reprinted in 1981 and 1984. In 1990, Gordon Wright Publishers produced a 63-page reissue of this pamphlet as *Greyfriars Bobby: The Real Story at Last*, revised and considerably improved by the 85-year-old Forbes Macgregor, who was still hale and hearty. Gordon Wright personally went to photograph various Greyfriars Bobby memorabilia, to make sure the book was properly illustrated. The book now achieved mainstream distribution and very respectable sales, particularly after being reissued by Steve Savage Publishers in 2002. It is still in print, and likely to remain so for many years to come.

As an influential Edinburgh author and scholar, Forbes Macgregor's pamphlets on Greyfriars Bobby won considerable critical acclaim. In a feature in the *Scots Magazine*, Forbes Macgregor explained how he had found out the truth about Greyfriars Bobby, more than a hundred years after the dog had expired. A hilarious illustration shows the dapper, kilted Forbes Macgregor explaining the story of Greyfriars Bobby to some rather cheeky-looking Italian students visiting Greyfriars. Forbes Macgregor's groundbreaking research effectively demolished Eleanor Atkinson's version of events, and proposed a new and outwardly credible alternative: the tiny Greyfriars Bobby had actually been a police dog! Forbes Macgregor sent two copies of the 1990 edition of his book to the Queen Mother, who was kind enough to write him a personal letter of thanks, which the royalist old Scot framed and treasured.[15]

Later authors on Greyfriars Bobby have tended to adhere to Forbes Macgregor's reinterpretation of the myth. John Mackay, whose *Illustrated True Story of Greyfriars Bobby* appeared in 1986, swapped the rustic Auld Jock for John Gray the policeman. Author Richard Brassey, who wrote a children's book about Greyfriars Bobby, also supported the theory of John Gray the policeman as Bobby's master, but eccentric local historian James Gilhooley disagreed. He instead presumed that Bobby had been keeping vigil by the wrong grave, since a farmer from the Borders named John Gray, who had come to Edinburgh for the market, had died in February 1858, and been buried in the East Preston Street cemetery. Gilhooley knew that dogs had telepathic abilities, and presumed that Greyfriars Bobby had used his psychic powers to find John Gray, but only to be thwarted because two men with that name had died within a week of each other in 1858.[16]

Mr John Thomson, a founder member of the One o'Clock Gun & Time Ball Association, was one of several Edinburgh local historians who appreciated Forbes Macgregor's research on Greyfriars Bobby, and their correspondence makes interesting reading.[17] Thomson found it difficult to reconcile the purported illustration of Greyfriars Bobby visiting Edinburgh Castle with the contemporary reports that Bobby seldom left the Greyfriars area and refused to accompany Sergeant Scott any further than the end of George IV Bridge, however. And did not the uniforms of the soldiers in the 1861 drawing look quite odd, with the 'warrant officer' wearing epaulettes and a leather belt with a cavalry pattern sword, and the sergeant not wearing the standard uniform of the Royal Engineers? Forbes Macgregor retained his belief in the *Good Words* illustration, however, responding that the artist had probably been careless with the uniform details. But when Thomson found out that Sergeant Scott's duties with the Ordnance Survey made it very unlikely that he had ever had anything to do with the time-gun and its management, Macgregor had to retreat. The two historians made plans to find Thomas Wilson Reid's elusive 'autobiography', but here they were thwarted; it would take until 2006 for another local historian, George Robinson, to finally solve the mystery of *Gabrielle Stuart*, as recounted earlier in this book.[18]

11

Greyfriars Bobby as a Cultural Icon

When they buried Bobby's master,
Still he never left his side:
By the grave in Greyfriars churchyard
Bobby watched until he died.
And the Edinburgh folk in wonder,
As such faith is rare to see,
Raised a statue in the city
To the doggie's memory.

So today man views his neighbour
With mistrust and hate and fear,
Cold suspicion, dark ambition
Seem to worsen every year.
Will that day be ever dawning
When all men shall brothers be?
Well, a humble Scottish doggie
Shows the way to you and me.

From the song 'Greyfriars Bobby'
by the Alexander Brothers, quoted by permission.

As is apparent from Table I, there has been a profusion of children's books about Greyfriars Bobby. Many of them have been inspired by the various films about the famous dog, although Forbes Macgregor's factual accounts have also played a part. Eleanor Atkinson's classic *Greyfriars Bobby* still rules the roost, although Ruth Brown's *Greyfriars Bobby* has also enjoyed good sales and widespread translation. Lavinia Derwent's *The Tale of Greyfriars Bobby* and Richard Brassey's *Greyfriars Bobby* also appear to have done well; the latter book is notable for its hilarious illustrations. On the other side of the spectrum of popularity, we have Hester M. Monsma's *Bobby Keeps Watch*, privately published in Grand Rapids, Michigan, and Anna de Raan's *Bobby van Greyfriars*, published in Afrikaans. Not a single copy of either of those two books is available for sale on the Internet, a predicament shared by Washiduka Sadanaga's *Etunporoui Papi*, published in Korean in 2004.[1]

TABLE I

GREYFRIARS BOBBY'S BIBLIOGRAPHY

A. FACTUAL ACCOUNTS OF GREYFRIARS BOBBY

Henry Hutton	Greyfriars Bobby	Edinburgh 1902 [improved 1931]
Forbes Macgregor	The Story of Greyfriars Bobby	Edinburgh 1981
	Authenticated Facts relating to Greyfriars Bobby	Edinburgh 1981
	Greyfriars Bobby: The Real Story at Last	London 2002
John Mackay	The True Story of Greyfriars Bobby	Edinburgh 1986
George Robinson	Rab, Greyfriars Bobby, Fiddy and Fan	Edinburgh 2004
	The Greyfriars Bobby A-Z: In Fact and Fiction	Edinburgh 2009

B. CHILDREN'S BOOKS ABOUT GREYFRIARS BOBBY

Eleanor Atkinson	Greyfriars Bobby	New York 1912
	Bobik od franciszkanow [Polish]	Poznan 1930
	Bobby [Danish]	Copenhagen 1980
	Yi quan bo bi [Chinese]	Shanghai 2000
	Gan dong ying guo [Chinese]	Beijing 2006
Anon.	Challenge to Lassie	London 1950
Anna du Raan	Bobby van Greyfriars [Afrikaans]	Cape Town 1970
Hester M. Monsma	Bobby keeps Watch	Grand Rapids, Mich. 1981
Lavinia Derwent	The Tale of Greyfriars Bobby	London 1986
Joy Graham-Marr	Greyfriars Bobby	Edinburgh 1992
Ruth Brown	Greyfriars Bobby	London 1995
	The Ghost of Greyfriars Bobby [US]	New York 1996
	Bobby, Der treue Hund [German]	Hildesheim 1995
	Bobby: En sann historia [Swedish]	Stockholm 1995
	Bobby [French]	Roy Yates Books 1996
	Bobi o pantotinos filos [Greek]	Athens 1999
	Sarangsuron Babi [Korean]	Seoul 2001
Michaela Morgan	Greyfriars Bobby	New York 1999
Richard Brassey	Greyfriars Bobby	London 2000
David Ross	Greyfriars Bobby	New Lanark 2001
Ian Macdonald	Greyfriars Bobby	Wigtown 2001
Washiduka Sadanaga	Etunporoui Papi [Korean]	Seoul 2004
Betty Kirkpatrick	Greyfriars Bobby	Edinburgh 2005
Linda Strachan	Greyfriars Bobby	Thatcham 2006
J. Abernethy	Greyfriars Bobby: Bobby's New Adventure	Broxburn 2008
Frances and Gordon Jarvie	Greyfriars Bobby: A Tale of Victorian Edinburgh	Edinburgh 2010

As the reader will already be aware, Greyfriars Bobby has also made an impact in poetry. The eloquent poem by 'E. E. S.' and the heartfelt Scottish effort by Mrs Boardman, both originally published in *Animal World* magazine, have already been quoted *in extenso* in this book.[2] The poem 'Greyfriars Bobby', privately published by Wm. A. Cribbes in 1950, is best left forgotten, as is the equally laboured effort

58. The Alexander Brothers, a photograph reproduced by permission.

by Alex Bruce, published in his *Rhymes and Notions: A Hantle of Verse*, a collection of poems in Scottish for children, contains the slightly more felicitous 'Greyfriars Bobby' by E. M. Sulley.[3]

Tom and Jack Alexander, two young Scottish labouring men, pursued a second career as entertainers. One of them plays the keyboards and the other the accordion, and both have good singing voices. In 1958, when the Alexander Brothers were in their early twenties, they took part in a talent contest, outclassing all other entrants. They soon got a recording contract and became professional musicians. Their 1964 hit single 'Nobody's Child' sold more copies in Scotland than did recordings by The Beatles. Their 1965 album *Married by the Bible* featured the single 'Greyfriars Bobby', which was yet another success for the Alexander Brothers. Its lyrics far outshine those of the insipid song featured in the Disney film, and the laboured poems referred to above; it has the rousing chorus:

> So when men boast of their honour,
> Of their faith and loyalty,
> Let us think of Greyfriars Bobby –
> Who could be as true as he?

The Alexander Brothers are still performing to this day, with success: in 2005, they both received MBEs from the Queen.

In 1992, a group of young Scots living in Vancouver, Canada, founded the punk band The Real McKenzies. In addition to writing and performing original music, the band recorded some traditional Scottish songs, giving them a new, punk-influenced sound. Their albums have met with considerable approval from the punk fraternity, and the eight-piece band's live performances, featuring two players of Highland bagpipes, have been widely praised. One of the songs on their 2008 album *Off the Leash* was 'The Ballad of Greyfriars Bobby'.

Founded in 1998, the One o'Clock Gun & Time Ball Association initially specialised in researching Edinburgh's historic time-gun service, but several members, like the aforementioned John Thomson and George Robinson, also have a strong interest in Greyfriars Bobby. Mr Thomson now lives in Canada, but George Robinson and other members have spent more than a decade researching the true history of Edinburgh's dog of mystery. Not the least important member of the Association is its canine mascot, the North Berwick ceremonial dog 'Bombardier Blue'. A handsome little Yorkshire terrier, he is quite a Greyfriars Bobby lookalike, and no Edinburgh parade staged by the Association is complete without him.

A present-day visitor to Edinburgh will find that the Greyfriars Bobby drinking fountain remains well looked after. The filling has been removed from the drinking basin, but suggestions that the water supply should be restored have not been acted upon. Nor have appeals from the One o'Clock Gun & Time Ball Association that the statue should be lit up at night, by a replica of the old streetlamp seen in some of the early picture postcards of the dog monument. Here the Edinburgh authorities were actually quite right, since the early illustrations of the drinking fountain, reproduced in this book, actually show that the lamp post appeared at a later stage.

Entering Greyfriars churchyard, Bobby's gravestone is straight ahead. In 1981, the Dog Aid Society of Scotland presented and erected a red granite memorial to Bobby himself, similar to the stone on Auld Jock's grave, on the triangular grass plot in front of the kirk, where reliable witnesses agree that Bobby was buried back in 1872. It has the inscription:

Greyfriars Bobby
Dies 14th January 1872
Aged 16 years
Let his Loyalty and Devotion
be a Lesson to us all.

Erected by the Dog Aid Society
of Scotland and unveiled by HRH
the Duke of Gloucester GCVO
on 13th May 1981.

After the gravestone had been unveiled by the Duke of Gloucester, there was a service with a children's choir. Greyfriars Bobby's gravestone has remained popular over the years. Many people leave wreaths, flowers, dog toys and biscuits, and other things they believe Edinburgh's dog saint would appreciate, on Greyfriars Bobby's grave.

Inside the church is John MacLeod's 1867 oil painting of Bobby, presented to the Kirk Session of Old Greyfriars. In a shopping area nearby, postcards, prints, tea towels, key rings and fridge magnets with the image of the famous dog enjoy very healthy sales. Those who have not had enough of Greyfriars Bobby merchandise can visit Bobby's Bothy, the dedicated souvenir shop situated in the old bothy just by the cemetery gates. Albeit small, the shop is crammed with Greyfriars Bobby memorabilia: thimbles, mugs, whisky glasses, paperweights, mouse mats, jigsaws and a multitude of other objects, including small replicas of the dog statue.

Any visitor to Greyfriars and Bobby's Bothy feeling thirsty after these exertions could do worse than to visit Greyfriars Bobby's Bar at the top of Candlemaker Row. Although there is evidence of a 'licensed house' on this site from a quite early date, the pub was extended in 1893, and given its present name at a later date.[4] Greyfriars Bobby's Bar has various Bobby-related objects on show, mainly some press-cuttings and stills from the Disney film. Further down Candlemaker Row is Auld Jock's Pie Shoppe, with a sign showing the kilted Jock holding a pie and Bobby jumping up to grab it. Mr Traill's former restaurant at No. 6 Greyfriars Place was long used as offices, with a small plaque inside noting its history. For a while, it was reopened as Better Baguettes, with a 'Bobby Baguette' for sale, but today it is a laptop repair shop.

The City of Edinburgh Museum at ancient Huntly House in the Canongate, situated within Edinburgh's Royal Mile, boasts an impressive collection of objects relating to Greyfriars Bobby, and a capacious archive of material relating to the famous dog. Some of the most interesting items are on permanent display in a large cabinet. Prominence is given to the full-scale plaster statue of Bobby by William Brodie, used for the original bronze statue of Edinburgh's dog saint. There is also an enlarged version of the original 1867 cabinet card of Greyfriars Bobby, given to Mr Traill by Walter Greenoak Petterson in 1868; two photographs of Bobby with the Traills; an original pencil sketch of Bobby given to Mr Traill by Gourlay Steell; a photograph of Traill's Temperance Coffee House by John Dickson; and an oil portrait of Mr Traill in 1895 by Oliver Morris. The Baroness Burdett-Coutts had dedicated her photograph to Mr Traill on 22 November 1873, 'the kind friend of poor faithful Greyfriars Bobby'; it is also on display, along with a copy of her scarce little biography of her dog 'Fan', which she had also sent to Mr Traill.[5]

Bobby's collar had been kept in the small bothy near the entrance to Greyfriars for many years, before being transferred to the old Town Museum in the City Chambers when it was opened in 1899. Since Huntly House was acquired as the new city museum in 1932, Bobby's collar has found a safe repository in the display cabinet there. In 1956, Mr Traill's granddaughter Mrs Mary Dickson donated Greyfriars Bobby's dinner bowl to the museum. In a letter accompanying her donation, Mrs Dickson vouched for the truth of the story that each day, as the one o'clock gun fired, Bobby left his master's graveside and jumped in through the back window of Mr Traill's restaurant, to have a meal from this very bowl. Mrs Dickson added that although she had kept several pets, none of them had ever been allowed

HUNTLY HOUSE, CANONGATE EDINBURGH
RESTORED BY THE CORPORATION IN 1931

59. A postcard depicting ancient
Huntly House, today home to an
impressive collection of Greyfriars
Bobby memorabilia.

to feed from this sacred relic of Greyfriars Bobby.[6] 'Greyfriars Bobby's Dinner
Dish' is also on display at Huntly House, but the story that it is marked with the
dates 1862–1872, to signify the years Bobby was fed by Mr Traill, is untrue. When
the water supply to the Greyfriars Bobby drinking fountain was cut off in 1957, the
remaining drinking cup was given to the museum, where it is still on display. Most
of the Traill material was donated by his granddaughters Mary Dickson and Joan
Leitch in 1962, after it had been used for the display to launch the Disney film. 'If
you are in Edinburgh you should pay a visit to Huntly House and see these things,'
Forbes Macgregor rightly recommended.[7]

Edinburgh became twinned with San Diego in 1978, an odd choice since the two
cities have very little in common. Lord Provost Eleanor McLaughlin donated
a copy of the bronze statue of Greyfriars Bobby, made using William Brodie's
plaster original at the City of Edinburgh Museum, to San Diego Mayor Maureen
O'Connor. After Bobby's statue had spent years outside the mayor's office, while
the Americans pondered what to do with this surprise gift, they finally erected it
next to the statue of their own canine celebrity, the dog Bum, in Gaslamp Quarter
Park.[8]

The San Diego dog Bum, presumed to be a St Bernard/spaniel cross, had an adventurous life. He had come to San Diego as a stowaway on a ship in 1886, and soon established himself as one of the city's rowdiest dogs, fighting other large dogs with good success, and killing many cats. He was friendly to human beings, however, and liked cadging food from the Main Street restaurants. This eccentric dog acknowledged no master and allowed no one to discipline him. Still, many people liked him, and since he was such a 'bummer', begging for food at the restaurants all the time, the San Diego people called him Bum. After being hit by a train while fighting a bulldog, Bum lost half his right foreleg and part of his long, bushy tail, but this did little to slow him down.

The distinctive three-and-a-half-legged Bum was declared San Diego's official town dog. Since this remarkable dog ate where he wanted, some enterprising San Diego restaurants boasted signs saying 'Bum Eats Here!' When dog licences were introduced, Bum was declared exempt and his image was printed on the dog-tax receipts. In spite of his hobo lifestyle and regular partaking of alcoholic beverages, as well as suffering from some kind of rheumatism, Bum lived on until 1898. The local children collected pennies for him to have a proper funeral.

In 1989, Bum and Greyfriars Bobby were officially declared 'Brother Dogs', and a copy of the statue of Bum was dispatched to Edinburgh. The Americans were keen to see it erected next to the Greyfriars Bobby monument, but the Edinburgh worthies did not share their enthusiasm. Firstly, there was simply not enough room; secondly, many people found it unsuitable for the statue of this obscure American dog to be anywhere near the monument to Edinburgh's dog saint. In the end, Bum's statue was put in Princes Street Gardens, where it still is today. In November 2010, the One o'Clock Gun & Time Ball Association held a ceremony for Bum. Suitably, Bombardier Blue was present, and a proclamation from the Mayor of San Diego was read out.

The only possible parallel between Bum and Greyfriars Bobby, the two 'Brother Dogs', is that both of them appear to have dispensed with the usual canine prerequisite of having a master. Just like Bum, Greyfriars Bobby was 'the dog of the town', who had many human friends, but acknowledged none of them as his master, until he was taken care of by the Traills in old age. Such independent dogs attracted a good deal of attention in Victorian times. The equally masterless 'travelling dogs' that delighted in long-distance travel on the railways were the pets of the railwaymen of a certain station. There were several of these strange railway dogs: 'Railway Jack' and 'Trotter' in Britain, and 'Railroad Jack' and 'Owney' in the United States.[9]

The considerable success of the 1961 Disney film prompted yet another remake of the old story, namely the 2005 film *The Adventures of Greyfriars Bobby*, directed by John Henderson. Filming had started already back in 2002, but the film company ran out of money later that year, and the work had to be suspended. A disgruntled columnist in the *Daily Express*, perhaps a reincarnation of Thomas Wilson Reid or

Councillor Gillies, commented that 'A plan to remake the movie *Greyfriars Bobby*, an ill-stuffed turkey even by the standards of the early sixties Disney, has been stalled by a budget crisis. If there's a better good news story around anywhere this week, I can't imagine what it could be.'[10]

The writers of the film script had clearly read Forbes Macgregor's book, since they make Bobby a police dog, on patrol with his master Constable John Gray. Both dog and master perform heroics when an infuriated bull threatens to go on the rampage, but in the next scene, both are injured trying to catch a pickpocket, and Gray later expires. After Gray has been buried at Greyfriars, Bobby begins his vigil on the grave. The rotund James Brown tries to keep him out, but the little dog makes use of various stratagems to gain entry, once hiding underneath the wide crinoline skirts of a lady visitor. Bobby's remarkable fidelity, and his ratting prowess, eventually endears him to Brown, who allows him to stay in the cemetery. One day, a villainous factory boss and his friend, the equally crooked local charity commissioner, point out to James Brown that dogs are not allowed in the cemetery, but Brown tells them Bobby is employed as the church's official rat-catcher. This rebuff fills the two villains with deadly hatred for Greyfriars Bobby, which extends to all the little dog's friends and supporters.

A shy, awkward-looking boy named Ewan befriends Bobby, but Ewan's mother dies when a tenement building collapses, and the charity commissioner makes his life a misery at the workhouse. Aware of the threat from the two villains, Constable Grey's widow takes Bobby away to Dunbar, but the dog sets off back to Edinburgh and rescues Ewan from the workhouse. The bad guys are not done with him yet, however; Bobby is caught and prosecuted for lacking a licence. Ewan joins up with the mad-looking street trader Coconut Tam, played by *Father Ted* actor Ardal O'Hanlon, to try and rescue Bobby.[11] In the end, the Lord Provost, played by none less than Christopher Lee, gives Bobby his collar and the Freedom of the City. Before accepting it, Bobby runs up to the wicked charity commissioner and cocks his leg.

In *The Adventures of Greyfriars Bobby*, all the old exaggerations are carried along, with a few novel inventions added for good measure. New characters are liberally added to the cast, whereas the stalwart Traill is unaccountably left out altogether. The annoying juvenile leads 'steal the show', whereas the good actors only make cameo appearances. Bobby's Edinburgh friends must have been appalled to see that the Edinburgh Castle scenes had been shot at nearby Stirling Castle instead. Not even the geography is right: when Bobby travels from East Lothian to Edinburgh, he passes what are obviously Highland hills and lochs! What really lets the film down is the incoherent plot, however. The realistic elements, like the collapsed slum tenement and the miseries of the workhouse, clash with the soppy sentimentality of the story. The characters do not develop: the bad guys are just pantomime villains, the children just stereotypical Victorian kids in over-large caps, and even the weirdo Coconut Tam does not do much that is funny or interesting.

For the Greyfriars Bobby purists, the worst thing of all about *The Adventures of Greyfriars Bobby* was that Bobby himself had been transformed into a dapper-looking West Highland white terrier. If Walt Disney, who was not known for his strict adherence to historical fact when there were a few dollars to be earned, could find and train the right breed of dog to play Greyfriars Bobby, then surely a British film company could make an effort to do so. 'Och, an *English* film company!' the disgruntled Scots murmured. When challenged by the Edinburgh newspapers, the filmmakers tried to bluster it out; it was not known, they asserted, what breed of dog Bobby really belonged to: he might have been a Cairn terrier or he might have been a Skye, so why could he not have been a West Highland white terrier? One very grainy photograph was the only contemporary image of Bobby, producer Christopher Figg claimed, quite wrongly, as we know; had he not even seen the dog statue on the drinking fountain, or the painting at Greyfriars?[12]

Bobby's Edinburgh friends were not amused by these newspaper shenanigans. The Skye Terrier Club had joined the fray to declare that Bobby had definitely been a drop-eared, dark-haired Skye. Sine Threlfall, a noted expert on the breed, stated that the psychology of Skyes and Westies was completely different: the Skye was very loyal and had an impressive memory, whereas the Westie would just attach itself to the next kind person coming by, after its master died.[13] In the end, the filmmakers had to recant, admitting that they had chosen the West Highland white terrier because they thought it was more photogenic. Since Skye terriers were by this time quite a rare breed, and in dire need of some good publicity, the Skye Terrier Club was understandably quite upset: to choose the wrong breed of dog was disrespectful to Greyfriars Bobby, the most famous dog in the world, and all club members would boycott the film. The *Sun* newspaper saw nothing wrong with having a Westie playing the part of Greyfriars Bobby, however; why, they could even have used a Great Dane, after the part of six-foot-six Scottish hero William Wallace had been played by five-foot-six Aussie Mel Gibson in the blockbuster film *Braveheart*. The journalist also knew about 'Greyfriars Boaby', a sex toy sold in some Edinburgh naughty shops; American visitors to the Scottish metropolis should take care not to mix them up![14]

The premiere of *The Adventures of Greyfriars Bobby*, held at the Vue Omnia cinema in Leith Walk, Edinburgh, was attended by Christopher Lee, Ardal O'Hanlon, and of course Bobby the acting dog. It was followed by a reception at Edinburgh Castle, attended by Jack McConnell, the first minister for Scotland. But if the film company had hoped that the newspaper debate about the film's inaccuracies would give them useful publicity and fill the cinemas, they were very much mistaken. Reviewers in the Scottish papers kept grumbling about the film's geographical gaffes. 'No Bobby Dazzler!' exclaimed the *Glasgow Daily Record*, pointing out that in a scene supposed to be at Edinburgh Castle, the Wallace Monument in Stirling can be clearly seen in the background. Reviews elsewhere ranged from the indifferent to the downright insulting. In the *Guardian*, Peter Bradshaw found the film old-fashioned with its saucer-eyed kids in absurdly large caps, and the laboured plot 'quite incredibly boring'. 'Mutt dressed as lamb!' exclaimed Donald Clarke in the *Irish Times*, pointing out that if you wanted to punish some very naughty children, taking them to see this gloomy and soul-withering film would do the trick! 'You might think Lassie was schmalzie garbage but this film enters the third circle of doggie hell!' sneered another canophobic critic. The *Daily Express* found this shaggy dog story pretty lame, and pointed out that a preview of the film at an international festival had met with an underwhelming reception: 'Greyfriars Bobby had just dropped a big dog pile in Cannes!'[15]

Apart from the dignified-looking Christopher Lee, whose cameo appearance as the Lord Provost was widely praised, the only other member of the cast to receive many accolades for his acting was the canine lead, the attractive West Highland white terrier Bobby One. This clever little dog was trained by Gerry Cott, former guitarist with Bob Geldof's band The Boomtown Rats, who had turned to animal training in middle age. Even the grumbling, sarcastic reviewers quoted above had to admit that Bobby One could in no way be blamed for the film's various other shortcomings. In addition to his understudy, Bobby Two, three other West Highland white terriers were used during the filming.

In 1999, the eccentric Edinburgh local historian James Gilhooley spoke out in several newspaper interviews with a confused theory that in spite of possessing psychic powers, Greyfriars Bobby had been keeping vigil in the wrong cemetery. His real master, the Borders farmer John Gray, had in fact died in February 1858, and been buried in a pauper's grave at East Preston Street cemetery. The ignorant London journalists were completely hoodwinked by these fantasies, which were featured even in the *Sunday Times*.[16] In particular, the irreverent *Sun* newspaper thought the story capital good fun. If the legend of Greyfriars Bobby was not true, then what about Greenfriars Polly, the faithful parrot who perched on her master's tombstone for fourteen years? Showing further disrespect to Edinburgh's canine saint, the journalist pointed out that if Greyfriars Bobby had had three 'poos' a day while keeping vigil on the grave, the grand total in fourteen years would have been 15,330, in an era long before 'pooper scoopers'; surely, the poor dog must have been resting on a huge mountain of 'poo'! Now, the Edinburgh local historians ought to investigate the legends of Lassie, Rin Tin Tin, Skippy and Flipper, before determining whether Edinburgh Castle had been built by Wimpey in 1963.[17] Bobby's Edinburgh friends must have ground their teeth with rage if they came across this deplorable tabloid squib ridiculing their favourite dog.

As the years went by, Greyfriars Bobby cemented his place in Scottish culture. The quaint dog monument became a symbol not just for canine fidelity, but for the 'good old days' depicted in Eleanor Atkinson's book and Walt Disney's film: in Bobby's time, dogs had been faithful and people had been loyal and kind. Supervised by the benign Lord Provost, stalwarts like Traill and Brown had been going about their business, and the children had been collecting pennies for their favourite dog instead of playing truant from school, taking drugs and getting pregnant. Clashes between Greyfriars Bobby and the unpleasant, dangerous Modern World are always headline news in the local papers. In 2003, there was anger when Greyfriars Bobby was crowded out by bin bags and wheelie bins; there should be no refuse anywhere near the statue! In 2005, there was further outrage when a 'sex beast' raped a woman just a few feet away from the Candlemaker Row dog monument. Two years later, *Playboy* magazine wanted to make it the scene for a nude photo shoot! The authorities put an end to this plan, however – not for reasons of piety but because they could not guarantee 'crowd control'!

In 2009, the programme for the rowdy Edinburgh International Festival had a picture of two 'Neds' vomiting and urinating into the Greyfriars Bobby drinking fountain. This disgusting image was much criticised by Bobby's Edinburgh friends: was it not a symbol of 'Nedinburgh', with its disrespect for the city's historical past, and drunken and mindless youth culture? In September 2009, there were again newspaper reports that Bobby's statue had been 'vandalised'. This time, some jolly young protesters against the American tycoon Donald Trump building a golf course in Scotland had put masks of Trump's face over the heads of various famous statues in Edinburgh, Aberdeen, Glasgow and Stirling. Although Greyfriars Bobby was just one of several statues defaced in this manner, he was the only one to make the news. Several old Edinburgh residents spoke of the shock they had experienced when they saw Trump's ugly face grinning at them from the Candlemaker Row dog monument. The same year, a map of Edinburgh made for the city's hotels had been manufactured by some very foolish and ignorant person: among a number of mistakes was the monument to 'Blackfriars Bobby'! In April 2010, the Greyfriars Bobby drinking fountain was damaged in yet another road accident; two months later, it was vandalised by three mindless youths, and the marble bowl cracked and damaged.[18]

The aforementioned One o'Clock Gun & Time Ball Association has remained a wholesome influence of good against these uncouth Edinburgh philistines. In April 2008, it arranged a dog parade through Edinburgh for fifty Skye terriers and their owners, ending up at Greyfriars, where an outdoor service was held by the assistant minister of Greyfriars kirk for the edification of both the dogs and their masters. In the first ever civic reception for dogs in Edinburgh, Lord Provost George Grubb joined them to raise a toast to Greyfriars Bobby. In January 2009, the little dog Bombardier Blue put down a wreath on Greyfriars Bobby's grave in a much publicised ceremony. Mr Brian McKenzie, the Chairman of the Association, played the part of Sergeant Scott in a Victorian uniform, a piper was playing, and George Robinson was interviewed on TV calling Greyfriars Bobby the world's most famous dog. Since Blue actually lifted his leg against Bobby's gravestone, the irrepressible *Sun* could not resist some further fun: 'It's RIP Greyfriars Bobby, rest in pees!' This ceremony was repeated in 2010 and 2011, as was another parade on World Animal Day, also featuring the popular ceremony dog. Bombardier Blue also played a leading part in the Association's mobile exhibition about Greyfriars Bobby, which toured a number of schools and libraries in 2009 and 2010.[19]

Where in the World is Carmen Sandiego was a popular, low-budget game-show for easily amused American children, airing not less than 295 episodes between 1991

60. An Edinburgh parade on World Animals Day 2009, led by Greyfriars Bobby lookalike 'Bombardier Blue', the official canine mascot of the One o'Clock Gun & Time Ball Foundation. Reproduced by permission of John and Kit Lovie. Note Greyfriars Bobby's Bar in the background

and 1995. Aimed to test the geographical skills of children aged 8–12, each episode involved the theft of some valuable and iconic object, such as Stonehenge, the Manneken Pis of Brussels, or the Leaning Tower of Pisa. The perpetrator is always a thief belonging to the organization V.I.L.E., run by the elusive female criminal mastermind Carmen Sandiego. It is the task of the 'good guy' organisation ACME to capture the thief, and three young 'agents' have to answer various geographical questions. In a series of challenges, one of them advances to capture the thief and to make sure the stolen object is recovered. In Episode 133, the action is set in Edinburgh, and I think the reader can guess exactly what was stolen, particularly when I reveal that the title was 'Little Dog Gone'. The thief Patty Larceny tries to tempt Greyfriars Bobby with a bone, but the dog statue (which is depicted as being alive) refuses to go with her, although he sniffs at the bone. She then fastens a lead to Bobby's collar and walks away with him. The juvenile agents make sure Patty is captured and Bobby restored to his position, however.

In 'Jurassic Bark' the seventeenth episode of the fourth series of the popular American animated series *Futurama*, the foolish but kind and sentimental Philip J. Fry encounters a Greyfriars Bobby of the future. Fry, an unremarkable pizza delivery boy, who fell into a cryogenic freezing tank in the year 2000, wakes up in 2999 and joins an outfit of various aliens and weirdos in the intergalactic delivery company Planet Express. When Fry takes his robot buddy Bender to a museum, he is shocked to find a fossilised dog on display, which he recognises as Seymour, his own pet from the 1990s! He manages to get his hands on the fossil, and the mad scientist Professor Hubert J. Farnsworth offers to produce a clone, complete with Seymour's personality and memory. But when Fry begins to prepare for the dog, the volatile and unpredictable Bender becomes jealous, especially when Fry refers to Seymour as 'my best friend'. Just when the professor is ready to clone Seymour, Bender grabs the fossil and throws it in a pit of lava, believing that destroying it will restore his friendship with Fry.

Fry is quite distraught at again losing his dog, and angry with the foolhardy robot. The professor explains that the fossil may not have instantly melted, as it was made of a particularly hardy mineral. Regretting his rash action, the robot Bender, claiming to be partly made from that very same mineral himself, dives into the lava and recovers the fossil! But when the professor begins the cloning process, his computer informs him that Seymour died at the age of fifteen, and thus that he lived for twelve years after Fry was frozen. Fry has a change of heart and aborts the cloning process, believing that Seymour must have moved on with his life, found a new owner, and forgotten about Fry altogether. But in a both disconcerting and unexpected ending to this somewhat silly and childish animated drama, it turns out that Seymour had faithfully obeyed Fry's last command, which was to wait in front of Panucci's Pizza until he returned. Like Greyfriars Bobby, Seymour keeps vigil at the pizzeria for twelve long years, waiting for his master to return. As the years pass by, the faithful dog, the pizzeria, and Mr Panucci himself begin to show their age. In the final shot, old Seymour lies down and closes his eyes.

The *Futurama* episode 'Jurassic Bark' was nominated for the 2004 Emmy Award for 'Outstanding Animated Program' but lost out to *The Simpsons* episode 'Three Gays of the Condo', although critic Dan Iverson remarked that the climax was 'one of the saddest endings to a television program that I have ever seen'.

12

What Do We Really Know about Greyfriars Bobby?

MOST loyal creature! whom no bribes can bend;
Still thou untaught thy Master doth defend,
Lov'st generous Actions, that will bear the Light,
irreconcilable to deeds of night.
To Thieves and Villains a professed Foe,
And what soe're doth hidden treachery know.
Ne're in distress didst leave thy wretched Lord,
But didst at Life's expense thy help afford.

Thomas Heydrick, 'On a Faithful Dog',
from his *Miscellaneous Poems*, 1691.

So, what do we really know about Greyfriars Bobby? What are the hard facts remaining after nearly 140 years of canine hagiography has turned the humble little terrier from Edinburgh into a cultural icon and a Hollywood megastar?

Firstly, were Rebecca West and her Informant right, and was Greyfriars Bobby just an invention, a hoax to make fun of the tourists? No, certainly not! I think the reader will agree. In the 1931–32 Greyfriars Bobby debate, the bold female journalist was answered, in no uncertain terms, by not less than five eyewitnesses who had seen, or even fed, the little dog themselves. When Greyfriars Bobby was debated in the *Scotsman* newspaper in August 1934, four more elderly Scots wrote letters to say that they had seen the famous little dog themselves, either at the churchyard or at Mr Traill's establishment nearby. As late as 1953, a very old lady declared that as a little girl, she had more than once seen Bobby accompany her father William Dow to Traill's eating house, where she had stroked Bobby, and held him in her arms.

One of the witnesses who rebutted Rebecca West in 1932 was none less than John Traill Leitch, who was understandably not particularly amused that the Baroness Burdett-Coutts, who had befriended his grandfather back in 1869, was depicted as a gullible fool, who did not even make sure the dog existed before donating money to erect his monument. Traill Leitch's comment that it was nowadays a common practice for popular authors to pose as authorities on subjects about which they knew very little, is just about right.[1] Although she was a novelist of repute, Rebecca West's journalism was sometimes dangerously careless. She would have done better to check the facts before dashing into print, misled by her equally ignorant and wrong-headed Informant, who at least took care to remain nameless in the 1931–32 debate.

Multiple independent sources agree that Greyfriars Bobby definitely existed. The many accounts of Bobby and his various antics, by reliable witnesses, already during the dog's lifetime, make it impossible to dispute that there was a resident dog at Greyfriars from (at least) 1864 until 1872. Bobby was definitely at Greyfriars in 1864, and he probably came there several years earlier, since the 1864 article in the *Inverness Advertiser* speaks of him having attained some degree of local fame already by that time. John Traill could remember feeding Bobby for a very long time, perhaps already back in 1862 when he took over the restaurant. In *Gabrielle Stuart*, which was probably written in 1880, since it was serialised already in May 1881, Thomas Wilson Reid dated the appearance of Bobby at Greyfriars twenty years earlier, thus perhaps already around the year 1860.[2]

The earliest mention of a dog living in the Greyfriars burial grounds is from May 1864, namely the *Inverness Advertiser* article stating that the little terrier named Bob had been staying there for some period of time, becoming quite well known locally. It was presumed that Bob had come from the country with a funeral cortege, but nobody knew whom he was mourning or whence he had come. This variant of the story also received support from William Chambers, who wrote that 'A stranger arrived in Edinburgh some years ago, bringing with him one of these rough-looking dogs. Nobody knew who the stranger was, or whence he came.'[3] Then, there was massive publicity about Greyfriars Bobby in April and May 1867, with the result that the sentimental story about the faithful dog evading the dog-tax gatherers was spread all over the English-speaking world. These articles mention nothing about a country funeral cortege, instead stating that Bobby had belonged to a poor man named Gray, who had lived in a quiet way in some obscure part of Edinburgh, before expiring eight and a half years earlier. James Brown was said to have remembered Gray's funeral, and also the dog being one of the most conspicuous of the mourners.[4] Thirdly, John Traill told his 1871 visitor Wilson MacLaren that Bobby's master had been a Midlothian farmer named Gray, who had expired in 1858.[5] Fourthly, we have the old soldier Robert Gray, referred to as Bobby's master by Baroness Burdett-Coutts' 1869 Informant.[6] Further mystery and suspicion is arisen when we reconsider that around 1880, when Dr Stables made inquiries in Edinburgh about Bobby's master, and in 1885, when a correspondent to *Animal World* made a pilgrimage to Greyfriars, no person could supply either of them with the name of 'the poor man' who had once been Greyfriars Bobby's master.[7]

If there is solid evidence that Bobby really existed, and that he stayed at Greyfriars for some considerable period of time, the four different versions about his master all appear very suspect. Firstly, Forbes Macgregor found out that John Traill's story about the old farmer having had luncheon in Traill's restaurant with his little dog back in 1858 must have been pure invention; Traill did not take over the restaurant in Greyfriars Place until May 1862. Nor had a Midlothian farmer, or an out-of-towner of any description, any business being buried in the Greyfriars burial grounds, since they were reserved for local inhabitants. There was no Cauldbrae farm, nor did any John Gray residing in Midlothian or Edinburghshire expire from 1858 until 1860. As for the old soldier Robert Gray, proposed as being Bobby's master in 1869, no such person was buried at Greyfriars in or near 1858. When searching for this elusive figure, the closest George Robinson got was a forty-year-old carter of that name, who died in Edinburgh Royal Infirmary on 25 January 1858, and was buried at East Preston Street cemetery on the south side of Edinburgh.[8] This Robert Gray was neither old nor a soldier.

As we know, several historians have searched the Greyfriars burial records for a more promising candidate to be Bobby's master, instead of the fictional 'Auld Jock'. Two men named John Gray are recorded as having been buried at Greyfriars kirkyard in 1858: a 45-year-old local policeman and the young son of a merchant. Forbes Macgregor considered John Gray the policeman a worthy candidate, and managed to find some useful information about his career, including that he was actually the local policeman: his beat included Greyfriars itself.

If we make two quite hazardous presumptions, firstly that the name 'John Gray' is really that of Bobby's master, and secondly that the vague reports that Bobby came to Greyfriars in 1858 are true, then Forbes Macgregor is probably right: Gray the policeman is the only likely candidate to be Bobby's master. But there are also strong arguments against this individual ever having anything to do with the dog. Firstly, the local policeman was a very well-known character in those days. Would it really be possible that the inhabitants of his beat would entirely forget about his identity just a few days after his death, when the dog appeared in the cemetery? Macgregor's hypothesis that Bobby had been John Gray's watchdog is also open to criticism. Firstly, there is no solid evidence that ordinary Edinburgh police constables kept watchdogs at the time. Secondly, would any sane person really employ a tiny Skye terrier as a police dog? If Constable Gray had got into a brawl with some sturdy fellows, it would have been enough for one of the combatants to tread on Bobby by accident for the 'watchdog' to be put permanently out of action. And thirdly, would not the locals remember such a singular police dog, patrolling the local beat for several years, when it turned up at Greyfriars to keep vigil on its master's grave?

A dog was not worth much money in Greyfriars Bobby's time, but it should be remembered that Constable John Gray's wife and son must have been in very straitened circumstances after the untimely death of the family breadwinner. Had Bobby been their property, there was no logical reason for them to give up ownership of him. Why did they not take care of the little dog, of whom they would be likely to have been quite fond if he had been staying with the family for some considerable period of time, or alternatively sell Bobby to the highest bidder? And if Bobby had really been a police dog, and there had been a local tradition concerning this in the Greyfriars neighbourhood, would this not have been a good argument to put forward at the Burgh Court in 1867?

TABLE II

GREYFRIARS BOBBY'S ICONOGRAPHY

ARTIST	TYPE	DATE	NUMBER
Gourlay Steell	Oil paintings Drawing	Mid-April 1867	16-18
W.G. Patterson	Photographs	Mid-April 1867	14, 27
Cormack Brown	Oil painting	Late April 1867	Lost
Robert Walker Macbeth	Oil painting	April or May 1867	19
Friedrich Wilhelm Keyl	Drawing	June 1867	1
Robert Sanderson	Oil painting	1867	21
John MacLeod	Oil paintings	1867	22
Unknown artist	Drawing	Unknown	5
Mr Burns	Photograph	Unknown	Lost
W.G. Patterson	Photographs	1871	25-26
William Brodie	Sculpture	1871	28-30, 33

It is a both important and long-neglected task to critically investigate Greyfriars Bobby's iconography (Table II), and to correlate it with the descriptions of him during life. The first, and most obvious, observation must be that the two existing oil portraits of Bobby, painted by Robert Sanderson in 1867 (Figure 21) and by John MacLeod in 1867 (Figure 22) clearly depict the same dog: a dapper-looking little animal, looking very much like a Skye terrier, black in colour with brown paws, and grizzled grey on his back. This tallies exactly with the contemporary description of Bobby in *Animal World*: 'a small rough Scotch terrier, grizzled black, with tan feet and nose'. The two drawings of Bobby from life, by Friedrich Wilhelm Keyl (Figure 1) and by an unknown artist (Figure 5) agree quite well with the two oil paintings of him, as does William Brodie's sculpture (Figures 28–30).

There is an obvious odd dog out in the iconography of Greyfriars Bobby, namely the alleged photograph of Bobby donated to the National Galleries of Scotland in 1984 (Figure 65), along with the large collection of photographs belonging to Mr Peter Fletcher Riddell. Skye terriers occur in two varieties: prick-eared and drop-eared. A prick-eared dog remains prick-eared throughout its existence; a drop-eared one remains drop-eared. Thus this 'recently discovered photograph of Greyfriars Bobby', attested to by many people who should have known better, and used on the cover of the 1990 and 2002 edition of Forbes Macgregor's pamphlet, and also in the Wikipedia article on Greyfriars Bobby, must be a falsification; it is

Above left: 61. The alleged photograph of Greyfriars Bobby. Reproduced by permission of the National Galleries of Scotland.

Above right: 62. Two prick-eared Skye terriers, an engraving by Harrison Weir from *Chatterbox* magazine, 3 June 1886.

63. A drop-eared Skye terrier saving another from drowning through grabbing it by the ear, another engraving by Harrison Weir from *Chatterbox* magazine, 8 October 1887. Drop-eared Skyes were in the majority until 1900, but today the prick-eared dogs are more common.

impossible that it depicts the dog painted by Sanderson and McLeod, and sculpted by Brodie.[9] The handwritten 'Grayfriars Bobby' on the photo might well suggest that some unscrupulous individual, with indifferent talents of spelling, had made up his own cabinet cards of the famous dog, for sale to gullible tourists, with the photograph of *another* Skye terrier.

It is crucial to analyse the original photographs of Greyfriars Bobby, taken by Walter Greenoak Patterson in April 1867. Two slightly different examples of this valuable photograph have been preserved at the City of Edinburgh Museum, Huntly House: the original 1867 cabinet card (Figure 14) and the enlarged version given to John Traill by Patterson in 1868 (Figure 27). Another copy of the 1867 cabinet card was kept in the Greyfriars Bobby ledger at the Edinburgh Room of the Central Library, but it was stolen a few years ago. George Robinson, who saw it there, finds no reason to suspect it looked any differently from the card at the City of Edinburgh Museum, including the text from the original *Scotsman* article on the back.

The dog in the Patterson photographs looks like an elderly terrier mongrel. It is likely to have an established cataract in at least one eye, since the pupils looks greyish and clouded, one more than the other. The fur colour appears to be grey or dark yellow, and the fur on the nose and paws is not lighter in colour than that on the dog's chest. The dog's face looks quite odd, with the eyes widely apart. The right nostril is considerably enlarged, and the right side of the face wider than the left one. This is a phenomenon known as facial asymmetry, a relatively uncommon congenital deformity in dogs, perfectly harmless, and probably caused by a partial split palate. The etching of Macbeth's portrait of Greyfriars Bobby (Figure 19) clearly depicts the same dog as the Patterson photograph, in a slightly different pose: all the facial peculiarities are there to be seen. In spite of their undoubted artistic merits, Gourlay Steell's drawing (Figure 16) and the engravings of his paintings (Figures 17–18) of Greyfriars Bobby are a less valuable source with regard to the analysis of canine facial characteristics, due to the dog's recumbent position, but the enlarged right nostril can still be observed.

It is impossible that the terrier mongrel photographed by Patterson and painted by Macbeth and Steell is the same animal as the Skye terrier painted by Sanderson and McLeod, drawn by Keyl and another, and sculpted by Brodie. So, was Bobby a dog enough for two? Did Greyfriars Bobby I, the dark-yellow terrier mongrel, described as elderly already in 1864, expire in May 1867, to be replaced by Greyfriars Bobby II, the Skye terrier, who then lived on until 1872? This iconoclastic version of events would also tend to explain Bobby's startling longevity. Since he was presumed to be an adult dog (2–4 years old) already in 1858, this would imply that he lived to be sixteen or even eighteen years old. A modern monograph on the breed claims that 10–12 years is a good lifespan for a Skye terrier.[10] They have relatively large heads and bodies in spite of their short legs, and do not live as long as the tiny Yorkshire terriers. In Greyfriars Bobby's times, the average lifespan for any dog would of course have been considerably shorter than for present-day

64. The Vennel, from an old postcard; did Greyfriars Bobby come trotting up this steep and narrow alleyway, in search of a better life for himself?

representatives of the same breed, due to the rudimentary veterinary attention available. It makes more sense for Greyfriars Bobby I to take up his position in the cemetery in 1860 (give or take two years) as an adult dog (2–4 years old) and then expire in 1867 aged between nine and thirteen. His successor, Greyfriars Bobby II, recruited in 1867 as an adult dog (aged 2–4 years), remained at Greyfriars for nearly five years. As we know, this angry little dog was noted for his propensity to fight other dogs, even if they were much larger than him, a most unseemly belligerence in a dog that is presumed to be seventeen years old, but perfectly natural in one aged around eight. Greyfriars Bobby II lived until January 1872, expiring between the ages of seven and nine, not from old age, as previously presumed, but from disease (cancer of the jaw), as proven by two independent sources.[11]

The hypothesis that Greyfriars Bobby was a dog enough for two also solves some of the other conundrums surrounding this dog of mystery. Firstly, the original description of the elderly Bobby in the *Inverness Advertiser* of 1864 and the *Ayrshire Express* of 1865 fit the dog in the Patterson photograph quite well. Secondly, the two Bobbys would explain some very enigmatic statements from the scoffer Thomas Wilson Reid, namely that Bobby died soon after being lionised in April 1867. After its investiture with the grand golden chain from the Lord Provost, the ugly old mongrel 'died of pure shame of itself', only to be transformed into the similitude of a pure Skye terrier.[12] Several early authors remarked on Bobby's ugly appearance: the *Inverness Advertiser* journalist, the 1871 *Leeds Mercury* journalist, Councillor Gillies himself, and also Samuel Dunlop, author of a book on the memorials of Greyfriars, who remarked that those who had seen Bobby agreed that he was nothing much to look at.[13] Others described him as a fine Skye terrier, adding that the statue on the Candlemaker Row dog monument was an excellent likeness.[14] In 1997, a perceptive correspondent to the *Scotsman* commented on the obvious discrepancy between the Patterson photographs and the Macbeth portrait on one side, and the statue of Bobby on the Candlemaker Row dog monument and the Greyfriars painting of Bobby by MacLeod on the other.[15]

The obvious instigators of a substitution of dogs would of course be James Brown and/or John Traill. Brown earned considerable sums from the tips and the sale of his cabinet cards; Traill found Bobby very useful to advertise his restaurant, and to attract customers who wanted to see the famous dog. Had the elderly Greyfriars Bobby expired in May 1867, these two would have been in a quandary. A dead Bobby would have been no good for them, but a living one would do the trick for many years to come. If Mrs Watson had known about the substitution of dogs, it would have explained her indignation at James Brown making money from exploiting Bobby. As originally expressed by an 1889 journalist, 'After the story got current, Brown was very solicitous about Bobby, and on account of the crowds who came to see him, it was not in the interest of several others in the neighbourhood, to minimise the circumstance.'[16]

The main objection to the hypothesis that Greyfriars Bobby was a dog enough for two is of course that both James Brown and John Traill appear to have been honest and upright citizens: would they really have had the audacity to substitute another dog after the original Bobby had expired? And surely there must have been people who had seen the two different-looking Bobbys before and after the substitution; would they not react when the living dog at Greyfriars looked quite unlike the animal in the cabinet cards they had previously purchased? Furthermore, the substitution of dogs must have been noticed by the locals living near Greyfriars; even if Brown and Traill had managed to swear most of them to secrecy, it would only have taken one mean-spirited person, like the cantankerous Mrs Watson, to leak the secret to the press, and let the cat out of the bag. And if there had been rumours among the local inhabitants that there had been two Bobbys, why were these not aired by Councillor Gillies or Bobby's other detractors? The dating of Macbeth's painting of Bobby I appears to be uncertain, and some sources claim it was done in 1868, but the scenario of two different Greyfriars Bobbys at large in the cemetery at the same time would tend to make matters insufferably mysterious.[17]

Is there any alternative hypothesis that might explain the two different Greyfriars Bobbys? There is, but only just. What if James Brown, who was stated to have been very much worried when Bobby was taken away to Gourlay Steell's studio, had panicked when he realised that some mean-spirited person might issue a pirated print or cabinet card of the little dog? And what if he had got hold of another dog and had it photographed when the real Bobby was 'sitting' for Gourlay Steell, so that he had some cabinet cards to sell to the throng of visitors. And what if (unlikely, I know) some of these bogus cabinet cards had survived to this day, whereas those depicting the real Bobby all perished. And finally, what if Macbeth painted his portrait of Greyfriars Bobby not from life, but using the cabinet card (of the other dog), provided by James Brown or some other person?

One myth regarding Greyfriars Bobby was exploded already by Forbes Macgregor: the dog did not keep vigil on the grave, but went around Greyfriars as he wanted, ratting inside the church, and visiting his various human friends. Bobby regarded the kirkyard as his territory, where he hunted rats, chased cats, and drove mischievous schoolboys away. Already at the time of the Burgh Court hearing in 1867, Bobby was an habitué at the 'Hole in the Wa'' tavern near Society, Bristo, and he was also fed at the small public house at the top of Candlemaker Row, just outside the cemetery.[18] Two years later, Mrs Denholm fed him when he came to visit the local butcher's shop, and Mrs Watson could well remember Bobby visiting her husband at his Bristo workshop. In spite of his independent nature, Bobby must have been an attractive, friendly dog who made many friends. Since Robert Ritchie, James Anderson, Mr Watson and Mr Traill all took care of Bobby, and allowed him to sleep indoors if he wanted to, the image of poor Greyfriars Bobby shivering on the grave in sleet and snow is likely to be equally fictitious: Bobby probably spent the majority of nights indoors.

Thus the assertion in the fountain inscription that Greyfriars Bobby 'lingered near the spot' is certainly false: the little dog roamed all over the district as it pleased him. Another curious matter concerns the location of the grave of 'the poor man Gray'. As we know, in the two oil paintings showing the dog keeping vigil on the grave, namely those by Gourlay Steell (Figures 16–18) and Robert Sanderson (Figure 21), Bobby is sitting or lying in the north-eastern part of the churchyard, with Edinburgh Castle in the background. This is far from Jean Grant's table-stone, where Bobby was reported to take refuge from the elements, and where the Americans erected Auld Jock's gravestone in 1925. Was this just artistic licence, or were there differing opinions, already during Greyfriars Bobby's lifetime, where the famous dog's elusive master had been buried?

As for the identity of Greyfriars Bobby's master, all that can be said is that it remains unknown; that is, if the dog (or perhaps rather *dogs*) ever had one. There are four different hypotheses regarding the identity of 'the poor man Gray'. The old Midlothian farmer John Gray (or Grey), also known as 'Auld Jock' can be discounted, since no such person died in or around 1858, and since an out-of-towner had no business being buried at Greyfriars. The latter objection can also be used to demolish the tale of the 'nameless stranger' being brought in a funeral cortege from the country; burial at Greyfriars was strictly reserved for the locals. Robert Gray, the old soldier who was pointed out to Angela Burdett-Coutts as Bobby's late master in 1869, does not appear to have existed either; at least, no person of that description was buried at Greyfriars during the relevant years. This leaves us with the 'man named Gray, of whom nothing was known, except that he was poor and lived in a quiet way in some obscure part of town', who was buried eight and a half years earlier, thus around October 1858. George Robinson has searched for a worthwhile candidate in the burial registers, but found none. As already pointed out, Forbes Macgregor's version of Bobby as Constable John Gray's police dog has many serious drawbacks, and entirely lacks support from contemporary sources.

TABLE III

GREYFRIARS BOBBY: A CHRONOLOGY

1858	Alleged year of death for 'the poor man Gray'.
1861	The One o'Clock Gun is set up at the Half Moon Battery, Edinburgh Castle.
1862	John Traill takes over the restaurant as No. 6 Greyfriars Place.
1864	Bobby's story appears in the Inverness Advertiser.
1865	Bobby is featured in the Ayrshire Express.
1866	Sergeant Scott leaves his lodgings in Candlemaker Row.
1867	Mr Traill is summoned before the Burgh Court, but the Lord Provost pays for Bobby's license. Bobby is featured in the Scotsman and many other newspapers. Bobby's master is said to have been a poor old Edinburgh man named Gray.
1868	James Brown dies.
1869	Angela Burdett-Coutts comes to Edinburgh to see Bobby. She is thwarted when she tries to persuade the Town Council to erect a headstone for 'Robert Gray'.
1870	Greyfriars Bobby is featured in Animal World.
1871	John Traill tells Wilsom MacLaren that Bobby's master was a Midlothian farmer named Grey. The Baroness Burdett-Coutts makes sure Bobby will get his monument. Bobby is attacked in the Leeds Mercury and other newspapers.
1872	Greyfriars Bobby dies.
1873	The Candlemaker Row drinking fountain is erected.
1874	Greyfriars Bobby is again featured in Animal World.
1882	The scoffer Thomas Wilson Reid attacks Greyfriars Bobby.
1889	The Town Council turns down an offer from Mr and Mrs Slatter to erect a memorial to Auld Jock. Councillor James B. Gillies attacks Greyfriars Bobby, and there is much debate in the Edinburgh press.
1897	John Traill dies.
1902	Henry Hutton publishes 'The True Story of Greyfriars Bobby'.
1912	Eleanor Atkinson publishes her novel 'Greyfriars Bobby'.
1924	Auld Jock's headstone is set up by the American Friends of Bobby.
1931	Rebecca West attacks Greyfriars Bobby.
1932	Greyfriars Bobby is debated in the Weekly Scotsman.
1934	Greyfriars Bobby is debated in the Scotsman newspaper.
1942	Eleanor Atkinson dies.
1949	MGM's 'Challenge to Lassie' film is released.
1960	Walt Disney's 'Greyfriars Bobby' is released.
1981	Forbes Macgregor published his pamphlets about Greyfriars Bobby.
1981	The Duke of York unveils Greyfriars Bobby's gravestone.
2005	The film 'The Adventures of Greyfriars Bobby' is released.

TABLE IV

SOME EYEWITNESS ACCOUNTS OF GREYFRIARS BOBBY

Thomas Wilson Reid first saw GFB in the cemetery	1860?	Gabrielle Stuart
William Dow's daughter Helen saw GFB accompany her father	1862?	Scotsman March 5 1953
A journalist saw GFB in the cemetery	1864	Inverness Adv May 10 1864
Mr Morham saw GFB in the cemetery	prior to April 1867	Weekly Scotsman Feb 9 1889
A journalist saw GFB at Gourlay Steell's house	April 1867	Scotsman April 18 1867
Journalists saw GFB ratting in the church	July 1867	Aberdeen J July 24 1867
Andrew Hislop many times saw GFB going to dinner	1868-1869	Scotsman Aug 2 1934
William Watson many times saw GFB at Mr Traill's	1868-1871	Weekly Scotsman Jan 2 1932
Mrs Denholm gave GFB milk at the butcher's shop	1869	Scotsman July 31 1934
Angela Burdett-Coutts and Hannah Brown saw GFB	October 1869	Town Council records
A. Watson used to see GFB trotting down to Mr Traill's	1869-1871	Weekly Scotsman Dec 26 1931
Mrs Martin saw GFB emerging from Mr Traill's	1870	Weekly Scotsman Jan 2 1932
William Albert Cunningham saw GFB at Mr Traill's restaurant	1870	Scotsman Aug 2 1934
Wilson McLaren met and fed GFB at Mr Traill's restaurant	1871	Scotsman Aug 11 1934

It is also notable that from a very early stage, some Edinburgh people 'in the know' voiced their opinion that the story of Greyfriars Bobby was entirely bogus. Already in 1867, the Edinburgh *Daily Review* disapproved of the *Scotsman*'s acceptance of the story of Bobby's long vigil. At the Town Council in 1869, Baillie Miller's attack on Greyfriars Bobby was entirely successful; after making inquiries, the Clerk concluded that Miller had been right. The 1871 onslaught on Greyfriars Bobby in the *Leeds Mercury* and other newspapers was never contradicted, and even when the Town Council reviewed Baroness Burdett-Coutts' second application to erect a monument, there were ribald comments doubting the authenticity of the tradition. But the time has come to pass judgment on Greyfriars Bobby; the legend of this extraordinary dog must be put into its proper context in European canine mythology, for the first time.

13

Legends of Canine Fidelity

Zantippus sayling from th' Athenian strand,
Was follow'd by his faithfull hound to land:
And Philips sonne (as Theopompe doth wright)
In faithfull Pertha tooke so great delight,
That being dead, who gaue him so much game,
He built a towne in honour of his name ...

Thomas Lodge, *A Fig for Momus*, 1595

The classical Greeks and Romans had a high opinion of their dogs. Pliny's *Natural History* tells the tale of King of the Garamantes, who was rescued by his 200 dogs after being captured by his enemies. The loyal animals escorted him home from exile and fought anyone who got in the way. These classical dogs were faithful as well as brave and sagacious. As an example of the affecting fondness of dogs for their masters, Plutarch told the story of the dog of Zantippus (or rather Xanthippus), the father of Pericles. This faithful animal could not endure being abandoned by his master, but leapt into the sea and swam alongside his master's vessel. The exhausted dog staggered ashore on Salamis, but only to collapse and die; the tomb of this canine prodigy was long pointed out by the old Greeks. 'Philips sonne', referred to by the old poet Thomas Lodge, was none other than Alexander the Great, who was very fond of his large mastiff-like dog named Peritas. When the dog died, Alexander led the funeral procession to the grave. He had a fine stone monument erected on the site, and ordered the locals to extol the dog's memory in annual ceremonies.

There is no shortage of other tales of classical dogs, and their willingness to make the most astounding sacrifices for their masters. Pliny writes that in the consulship of Appius Junius and P. Silius, when Titus Sabinus was put to death, together with his slaves, for assaulting Nero, the son of Germanicus, it was found impossible to drive away a dog, which belonged to one of them, from the prison. After the dog's master had been executed, nor could the animal be forced away from the body, which had been cast down the Gemitorian steps. There the dog stood howling, in the presence of vast multitudes of people; and when someone threw a piece of bread to it, the animal carried it to the mouth of its master. Afterwards, when the body was thrown into the Tiber, the dog swam into the river and endeavoured to

65. Ulysses is recognised by his old dog Argos, from A.-F.-J. de Fréville's *Histoire des Chiens Célèbres*.

66. Ulysses and Argos, from Emile Richebourg's *Histoire des Chiens Célèbres*.

67. The ailing Saint Roch is fed by his faithful dog, from Emile Richebourg's *Histoire des Chiens Célèbres*.

raise the body out of the water. Many people saw and admired this remarkable instance of an animal's fidelity, Pliny assures us.

A Roman named Theodorus possessed a very faithful dog; after he died, the dog lay down by his coffin after it had been put in the tomb. A certain Agnestis Corsus went hunting with his dog, but froze to death in a blizzard; the faithful dog remained by his corpse for three days. When Ulysses returned from his long journeys, he was recognised only by his faithful dog Argos. Overjoyed at the return of his long-lost master, the old dog expired at his feet. When Saint Roch, the patron saint of those suffering from the plague, withdrew into the woods to die after contracting the pestilence himself, his faithful dog refused to abandon him and provided him with a loaf of bread daily.[1]

From classical antiquity, there are several versions of a legend of a man being murdered by jealous enemies, with his dog as the only witness. In his *Scripta Moralia*, Plutarch wrote of King Pyrrhus of Epirus, who saw a dog that had kept vigil over its murdered master's corpse for three days without access to food. The King made sure the man was decently buried, and took care of the faithful dog. At an army review, the dog started barking at two soldiers, and they promptly confessed to the murder. When Hesiod, called the Wise, was murdered, his faithful dog brought to justice the sons of Ganyctor of Naupactus, who had murdered him.[2]

When an officer named Hecati was murdered in Antioch, his dog was the only witness. According to St Ambrose's *Hexaëmeron*, the sagacious canine later identified the murderer, and grasped him with its powerful jaws until he confessed. Another legend told of a certain Sir Roger, a knight at the court of the King of Aragon, who was mortally wounded and left to die by his enemy Sir Mardock.

68. The Dog of Montargis, from A.-F.-J. de
Fréville's *Histoire des Chiens Célèbres*.

Roger's faithful greyhound remained with him until he died, and then it scraped a
pit for his body and covered it with grass and leaves. After keeping vigil over Roger's
remains for seven years, the gaunt dog went to the King's palace on Christmas Day,
where it was recognised and given a meal. Cheered by such festive generosity, the
dog returned the following day, but this time it encountered the hated Mardock,
whom the faithful animal promptly dispatched. The greyhound then led the King's
soldiers to Roger's grave. His remains were dug up and given a proper burial in
consecrated grounds. A proper monument for Roger was erected, at the foot of
which the faithful dog soon after expired.

Giraldus Cambrensis adds another dramatic development to the legend, namely
that after the dog had detected its master's murderer, it was allowed to fight a
judicial duel against this miscreant. This twelfth-century *chanson de geste* 'La
Reine Sibile' took place at the court of Charlemagne, but it reoccurs in the legend
of the Dog of Montargis, set in 1371 during the reign of Charles V of France.
When the officer Aubry de Montdidier is passing through the Forest of Bondy
near Montargis, he is attacked by two jealous enemies, the Chevaliers Landry and
Macaire. He is defended by his large greyhound, but Macaire is able to dispatch
Aubry when the dog is busy biting the other villain. The Dog of Montargis kept
vigil over Aubry's body until hunger forced it to come into town. Whenever it
saw Landry and Macaire, it growled and tried to attack them. This made the King
suspicious that these two had murdered Aubry, and the dog was allowed to prove
its accusation like a gentleman, in a judicial duel.

69. The Dog of Montargis
in action, from Emile
Richebourg's *Histoire des
Chiens Célèbres*.

One version has the duel between Macaire and the Dog of Montargis take part at Charles V's court in Montargis, another places it at 'l'ile Notre-Dame' in Paris. Both agree that a plentiful company of ladies and gentlemen were present at the arena, to cheer the combatants on. The distribution of arms for this strange duel was distinctly unfair: the sturdy Macaire was provided with a large shield, with which to ward off the dog's attacks, and a heavy cudgel, with which to belabour it. The Dog of Montargis was given only a large barrel, in which to take cover against the Chevalier's assault. But the faithful dog eschewed such defeatism, and went for Macaire's throat like a bullet. Forced to confess his crime, the Chevalier was later executed as a murderer. The tale of the Dog of Montargis was long believed to be historical, but competent antiquaries have disproved it as one of several versions of a long-lived ancient myth.[3] The Dog of Montargis is immortalised in a dramatic bronze sculpture of the duel, by Gustave Debrie, situated in front of the Girodet museum in central Montargis.

In Paris, the drama *Le Chien de Montargis, ou la Forêt de Bondy* premiered in 1814, and had an uninterrupted run in until 1834. Translated into English as *The Dog of Montargis, or the Forest of Bondy*, and staged at the King's Theatre, it was to remain the staple item for canine thespians for many years. In a remote forest, the officer Aubri is murderously attacked by two enemies, Macaire and Landri. He is valiantly defended by his large dog Dragon, but when the faithful animal is kept occupied by Landri, the second villain gives Aubri the fatal wound. Later, an innocent deaf-mute simpleton is 'framed' for the murder, but Dragon saves him

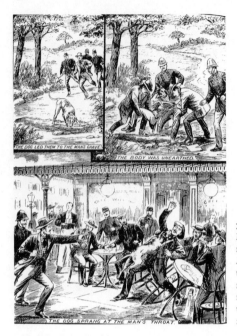

70. The legend of the Dog of Montargis reworked as a newspaper myth, from the *Illustrated Police News*, 18 August 1906. In Valencia, the master of a brave Spanish dog is murdered by some miscreant. The faithful dog leads the master's son to the corpse, and later attacks the murderer in a tavern.

by producing a sash he has torn off Macaire's uniform. Each time Dragon sees the murderers, he growls and tries to attack them. After the King gives the brave dog the right to trial by battle, the faithful animal seizes Macaire with his powerful jaws, and forces him to confess the murder. This scene introduced the trick of 'taking the seize', in which the acting dog leaps up onto the villain and seizes him by the throat. The actor playing the villain had to wear protective padding round his neck, and yell 'Take off the dog!' once he was brought down. With its racy plot and exciting fight scenes, *The Dog of Montargis* would remain a staple item of dog drama for decades to come. In spite of this, the play did not always come off as planned; it is recorded that once, the friendly acting dog stood watching the audience and wagging his tail, instead of 'taking the seize'. The infuriated villain desperately tried to induce him to attack; in the end, he had to fly at the placid dog himself and lift the animal up to his throat.[4]

Perhaps the most famous legend of Wales is that of Prince Llywelyn the Great and his faithful wolfhound Gelert.[5] Llywelyn ap Iorwerth, also known as Llywelyn Fawr (the Great), was an early thirteenth-century Prince of Gwynedd who dominated Wales for forty years. He married Joan Plantagenet, the daughter of King John of England, but this did not prevent him from successfully waging war against the English, and becoming the ruler of large parts of Wales.

71. Gelert fights the wolf, from
Chatterbox magazine, 16 November 1879.

The wolfhound Gelert was the favourite of all Prince Llywelyn's dogs. He had been a present from King John when the two princes had been on friendly terms, and was a dog of uncommon size and beauty. Gelert always used to accompany the Prince and his followers when they went hunting. But one day, Gelert was nowhere to be seen. Prince Llywelyn blew his horn but no dog came. Returning from the hunt, he was pleased to see Gelert coming, as the poet William Robert Spencer expressed it:

> But when he gains his castle door,
>   Aghast the chieftain stood;
> The hound all o'er was smeared with gore,
>   His lips, his fangs, ran blood.

Seeing that his young son's cradle has been overturned, Prince Llywelyn becomes furious:

> 'Hell-hound! my child by thee devour'd!
>   The frantic father cried;
> And to the hilt his vengeful sword
>   He plung'd in Gelert's side.

But after committing this rash canicide, Prince Llywelyn hears his little son cry! It turns out that he is alive and well, lying next to the cradle in a bundle of clothes; next to him is the torn body of a large wolf.

Llewellyn's Grief after killing his favourite Hound.

Right: 72. Prince Llewellyn mourns the martyred dog, from *Chatterbox* magazine, 11 November 1888.

Below: 73. Gelert's grave in Beddgelert, a postcard stamped and posted in 1904.

Beddgelert.

> Ah, what was then Llewelyn's pain!
>   For now the truth was clear:
> His gallant hound the wolf had slain
>   To save Llewelyn's heir.

Stricken by remorse for killing his faithful dog, Llywelyn had Gelert buried with much ceremony; the village where the martyred wolfhound was laid to rest was

74. The knight, the faithful dog, the serpent and the child, from an early edition of the *Directorium Humanae Vitae*.

named Bedd Gelert (The Grave of Gelert) in his honour. Since the late eighteenth century at least, Gelert's grave in Beddgelert, as the village is still known today, has been a tourist attraction. Ignoring the many quaint local villages, the historic castles, and the magnificent natural scenery of the Snowdonia mountains nearby, many tourists have come to see the martyred Gelert's grave.

In his *Curious Myths of the Middle Ages*, the antiquary Sabine Baring-Gould exposed the tale of the knight and the martyred dog as a version of a widespread medieval legend. The earliest version was found in an ancient Indian book, the Sanskrit Pantschatantra, complied about AD 540. A Brahmin named Devasaman had a wife, a son, and a pet mongoose. One day, when the Brahminee went to fetch water, she asked her husband to look after the baby, so that he was not injured by the mongoose. But the thoughtless Brahmin went out begging, leaving the house deserted. When a black snake came slithering in and attempted to bite the child, the faithful mongoose tore it to pieces. But when the returning Brahminee saw the bloodstained creature, she rashly concluded that it had injured the baby, and threw her water-jar on it with lethal results. She then discovered her mistake, mourned the brave mongoose, and berated her foolish husband for deserting his post.

The story evolved as it travelled all over the cultural world. The Faithful Animal, which had originated as a mongoose, developed into a cat, a falcon, or even a tame lion, before ending up as a dog guarding the cradle of its master's young child. The Bad Animal, a snake or a wolf, approaches the cradle with evil intent, but the Faithful Animal kills it after a fierce fight, only to succumb to the rash and irate master's sword. The fate of the dog's master varied widely. In the bloodthirsty versions, he kills himself or goes mad; in others, he never speaks again, or becomes a recluse. In the more benign variants, he learns the medieval equivalent of anger management, refrains from further rash canicides, and lives happily ever after. In a German version of the tale, an angry knight beats his faithful dog to death with a long cudgel, and then disembowels himself when he sees the dead snake; the crying

Dieux!... quelle horreur!... jefremis

75. The bludgeon-wielding father, the child (screaming), the dog (dead) and the snake (in little pieces), from the pamphlet *L'Enfant sauvé du danger par la fidelité du Chien*.

little child is the only survivor of this fierce encounter. In Russia, a tale closely resembling that of Prince Llewelyn was told about a certain Czar Piras. The moral of the tale is always that rash wrath can have disastrous consequences.

The most famous of these martyred canine babysitters was the greyhound Guinefort, killed by a rash nobleman in medieval France. When the superstitious local peasants heard the story of the martyred dog, they seem to have reasoned that if the noble greyhound had died to save the life of a child, then the site where the canine martyr had been buried surely must have magical powers to heal sickly children, and they began worshipping there. In weird rituals, the mothers exposed their ailing offspring to the cold, and passed them through an opening between the trunks of two trees. They later plunged the children into a nearby river, reasoning that if they survived, Saint Guinefort, as the martyred dog was called, would surely make the surviving children strong and healthy. The Dominican Etienne de Bourbon, an enemy of superstition, wanted to suppress the cult of the dog saint. He had the gravesite destroyed, the trees cut down, and the dog's bones burnt and scattered. He threatened the peasants that if they kept worshipping at Saint Guinefort's wood, they would be severely fined. The forthright Dominican believed these harsh measures had enjoyed the desired effect, but here he was very much mistaken: the cult of Saint Guinefort withstood every attempt to suppress it for more than six centuries, and as late as the 1920s, a witch-like old woman had worshipped the dog saint at the cult site, and taken sickly children there.

76. The faithful dog fights a huge snake to save the sleeping child – a fanciful drawing from Emile Richebourg's *Histoire des Chiens Célèbres*.

The 'Martyred Dog' legend is an example of a medieval *historia valde memorabilis*, a short memorable tale with a moral, told and retold throughout the cultural world with different protagonists. Saint Guinefort's wood, Gelert's grave monument, and the various tombs and shrines erected for some faithful dogs in India, connect the different versions of the legend with certain visual landmarks. Although the 'Martyred Dog' legend is certainly very old, in Wales as well as in continental Europe, its association with Prince Llywelyn the Great, the dog's name Gelert or Cylart, and the village of Beddgelert, is a relatively recent invention. There are several eighteenth-century works on the topography and history of West Wales, but none of them mentions anything about any colourful origin of the name Beddgelert. In fact, there is a strong case to be made for the village to have been named after an early Christian missionary named Celert (or Cilert) who was active in these parts during the eighth century.

The 'Martyred Dog' legend has more than once been reported as news in the twentieth century. As late as the 1990s, a Belgian paper reported that a man had left his young son in the car, after he had gone shopping. Returning, he saw his bloodstained son and the bloody jaws of the dog, which he threw to the ground and killed. Aghast, he then discovered the body of a large rat, which was presumed to have emerged from a sack of potatoes and attacked the child, only to be dispatched by the canine martyr. Gelert and Saint Guinefort must have wagged their holy tails up in heaven when they heard that one.

77. After losing his master (a Scottish gunner) on the battlefield at Fontenoy in 1745, the faithful dog 'Mustapha' opens fire at the enemy. An oft-repeated French tale, from A.-F.-J. de Fréville's *Histoire des Chiens Célèbres*.

78. Mustapha opens fire, from Emile Richebourg's *Histoire des Chiens Célèbres*.

> But of their faith, what stories cannot boast?
> Lisimachus, when as his life was lost,
> And funerall prepar'd, and herse arrai'd,
> And faire addrest, & frends with griefe dismai'd;
> Began to burne his corse with many teares,
> His faithfull dog that seru'd him many yeares,
> In selfesame fire, that burnt his kingly corse,
> Consum'd to dust, freely without inforce:

When he was to illustrate yet another example of extreme canine fidelity in *A Fig for Momus,* our old poetical friend Thomas Lodge chose the dog Hyrkanus, belonging to King Lysimachus of Macedonia. A controversial ruler even by ancient Greek standards, Lysimachus had been killed by a well-aimed javelin throw at the Battle of Corupedium in 281 BC. It was said that his faithful dog had kept vigil by his corpse, protecting it from the birds of prey until it was found by the Macedonian soldiers. When the body of King Lysimachus was to be burnt on the pyre, the mourning Hyrkanus howled and whined, before leaping headlong into the flames to rejoin his royal master. Another excessively faithful dog, belonging to King Hiero of Syracuse, committed suicide in exactly the same manner after its master's death.

In the nineteenth century, canine suicides became part of the cultural construction of dogs as popularised symbols of the faith and devotion many people found to be lacking in human relationships. It was considered perfectly possible for a dog to throw itself out through the upper-floor window and commit suicide from grief after its master had expired. When some French rationalist was scoffing at the story of the faithful Hyrkanus destroying himself on the pyre, he was answered by M. Jean Robert, who had once known an old forester whose dog was excessively fond of him. When some jolly and careless young people dressed a mannequin in the forester's clothes and burnt it on top of a bonfire, the dog made a near-disastrous error of judgment, or so at least M. Robert claimed. Barking frantically, the poor dog tried to hurl himself onto the fire to rejoin what it perceived to be its lost master; when held back by some kind individuals, the frenzied animal bit them hard.[6]

In 1845, the *Illustrated London News* could report a 'Singular Case of Suicide by a Dog': a frenzied Newfoundland dog had thrown himself into water and drowned.[7] The RSPCA's *Animal World* had several other instances of animal suicides to report: a cat hanged herself after the loss of her kittens, an old horse leapt into a canal and destroyed itself, and a maltreated, old and infirm dog drowned itself in a river. Noble stags deliberately leapt from high precipices to escape pursuing packs of hunting dogs.[8] The *Bulletin* of the Société Protectrice des Animaux, the journal of the French equivalent of the RSPCA, had some very spicy newspaper stories about suicidal animals to add: several dogs had died from grief when their masters had expired, and another dog had drowned itself in the Seine. A little dog named

79. A suicidal monkey, from the
Illustrated Police News, 11 May 1889.

Chéri, belonging to a pensioner named Mme B., gave plaintive cries of distress and refused all nourishment after the old lady had expired. A niece took care of Chéri, but when she invited the little dog to sit on her lap in Mme B.'s favourite chair, where the pensioner had used to sit with her dog, Chéri was overcome with grief. In a fit of despair, the little dog leapt headlong out of the window, falling to her death in the street far below.[9] By granting dogs and other animals the capacity to commit suicide, they were given emotion, consciousness and intelligence.

The Scottish psychiatrist William Lauder Lindsay believed that the mind was essentially the same in humans and in other animals, and he collected case studies of animals committing suicide to bolster his arguments. A cat might destroy itself after its kittens had been killed, he argued, just like a woman might be driven to suicidal despair if she lost her child. And just like a sick, worn-out old man might blow his brains out, an overworked, ill-used old carthorse might end its misery by leaping into water.[10] Other scientists disagreed, however. Psychiatrist Henry Maudsley accused Lindsay of anthropomorphic reasoning, and criticised his odd case reports severely: some came from unreliable continental newspapers, others might well have depicted an animal driven to despair by pain and illness making a frantic rush that resulted in its death.[11] The 'suicidal' Newfoundland probably suffered from rabies, a disease not uncommon at the time. The newspaper stories of suicidal dogs often emanated from 'funny' French or Belgian papers. The typical version is that some emotional and dog-owning Paris banker (or actress) is ruined (or jilted). Seeing its master (or mistress) leap out through the window, the faithful dog leaps after him (or her), with a dismal howl. Another tall story concerns the faithful pet monkey, whose desperate and suicidal master blows his brains out with a pistol. The grieving primate grabs the pistol, aims at its own temple, and …[12]

Present-day zoologists and psychologists agree with Maudsley and his adherents: suicide is a distinctly human act.[13] Dogs and other non-human animals have a powerful instinct for self-preservation, and do not destroy themselves. Even the scorpion, said by Lord Byron in *The Giaour* to sting itself in the back when surrounded by fire, does not make use of its formidable weapon against itself even when cruelly provoked; in fact, the creature has some degree of immunity against its own venom.

The reader will appreciate that here we have a group of interlinked legends of canine fidelity, dating back to classical times, and founded on fancy rather than fact. The myth of the 'Dog on the Master's Grave' is yet another member of this group. It was said that Eupolis, a Greek comic poet who flourished about 435 BC, had a Molossan dog named Augeas, which was very fond of him. This dog had been a present from a friend of the poet, also named Augeas. Once, the canine Augeas spotted a dishonest slave purloining one of Eupolis' manuscripts; the faithful animal attacked the thieving menial and bit him to death. There are differing accounts of how Eupolis met his death; the most dramatic was that, having been lampooned in one of the poet's comedies, his enemy Alkibiades grabbed Eupolis and flung him headlong into the sea, exclaiming, 'As you drenched me in the theatre, I will now drench you in the sea!' Poor Augeas kept vigil at the poet's grave, howling and wailing from grief. The faithful animal refused all food, and died of grief and starvation on its master's tomb.[14]

William the Silent, the first Prince of Orange, had a little pug dog named Pompey. Once, this dog saved him from assassins through scratching and jumping on his face when it heard the villains approaching. In 1584, when the heroic Pompey was not present to give the alarm, another assassin shot Prince William dead, however. The little dog died of grief on its master's grave not long after, or so it was alleged; little Pompey was depicted lying at its master's feet on William's grand mausoleum in Delft. None less than Miguel de Cervantes, in his short 1613 novel *Dialogues of the Dogs*, wrote:

> I know well enough that there have been dogs so loving that they have thrown themselves into the same grave with the dead bodies of their masters; others have stayed upon their masters' graves without stirring a moment from them, and have voluntarily starved themselves to death, refusing to touch the food that was brought them.

There are several similar yarns from sixteenth- and seventeenth-century France and Italy. The 1663 edition of Samuel Bouchart's *Hierozoicon* alludes to a story well known in Paris at the time: a dog had kept vigil by its master's grave for three years. Supported by the people living near the cemetery, the faithful dog had braved the rigours of several winters. At about the same time, another dog near Lisle was also keeping vigil on its master's grave. The kind and dog-loving local inhabitants

Above: 80. Mr Stewart's dog on his master's grave, from F. C. Woodworth's *Stories about Animals*.

Below: 81. A dog mourning on its master's grave, from *Kind Words*, 28 June

Above left: 82. A desperate-looking dog mourning on its master's grave, from *Animal World*, 1 November 1869.

Above right: 83. A faithful poodle mourns its master, from the children's book *Memoires d'un Caniche.*

erected a comfortable kennel over the grave, and fed the faithful dog regularly, until the animal expired nine years later.[15]

The next incarnation of the 'Dog on the Master's Grave' surfaces not far from Greyfriars Bobby's home territory. In 1716, a certain Mr Stewart, of Argyleshire, died suddenly from 'inflammation in his side'. His faithful Highland greyhound (an old name for the Scottish deerhound) followed the remains of his master to the cemetery. Every evening afterward, about sunset, this dog walked the ten miles to the graveyard, lay down on his master's grave and spent all night there, before returning home in the morning. The local children befriended the dog and brought him some morsels of food, but the unhappy dog refused them. He could not be persuaded to eat a morsel, and frequently uttered long and mournful groans.[16]

14

Cemetery Dogs

'He will not come,' said the gentle child,
And she patted the poor dog's head,
And pleasantly call'd him, and fondly smil'd,
But he heeded her not, in his anguish wild,
Nor arose from his lowly bed.

'Twas his master's grave, where he chose to rest,
He guarded it night and day,
The love that glow'd in his grateful breast
For the friend that had fed, controll'd, caress'd,
Might never fade away.

Thus begins 'The Dog on the Master's Grave', a poem about a gloomy cemetery dog, written by Mrs Lydia Howard Sigourney and published in her popular collection *Poetry for Children* in 1834.[1] When a youthful Anne of Green Gables was once asked to recite a biblical paraphrase in her Sunday school, it turned out that her neglected religious education meant that she was the only girl incapable of this feat. The resourceful lass instead offered to recite 'The Dog on the Master's Grave', since she thought that although it was not a truly religious poem, it was so very sad and melancholy that it might well have been.

And when the long grass rustled near
Beneath some traveller's tread,
He started up with a quivering ear,
For he thought 'twas the step of that master dear
Returning from the dead.

And sometimes, when a storm drew nigh
And the clouds were dark and fleet,
He tore the turf with a mournful cry,
As if he would force his way or die,
To his much lov'd master's feet.

Le CHIEN des Tombeaux
Durant ~ années il demeura constamment couché
sur la tombe de ses Maîtres.

84. 'Le Chien des Tombeaux' mourning
its master, from A.-F.-J. de Fréville's
Histoire des Chiens Célèbres.

France has a rich lore of 'Dog on the Master's Grave' stories. One of the best-known
of them emanated from Marseille. When this city was struck by the plague in 1720,
an entire family was wiped out: the father, mother, two grown-up daughters and
three young sons. The only survivor was a Barbet, or French water dog. Although
given another home, the grieving dog refused to stay there: he kept vigil at the
tombs of the family, preferring that of the seven-year-old son, who had always
been very good to the dog. 'Le Chien des Tombeaux' lamented without cessation,
the sentimental French dog historian Anne-François-Joachim de Fréville asserted,
and he tried to dig with his frail paws to rejoin his young master in the grave. The
cemetery dog kept vigil night and day for not less than seven years, and could only
be persuaded to eat with the greatest difficulty. The dog became a local celebrity
for his devotion, and on Sundays and holidays, people came to see and feed him.
According to M. de Fréville, they used to contrast the faithful dog to the greedy
heirs who were only too keen to see their *tante d'heritance* put into the cemetery!
Mothers used to bring their daughters to see the cemetery dog, and exclaim,
'*Voyez-vous, mes enfants, voyez-vous le Chien des Tombeaux!*'[2] According to another
source, the cemetery dog was popular throughout the district: people regularly fed
and cared for him, and people travelled from distant villages to point out the dog
to their children, and exclaim, 'Mes *enfants, admirez le Chien des Tombeaux, et ne
l'oubliez jamais!*'[3]

> So, there through the summer's heat he lay,
> Till autumn nights were bleak;
> Till his eye grew dim with his hope's decay,
> And he pin'd, and pin'd, and wasted away,
> A skeleton gaunt and weak.
>
> And pitying children often brought
> Their offerings of meat and bread,
> And to coax him away to their homes they sought,
> But his buried friend he ne'er forgot,
> Nor stray'd from his lonely bed.

At about the same time the Marseille cemetery dog held court, a young Montpellier student named Renaudin expired in a hunting accident. The student had a faithful wolfhound that was very fond of him. When Renaudin's body was brought to his lodgings, the dog mourned him intensely, wailing and howling with grief. When the student's body was put in a coffin, the dog wanted to share it with him. At the funeral, the dog was the chief mourner, and a few days later, the other students could see it keeping vigil at Renaudin's tomb. They made the dog a comfortable kennel and kept it well fed. During its five-year vigil, the dog was never more than twenty steps away from Renaudin's tomb. It is recorded that the other dogs of Montpellier often came to visit the wolfhound in its snug kennel, to try to cheer the gloomy old cemetery dog up! In Montpellier, this dog became a byword for fidelity in friendship; it might be said about some person, '*Ah! pour celui-là, il ne vaudra jamais le Chien de Renaudin!*'[4]

> Cold winter came with an angry sway,
> And the snow lay deep and sore;
> And his moaning grew fainter day by day,
> Till there, on the spot where his master lay
> He fell, to rise no more.
>
> And when he struggled with mortal pain,
> And death was by his side,
> With one loud cry that shook the plain,
> He call'd for his master, but all in vain,
> Then stretch'd himself and died.

In Paris, many people had seen 'Le Chien des Innocents' keeping vigil on the tomb of his late master in this famous old cemetery for several years. In Lyons, a dog was said to have died of grief, lying on the grave of his master, a nobleman guillotined during the Revolution.[5] In January 1799, a student named Beaumanoir wanted to cross the frozen Seine, but the ice was too thin and he drowned. His little dog, which had seen him struggle in the water, kept vigil on the ice. When a soldier tried to carry the dog

85. 'He is always waiting', a 'funny' cartoon from *Charivari* magazine, inspired by the sad tale of the student Beaumanoir and his faithful dog.

off, he was bitten by the faithful animal; enraged by this ingratitude, the soldier instead shot the dog with his rifle! In one version of this yarn, the dog dies and is thrown onto a pile of refuse, whereas the soldier lives happily ever after; in another, the soldier dies from the infected dog bite, and the dog is nursed back to health by a kindly old woman. A 'funny' cartoon depicted the mournful-looking dog sitting near the hole in the ice, next to its master's tall hat, with the caption: 'He is always waiting.'[6]

According to the reminiscences of the executioner Sanson, an imprisoned deserter named Notter had a dog that kept vigil at the prison door. When Notter was brought to be executed at the Place du Trône, the dog followed the prison-cart. Notter patted his dog one final time, but it still insisted on following him up onto the scaffold. When pushed down, it leapt up again, howling dismally, until a gendarme pinned it with his bayonet. The mob pelted the gendarme with stones and he narrowly escaped with his life. The dog was rescued by a workman, but Notter was decapitated by the guillotine.[7] Here this section ends, with Mrs Sigourney's cemetery dog, but there are more of them to come, in poetry and prose!

> With gentle tread, with uncovered head,
>   Pass by the Louvre gate,
> Where buried lie the 'men of July,'
>   And flowers are hung by the passers-by,
>   And the dog howls desolate.
>
> That dog had fought in the fierce onslaught,
>   Had rushed with his master on,
> And both fought well;
> But the master fell,
>   And behold the surviving one!

86. The best-known engraving of Médor, the Dog of the Louvre.

Thus begins Ralph Cecil's translation of the French poet Casimir Delavigne's celebrated poem 'Le Chien du Louvre', said by many to be his masterpiece.[7] In July 1830, the unpopular King Charles X of France was persuaded by his reactionary ministers to change the constitution to the detriment of all but the rich and noble. Since the Parisians of course objected to these measures, there was widespread rioting, with barricades in the streets. The royalist troops were defeated after three days of fierce fighting. Charles X, whose obdurate mind had not been able to appreciate the lesson so harshly taught to his forefathers, that an angry Parisian mob is not to be underestimated, had to abdicate, and the Duke of Orléans took over the throne as King Louis Philippe I.

> By his lifeless clay,
> Shaggy and gray,
>   His fellow-warrior stood;
> Nor moved beyond,
> But mingled fond
>   Big tears with his master's blood.
>
> Vigil he keeps
> By those green heaps
>   That tell where heroes lie.
> No passer-by
> Can attract his eye,
>   For he knows it is not He!

87. Another fine engraving of the Dog of the Louvre.

During the fierce fighting near the Louvre, which was of course a royal palace in those days, not a museum, many revolutionaries fell in the hail of royalist bullets. As shown in Jean-Alphonse Rœhn's painting at the Musée Carnavalet in Paris, they were buried in a mass grave at the Place du Louvre, surrounded by a low wooden fence, and with a suitable monument. Overjoyed at the dethroning of Charles X and the fall of his unpopular government, the Parisians were inflamed with patriotism. It became popular to visit the resting place of the 'Heroes of the Louvre', whose blood had been shed to overthrow the tyrant. One day, these Parisians saw that they were not alone. Inside the wooden fence, asleep near the grave, was a large, white and brown, poodle-like dog!

Everybody of course realized that this was the Dog of the Nameless Brave, who had come to keep vigil at the grave of his fallen master. As a result, Médor, the Dog of the Louvre, became nothing less than a national celebrity. The sixth legion of the National Guards, stationed nearby, took an interest in Médor. They built him a comfortable kennel, with the sentimental inscription:

> *Depuis le jour qu'il a perdu son maitre,*
> *Pour lui la vie est un pesant fardeau;*
> *Par son instinct il croit le voir paraitre;*
> *Ah! Pauvre ami, ce n'est plus qu'un tombeau!*

Outside the Louvre monument stood the sellers of prints and pamphlets about this extraordinary dog. One of the pamphlets asserted that Médor had belonged to a young mason named Jacques-Léon Duhamel, who had bit the dust near the

88. Another contemporary engraving of the Dog of the Louvre, unfortunately very worn.

barricades at the Rue des Deux Ecus, along with his cousin, another revolutionary. The patriotic dog had also taken active part in the fighting, this pamphlet alleges, and shed his blood for the glory of France after receiving some minor bullet wounds. The other pamphlets mention nothing about these excesses, however; if the name of Médor's master had been known, how could he then have been referred to as the Dog of the Nameless Brave?[9]

> At the dawn, when dew
> Wets the garlands new
>   That are hung in this place of mourning,
> He will start to meet
> The coming feet
>   Of him whom he dreamt returning.
>
> On the grave's wood-cross
> When the chaplets toss,
>   By the blast of midnight shaken,
> How he howleth! hark!
> From that dwelling dark
>   The slain he would fain awaken.

The Parisians brought plenty of cakes, bread and sausages for Médor, with the result that the half-starved cemetery dog soon developed into a very sturdy, well-nourished specimen. Sometimes, people were disappointed to see the Dog of the Louvre sleeping peacefully in his kennel, or waddling around the enclosure looking quite jolly and carefree. Surely, he should be weeping profusely on the grave of the

89. An odd-looking image of the Dog of the Louvre, from the pamphlet *Médor, ou le Chien du Louvre* (Paris 1831).

Nameless Brave, and scraping the ground with his feeble paws, as the newspapers and pamphlets had told that Médor would be doing.

The francophile German journalist and traveller Ludwig Börne of course had to visit Médor, whom he described as a stout-looking white poodle. Médor was the Emperor of Dogs, Börne wrote, the most famous canine inhabitant of Paris, for his heroism in the July Revolution. Arriving at the Place du Louvre, Börne could see that Médor had already found his Plutarch: from the peddlers surrounding the fenced cemetery, he purchased a pamphlet on the Dog of the Louvre, a song about his heroism, and the dog's portrait from life. Börne wanted to stroke Médor, but the cemetery dog did not like him, perhaps because it offended the radical political sympathies of the Dog of the Louvre to have anything to do with a well-dressed foreigner.[10]

> When the snow comes fast
> On the chilly blast,
>   Blanching the bleak church-yard,
> With limbs outspread
> On the dismal bed
>   Of his liege, he still keeps guard.
>
> Oft in the night,
> With main and might,
>   He strives to raise the stone;
> Short respite takes:
> 'If master wakes,
>   He'll call me,' then sleeps on.

In late 1830, there was scandal when the cemetery attendant Auguste Marchal reported that an Englishman had tried to bribe her with 200 francs to look the other way when he stole the Dog of the Louvre! Outraged that Médor, the most famous dog in France, might be taken abroad to be exhibited for money, the French authorities had the Englishman arrested. Nine months later, he was still in prison. In the meantime, there was further drama when M. and Mme Martin, who owned a property near Vitri, claimed that Médor belonged to them. When they were reminded that he was the Dog of the Nameless Brave, and refused access to the dog, their response was to drive up to the Louvre in their carriage, grab Médor, and drive off with him. The feeble cemetery guardians were lambasted for losing the most valuable dog in France; surely, it was a crime that cried out to Heaven for vengeance to abduct the mourning dog from the grave of the Nameless Brave! The French authorities again acted with commendable resolution: a search order was issued for the Martin premises in Vitri, a swift dawn raid carried out, and the Dog of the Louvre recovered. When Madame Martin claimed she could find witnesses to testify that Médor was really her dog, she was severely reprimanded: she would go to prison if she kept insulting the Dog of the Nameless Brave!

The senior cemetery attendant, Madame Troiedul, was wholly unamused by these shenanigans. She objected that it was very unwise to allow this valuable dog to sleep outdoors in a cemetery, guarded only by an old woman and a couple of soldiers. She herself offered to take care of '*cet incomparable animal*', as she called him, and to stand guard at the cemetery gates during daytime to deter dog-thieves. She would also keep Médor in her house at night, where he would be safe from the foreign riff-raff with designs to kidnap him and take him abroad. The sentimentalists feared that Médor would become desperate with grief when he was parted from the remains of the Nameless Brave, but the cemetery dog and Madame Troiedul soon became firm friends.

To prevent Médor being given unsuitable food, or gorging himself on the delicacies provided by his visitors, all the people who wanted to feed the Dog of the Louvre had to apply at Madame Troiedul's house. The forthright Parisian lady was understandably most indignant when another cemetery attendant, jealous of her status as Médor's keeper, accused her of putting the tastiest *tartelets* and *gateaux* aside for her own consumption! She showed the cemetery dog to the National Guards officers to prove that he was a very well-nourished specimen; in fact, he might burst if he ate everything that was provided for him!

Later, Madame Troiedul was again in trouble after being accused of fiddling the accounts for the sale of pamphlets and prints about Médor. The outcome was that although she was allowed to keep the dog in her house at night, she was ordered to share the daytime care of the Dog of the Louvre with Madame Détot, the official pamphlet-seller, and the concierge of the cemetery.

Throughout 1831, Médor remained one of the curiosities of Paris. When the pamphlets about him were reissued, there was some squabbling as to how much of the profit should go to the widows of the deceased 1830 revolutionaries. One of the pamphlets included a poem in praise of the cemetery dog:

> *Quand tout Paris l'admire et le contemple,*
> *Quand son renom augmente tous les jours,*
> *ce chien célèbre offre au monde un example*
> *Que les humains ne donnent pas toujours:*
> *Vous, ses pareils , illustres dans l'histoire,*
> *Cédez la palme au chien du Parisien!*
> *C'est à Médor qu'appartient la victoire:*
> *trois fois honneur à ce fidèle chien.*

After December 1831, there is no mention of the once-so-famous Dog of the Louvre, however. Did Médor die in midst of his fame, or did the Parisians finally get fed up with him? Perhaps he ended up as just an ordinary dog, chewing bones, chasing cats, and going for walks with Madame Troiedul. M. Robert Lestrange, author of *Les Animaux dans la Littérature*, claims that Médor died of grief on the grave, but his fanciful book can hardly be considered a reliable factual account. M. Rodolphe Trouilleux, author of the excellent *Histoires Insolites des Animaux de Paris*, has no suggestion as to what happened to the once-celebrated cemetery dog.[11] But irrespective of his ultimate fate, the Dog of the Louvre will live forever in Casimir Delavigne's poem:

> He'll linger there
> In sad despair,
> And die on his master's grave.
> His name? 'Tis known
> To the dead alone –
> He's the dog of the nameless brave!
>
> A tear for the dead! for the dog some bread!
> Ye who pass the Louvre gate!
> Where buried lie the men of July,
> And flowers are flung by the passers-by,
> And the dog howls desolate.

The Dog of the Louvre had many successors in the nineteenth-century francophone world, where some very queer notions of excessive canine fidelity flourished among the well-to-do bourgeois dog-lovers, as evidenced by a decidedly odd publication, the aforementioned *Bulletin* of the Société Protectrice des Animaux, the journal of the French equivalent of the RSPCA.[12] Just like their London colleagues at *Animal World*, the editorial team of the *Bulletin* trawled the newspaper press to find interesting titbits about animal protection and animal behaviour. But as we have already seen in the section about canine suicides, their good judgment often failed them and they reproduced what were obviously newspaper canards.

In 1858, the *L'Yonne* newspaper reported that after the death of a forest constable named François Prévot, of the Saint-Bris commune near Auxenne, his little dog

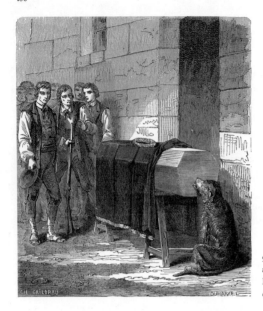

90. A mourning French dog
and its master's coffin, from
Emile Richebourg's *Histoire
des Chiens Célèbres*.

bit the timbers of his coffin, and gave plaintive cries of distress. The third day after the funeral, the dog rested on the grave of Prévot, and remained there. Prévot's successor as forest constable tried to tempt or bribe the dog away, but the dignified cemetery dog did not allow caresses or food to distract it from its grief.

In 1862, the *Indépendence Belge* newspaper had an even more affecting story, seized upon with glee by the editor of the *Bulletin*. An old man living in the Schaerbeek suburb had a common-looking dog, which never left him for a moment. When the old man died after a short disease, the dog had to be driven away from the cadaver. The mourning dog refused all food, '*en jappant d'une manière désespérée*'. The next day, the dog found its master's grave and lay down upon it, whining and crying, as if calling for help. Since then, there had not been a day that this poor animal has not visited its master's grave. It arrived at the cemetery with its nose to the ground and its tail low, behaving with the greatest decorum. On the grave, the dog crouched down in silence, feebly trying to dig the ground with its paws. After spending around a quarter of an hour mourning its master, the part-time cemetery dog left the graveyard and went on with its daily business, only to return the next day. People living nearby took care of the dog and kept it well fed; 'Le Chien de Schaerbeek', this part-time cemetery dog, was often pointed out for its intelligence and fidelity.

In 1874, the Société Protectrice des Animaux faced a crisis when the Paris cemetery authorities issued an edict excluding dogs from the grounds. The appropriately named M. Cheval, a member of the governing council of the Société,

91. A Parisian dog howling on its master's grave, from Henri Coupin's *Les Animaux Excentriques*.

was worried that it would have very harmful consequences for the cemetery dogs to be banned from mourning their dead masters. He knew for a fact that many dogs visited the great Paris cemeteries daily, to mourn their dear departed; there was an increase in their number on All Soul's Day. He claimed that he had himself several times seen a dog prostrate in grief on its master's tomb in the Cayenne cemetery, Quartier Clignancourt.

When a celebrated Paris cemetery dog, 'Le Chien de Montparnasse', was forced to interrupt its vigil on its master's grave by this novel legislation, the Société decided to act resolutely to save the poor mourning animal. This dog, which had been repudiated by the relatives inheriting its master, used to spend much time mourning him in the Montparnasse cemetery. When M. Cheval and the others officials of the Société arrived at the cemetery, the dog stood outside its gates, howling piteously. M. Cheval explained to the verger that this was a proper cemetery dog, with a very sensitive nervous system; it would certainly die from a broken heart if excluded any longer. When the dog was let in by the apologetic verger, it ran straight to the grave of its master, where *le gardien-chef* of the Montparnasse cemetery kept it well fed and cared for. Another tender-hearted Frenchman, M. Humbert, suggested that Paris should have a home for cemetery dogs, where the poor animals could be well looked after, and accompanied to the graves of their masters by an attendant.

Not all of the sentimental French dogs featured in the *Bulletin* became cemetery dogs after the demise of their masters. As we know, some of the more rash of these excitable animals actually committed suicide. Others kept vigil at the hospital where they had last seen their masters, or at the hotel where he had last stayed, or at the railway station or ferry pier where it had last seen the coffin. Some of these dogs also became minor celebrities; an example was 'Le Chien de Notre-Dame des Champs'. This dog had once belonged to the popular young painter Charles

92. The frontispiece of Emile Richebourg's *Histoire des Chiens Célèbres*; note the cemetery dog to the right.

Brentard. After he had died from pleurisy, the dog kept vigil at the hospital doors for two years; it was kept warm and well fed by the kindly porters and nurses.[13]

An even more pathetic French newspaper yarn of excessive canine fidelity is that of the 'Chien de Boulogne'. The *Petit Journal* could report that a big black ownerless retriever dog was the canine celebrity of Boulogne-sur-mer. Its unknown master, presumed to be a Norwegian baron, had one day departed and left his dog behind, or so it was presumed, and the poor animal had kept vigil on the jetty ever since. When the steamer arrived, he bounded out full of hope, to scan the passengers. Only when the last of them had filed past him did the disappointed dog lay down to resume his vigil. 'That steamer,' he seemed to think, 'did not come from Norway.' After three disappointments a day for 700 days, the Dog of Boulogne still kept vigil at the jetty. The newspaper writer wondered how many ladies had told the Norwegian baron that they adored him, and how true their affection had been in comparison to that of the big black dog: 'Man's nature stands confounded before the spotless fidelity of a dog.'[14]

Stockholm had its own 'Dog on the Master's Grave'. In the late 1830s, a dog lived in the Maria cemetery just south of central Stockholm. The Swedes presumed that the faithful animal, appropriately named Fidèle, was keeping vigil on the grave of his master. The name of this individual was unfortunately not known, but since the dog looked like a foreign breed, the master of Fidèle was presumed to have been an English skipper. There was a vague tradition that a troop of sailors had carried his coffin to the grave, followed by the faithful dog, the only other mourner at his funeral.

93. A French dog on its master's grave, from Emile Richebourg's *Histoire des Chiens Célèbres.*

In November 1840, the poetess Julia Nyberg published a lengthy poem in praise of the faithful dog, containing the following verse:

> Though winter winds scatter the leaves
> On his master's grave, the poor dog grieves
> Both day and night, in snow and ice
> By the grave stone, he always lies.

She claimed that Fidèle had kept vigil at the master's tomb for not less than fifteen years, braving many a cold Scandinavian winter. The sentimental Swedes liked to visit and admire the cemetery dog, and give him a treat. After Julia Nyberg's poem had been published, the flow of visitors to Fidèle increased very considerably.

One of them was the dilettante artist Baron Carl Stephan Bennet. A military man turned courtier in middle age, he was fond of dogs, and a competent painter of various Stockholm scenes. Carl Stephan Bennet's painting of Fidèle shows the cemetery dog sitting on his master's grave. A furry, rotund figure, the dog's mournful dark eyes look straight back at the viewer of the portrait. In the background is the wintry cemetery, the western side of the Maria church, and a lone woman dressed in black, her hands clasped like in prayer. The viewer of the painting is left wondering if she is just another visitor to the church, or if she is going to take care of the gloomy cemetery dog.

Carl Stephan Bennet's portrait of Fidèle was engraved at least three times in 1841. Two of the engravings had some explanatory notes about the cemetery dog.

94. Fidèle, the Stockholm cemetery dog, from an engraving of Baron Carl Stephan Bennet's portrait, dated 1841.

The first one points out that the faithful dog had been observed to keep vigil at the grave as early as 1825. The verger, the old dog's only friend, was looking after the pathetic animal. He was the only human contact the mourning cemetery dog would accept. Fidèle was always resting by the same tombstone, apathetic and dead to the world, thinking only of his departed master. Indeed, the almost human look in his mournful eyes was enough to make you believe in the transmigration of souls.

The second engraving presumes that Fidèle's master had been a foreign sea captain, since there was a tradition to that effect, and since the dog was clearly a foreign breed. Fidèle sometimes received his daily nourishment at a butcher's shop nearby, but he was also visited and fed each day by a very charitable Stockholm lady. She had once tried to entice Fidèle into her house, but the mourning dog had howled dismally and refused all food, until allowed to return to the cemetery. The lady had to be content with providing Fidèle with a pillow and a warm fur fleece to protect the little dog against the bitter Scandinavian winter. She is likely to be represented by the lone female figure in the background of Baron Bennet's painting. But after the engravings of the Baron's painting had been issued, and Julia Nyberg's poem published, the dog received visits from the curious every day, and nobody went to see the popular cemetery dog without feeding him some titbits; far from dying of grief, the animal was in serious danger of dying from indigestion![15]

Fidèle was remembered in various Swedish popular books on natural history. One of them, published in 1867, confidently stated that

> No animal shows such affection for the human being as the dog. There are examples of dogs which, after the death of their masters or mistresses, have refused to leave the corpse, or even kept vigil on their graves until they died of grief. Around thirty years ago, a dog was always resting on the same grave in the Maria cemetery in Stockholm.[16]

In 1982, Baron Bennet's painting of Fidèle was one of the leading exhibits at a large art exhibition in Stockholm; there was immediate newspaper interest in this half-forgotten canine celebrity. But when the historian Gunnar Jungmarker investigated the legend of Fidèle, he found that the story was more fancy than fact; even the dog's existence was very much open to doubt.[17] It was impossible that Fidèle's master had been an English skipper, since foreigners were buried in the south-eastern part of the cemetery, and Bennet's painting clearly showed Fidèle keeping vigil in the north-western part. Jungmarker found the various pamphlets about Fidèle more than a little flippant, and there were no contemporary newspaper accounts of the cemetery dog. He consulted the Norwegian cynologist Olaf Roig, who told him that

> the legend of the dog on the master's grave is reproduced in several old British dog books. The location varies from Edinburgh to various towns in Northern England; the length of the vigil varies from 10 to 15 years. It is often added that the dog pays a daily visit to a pub, where it is fed. This vulgar legend, which is widespread all over Britain, suits the romantic view of dogs prevalent among the inhabitants of those parts.

And this forthright Norwegian dog expert is not far wrong. There are versions of the 'Dog on the Master's Grave' legend from all parts of the British Isles. The old dog author Joseph Taylor, writing in 1804, knew of a dog that had been bemoaning the loss of its beloved master for eleven years, living in a cavern at St Olave's cemetery, Southwark. The dog was fed regularly, and pointed out as 'a striking example of the faithfulness and gratitude of a poor Dog, whose fidelity is not to be shaken, even though his departed master is no more'.[18] In 1827, a dog was constantly to be seen in St Bride's churchyard in Fleet Street. This dog had, for two years, refused to leave its master's grave. People were a little disappointed the dog did not look at all miserable. The inhabitants of the houses round the church fed the faithful dog daily, and the sexton provided him with a kennel.[19] No person knew the identity of the masters of either of these two cemetery dogs.

At Newcastle-upon-Tyne in the 1820s, a gentleman had a dog that was very fond of him. When he died and was buried, the dog kept vigil on the grave. The gentleman's widow wanted to retain the dog, but it refused to go with her. The poor

A FAITHFUL FRIEND. (See p. 154.)

95. A drawing of the sad-looking cemetery dog at St Margaret's church, Lee, from an undated extract from *Little Folks* magazine.

dog was brought food and water by kind people, but still expired 'worn away by pining, and by rain and cold'. Pondering this poor dog's fate, a religious children's magazine exclaimed:

> How does this poor brute shame us! We have a master Jesus Christ, who died for *us*, in our stead. Should we not then love him? think of him? serve him always? and if called upon, be willing to die for his sake?[20]

In the 1830s, there was a 'Dog on the Master's Grave', presumed to have belonged to an Italian, in the cemetery of the Catholic chapel in Scotland Road, Liverpool. Every day, this dog went to the nearby Throstle Nest tavern to be provided with a meal. The cemetery dog slept in the tavern, but each morning he set out to mourn his master, or so at least it was presumed.[21] Another faithful old dog lived in the cemetery of St Margaret's church, Lee, not far from London. After spending eighteen months mourning at his unknown master's grave, he was given a collar with the inscription: 'The Little Wonder, of Saint Margaret's Church, Lee'. There are many similar versions of the legend, from every part of the British Isles.[22]

A well-known Dublin monument is the statue of Captain John McNeill Boyd in St Patrick's Anglican Cathedral. The heroic Captain Boyd was lost at sea while attempting to rescue the crew of another stricken ship in the Irish Sea during the terrific gales of February 1861. According to tradition, his Newfoundland dog was the sole survivor, and this dog walked alongside his coffin to the Glasnevin cemetery. Here, the faithful Newfoundland refused to leave the grave and died of hunger. Rationalists have doubted this story, objecting that to commit suicide would have been a strange thing to do for a dog that had recently narrowly escaped death at sea, and also expressing doubts whether Captain Boyd was really buried in this cemetery. Aficionados of Irish ghosts have retorted that a spectral Newfoundland dog has often been seen in the cemetery, or even sitting at the base of Captain Boyd's statue in the cathedral.

The Hyndman memorial in the Clifton Street cemetery in Belfast has the statue of a mournful-looking little dog. According to local tradition, this statue would represent Hyndman's faithful dog, which lay down on the grave and starved to death, but historians of that cemetery have proven this story entirely without foundation. Dog-loving Victorians sometimes wanted a statue of their favourite pet on their tombs or memorials, and these have occasionally given rise to 'Dog on the Master's Grave' stories.

In Victorian times, canine virtue and fidelity were often portrayed in art. Paintings of heroic Newfoundland dogs plunging into the sea, and shaggy St Bernards rescuing distressed travellers, were never short of buyers, to the benefit of the wallets of Sir Edwin Landseer and other popular animal painters of the period. The theme that dogs are more capable of loyalty and affection than human beings also often occurs in Victorian art and poetry.

96. A dog keeping vigil on its master's tomb, from George R. Jesse's *Researches into the History of the British Dog*.

97. A mournful-looking cemetery dog, from George R. Jesse's *Researches into the History of the British Dog*.

98. When a Southend gentleman committed suicide by drowning himself in 1894, his faithful dog kept vigil at the spot afterwards, howling dismally. From *Illustrated Police News*, 3 March 1894.

99. Fido falls to his death, an engraving by William
Blake for William Hayley's *Ballads, founded on
Anecdotes relating to Animals*.

> Of all the speechless friends of man
>   The faithful dog I deem
> Deserving from the human clan
>   The tenderest esteem.

Thus begins William Hayley's *Ballads*, published in 1805 and adorned with a remarkable frontispiece: a naked man is standing on a precipice, watching a dog falling through the air, into the jaws of a waiting crocodile. The man is Edward, a careless fellow wanting to take a bath in a river infested with crocodiles. The faithful dog Fido perceives the danger and tries to stop him from jumping in, but at the cost of himself falling into the river and perishing inside the reptile's jaws. Lucy, the owner of Fido, and also Edward's sweetheart, mourns the heroic dog, but Edward puts a statue of Fido in her chamber. They marry, and

> The marble Fido in their sight
>   Enhanc'd their nuptial bliss;
> And Lucy every morn, and night,
>   Gave him a grateful kiss.

As we have seen, the cemetery dog made its first appearance in art and poetry already in the eighteenth century. When the auctioneer Peter Coxe's long poem *The Social Day* was published in 1823, one of its engravings depicted the faithful spaniel Chère keeping vigil at the tomb of her deceased mistress Ellen, with the lines:

100. The faithful spaniel Chère keeps vigil on the tomb of her mistress, one of the illustrations for Peter Coxe's *The Social Day*, an etching by John Scott from a painting by James Ward.

> She stole from home, there vigil kept;
> And could she weep, then Chère had wept.

It is just possible that Sir Edwin Landseer had come across the illustration to Coxe's poem, or alternatively one of the plates of faithful dogs in M. de Fréville's *Histoire des Chiens Célèbres*. The inspiration for his remarkable 1829 painting *The Poor Dog*, also known as *The Shepherd's Grave*, may also have come from some newspaper report of a cemetery dog. Landseer's *The Poor Dog* shows a mournful-looking dog keeping vigil on what must be presumed to be its master's grave. The stonecutter's tools left by the tombstone, and the unfinished inscription, indicate that the grave has been recently dug. The loneliness of the spot, and the distance from the church spire in the background, add to the impression that the nameless old shepherd has been forgotten by all of humankind: he is remembered only by his faithful dog. In 1837, the prolific Landseer improved on the same theme in his masterpiece *The Old Shepherd's Chief Mourner*. It shows a dark Scottish bothy, inside which a collie keeps vigil by the coffin of its master, an old shepherd. The mourning dog rests its head on the coffin, and one paw is slightly raised, as if it had been scraping the coffin wall.

Landseer's *The Old Shepherd's Chief Mourner* was very well known in Victorian times: framed prints of this famous painting were hanging in many a classroom and Sunday school. Mr Traill, James Brown, and many another Scot must have come across Landseer's powerful imagery of the collie and the old shepherd's coffin. In fact, it does not seem unlikely that Landseer's painting influenced the

101. An engraving of Landseer's *The Poor Dog*, by G. Sidney Hunt, from the 1884 *Library Edition of the Works of Sir Edwin Landseer*, R.A., 1st series.

legend of Greyfriars Bobby, and that the Old Shepherd was the original incarnation of the spectral Auld Jock. After all, the original account of Bobby's master mentions nothing about him being a shepherd, and an out-of-towner had no business being buried at Greyfriars; still, when Mr Traill and others were adding to the Greyfriars Bobby lore, they found it natural that the faithful dog's master had been a nameless old shepherd, and that Bobby had been a prominent mourner at his funeral.

Nor did the 'Dog on the Master's Grave' legend fail to cross the Atlantic. In Rose Hill cemetery, the oldest public cemetery in Washington County, is the stone statue of the dog Rollo, who kept vigil on his unknown master's grave for several years. The cemetery opened in 1865 and the dog statue is said to be nearly as old as that. People living near the cemetery tried to entice Rollo away from the grave, but without success; they instead provided the mourning canine with food, water and shelter in cold weather. When Rollo died, a marble statue was subscribed to by the kind, dog-loving locals. Although the name of the dog owner is long since forgotten, the head of Rollo's statue is worn smooth by thousands of sentimental visitors patting him on the head; nor does the grave ever lack fresh flowers, usually yellow roses.[23]

Another variation of the tale comes from Fort Benton, Montana, where an old sheep-farmer expired in 1936. The reader will be surprised (or perhaps not) that no person could recall his name. After his coffin had been loaded onto a train in Fort Benton, a sheepdog appeared at the station. Everyone presumed that it must be the sheep-farmer's faithful dog, which had come to mourn him. The animal was well fed by the railway staff and passengers, and made the station his permanent home. Already during his lifetime, he became a local celebrity: fan mail poured in after

Above: 102. An engraving of Sir Edwin Landseer's *The Old Shepherd's Chief Mourner*.

Right: 103. After the death of King Edward VII in 1912, his favourite dog Caesar was said to have been disconsolate. There was a book entitled *Where's Master?*, featuring the mourning dog, and Maud Earl's painting *Silent Sorrow* had Caesar resting his weary head on the late King's favourite chair, in a similar pose as *The Old Shepherd's Chief Mourner*. Caesar was led along in the King's funeral procession, and postcards depicting him sold well. Caesar is featured in *Greyfriars Bobby Magazine*, December 2006 – February 2007, 10–1.

104. The statue of Rollo, the American cemetery dog.

the dog had been featured by Ripley's *Believe it or Not*, schoolchildren sent him Christmas gifts, and rail travellers took detours to stop at Fort Benton and see him. 'Old Shep', as the dog was called, even appeared on TV, doing some simple tricks and playing with the station agent. In 1942, the elderly and deaf Old Shep was run over and killed by a train. He was given a grand funeral, with pallbearers and an honour guard; it was attended by hundreds of people. Old Shep is commemorated by an obelisk at his grave, and by a statue; his collar and bowl are on permanent display. A children's book based on his exploits became a healthy seller, and Old Shep also inspired a popular Country & Western song.[24]

Japan has its own Greyfriars Bobby, an Akita named Hachikō. This dog belonged to a university professor, and used to meet him at the local railway station. One day in 1925, the master did not turn up, since he had died from a stroke. Hachikō was given away, but he did not like his new owner, escaping and returning to his old home, and then visiting the railway station. Every day, he appeared at the station, just in time to meet the train his old master had used to travel on. The other passengers recognised the dog and began giving him food and other treats; this went on for several years, making the dog into a newspaper celebrity. His faithfulness to his master's memory impressed the people of Japan as a spirit of family loyalty that all should strive to achieve. Teachers and parents used Hachikō's vigil as an example for children to follow. Already before the old dog had died in 1935, his statue was unveiled at the railway station. Although there have been murmurations that Hachikō's story had been 'improved' to be made use of in Emperor Hirohito's pre-war Japan, in order to inspire loyalty to the state until the bitter end, the railway station dog has remained famous. There have been several books, and at least two films, about him.[25]

105. A ceremony to celebrate Hashikō, the Japanese faithful dog.

In January 1977, the *Komsomolskaja Pravda* newspaper had a story about a Russian 'Old Shep', a German Shepherd bitch that had been left behind by her owner at the Vnukovo airport near Moscow. The dog remained near the airport runway, and seemed to run to meet the planes as they landed. Clearly, this faithful dog was hoping that her dear departed master would return, the Russian sentimentalists speculated. The old Soviet state was good at keeping records of its citizens, both two- and four-legged, and the airport dog's owner was actually tracked down to a farm in Siberia. He admitted abandoning the dog because he had no veterinary certificate for her. The newspaper received a total of 3,470 letters from kind, dog-loving Russians offering to give the 'faithful mourner' a home.[26]

The 'Dog on the Master's Grave' legend has enjoyed considerable staying power, although the stories have often tended to crumble when examined more carefully. In 1908, a very large black dog was seen keeping vigil at the Muswell Hill omnibus terminus in London. The handsome animal was befriended by the omnibus conductors, and fed by the passengers. There was much speculation whether the dog's master might have been a person killed in an accident nearby. Or perhaps he had been callous enough to desert his dog at the terminus, for the faithful Dog of Muswell Hill to wait for him week after week. After featuring the story, the *Daily Mirror* was inundated with letters from people showing sympathy for the dog's extraordinary fidelity, many of them enclosing biscuits and other treats. Some of the readers offered to give the dog a new home. But when a Hackney dog fancier saw the photograph of the Dog of Muswell Hill, he recognised her as his fine Great Dane bitch, who had strayed two weeks earlier after a door had been left open. She was a young dog, and apt to make friends with everyone. The dog's master had not been anywhere near Muswell Hill. When visited by a *Daily Mirror* journalist, the Great Dane was sleeping hard, reclining comfortably at full length in a back room, evidently happy to be home after two weeks of masquerading as London's pathetic omnibus station dog.[27]

In Malmö, Sweden, a wealthy factory owner named Wadman died in the early 1920s, and was buried with much pomp. A few days later, a large brown dog was observed near his grave. The local people believed that Mr Wadman's dog had come to the cemetery to mourn him, and a conservative newspaper published the cemetery dog's photograph. But when interviewed in a socialist paper, Wadman's former coachman denied that his master had ever owned a dog; in fact, the old Swede had always had the greatest aversion to these animals. An old woman who kept a dairy shop recognised the cemetery dog from its newspaper photograph: it was her own watchdog, which had been let out of its yard by some mischievous youngster. This dog had no connection whatsoever with Wadman. The socialist newspaper mocked its conservative rival paper: was it not very foolish to believe these old yarns about dogs keeping vigil on the graves of their masters? In particular, no right-minded member of the canine tribe was likely to have much sympathy for such a money-grubbing capitalist as Wadman, who had been well known for firing his workmen if they belonged to the trade union![28]

In 1930, Mrs Elizabeth Smith, of Buffalo, was buried at Pine Hill cemetery. The day after, workmen were surprised to see a black collie dog lying disconsolately near the grave, howling dismally. Many people went to admire the devoted dog, and bring it food. The American SPCA took the dog away to their pound, where it was seen by Mrs Smith's flabbergasted relatives; they had never seen the 'faithful mourner' before, and Mrs Smith had never owned a dog! But the dog's newspaper photograph was seen by another Buffalo citizen, who had lost his fine collie Rex a few days earlier. When he arrived at the pound, Rex jumped up, yelping with delight. Since the dog had never even seen Mrs Smith, his alleged 'faithful mourning' had just been sentimental misinterpretation from the cemetery workmen.[29]

There were American newspaper stories of cemetery dogs from 1909, 1922, 1932 and 1954 (two). In one of the 1954 yarns, there was consternation when it turned out that the mongrel Brownie, presumed to have travelled 16 miles to keep vigil on the grave of his only real friend, his seven-year-old master, had selected the grave of a pensioner by mistake. In the other one, a stray dog had appeared after a funeral in a Hartford, Connecticut, cemetery. The local people presumed it had come to mourn its departed master, but again it turned out that the dog was 'keeping vigil' on the grave of a perfect stranger, and enjoying a comfortable life as a cemetery dog.[30]

106. Winston, the cemetery dog
impostor.

In 1971, a stray golden retriever attracted attention in the West Country town of Bradford-on-Avon, by stationing himself at a busy crossroads near the district hospital. Since the forlorn-looking dog was gazing wistfully at passing cars, people soon suspected that his master had been killed in a road traffic accident at the crossroads, and that the loyal canine was keeping vigil at the spot. An alternative hypothesis was that the dog had been abandoned by his callous owners, and that he was faithfully waiting for them to return. There was widespread sympathy for Winston, as the dog was called. A snug kennel was built for him at the crossroads, and another in the hospital grounds. Every day, he was given a hearty meal at the hospital canteen. The nurses pampered him, and the local children gave him bones and other treats.

After Winston had become a newspaper celebrity, and even appeared on television, the faithful dog received treats and gifts from sentimental dog-lovers all over the world. At Christmas, the crossroads were inundated with cards and gift-wrapped presents. As a leading local celebrity, Winston enjoyed police protection: the local constable stopped the traffic if the old dog decided to take a stroll along the High Street. In December 1977, plans to move the hospital to another site were put on hold, since the hospital's league of friends refused to go unless Winston and his kennels moved also. 'The hospital wouldn't be the same without him,' an old porter who looked after Winston told a *Daily Mirror* journalist.

Winston died of old age in October 1978, after having enjoyed more than seven years of complete independence and security; his funeral, at the Claverton Dog

Cemetery, was a grand affair. But in the local newspaper, quite a different story emerged. It turned out that Winston had once belonged to a Devon hunt, where he had been too gun-shy and unreliable to be of any use. Mr Alex Moulton, a Bradford-on-Avon inventor, offered to give Winston a home, but the dog did not appreciate his intervention, and ran away as soon as the trailer door was opened. Mr Moulton pursued him, but the determined dog swam the River Avon and disappeared. Winston later turned up at a farm nearby, where the eccentric dog was fed and allowed to sleep in a hay barn. Winston had higher aims in life, however, and ended up as Bradford-on-Avon's most popular dog. He is yet another example of a 'Dog on the Master's Grave' where the story of his alleged faithful mourning has been definitely disproved.[31]

In one of his darker and more macabre poems, Thomas Hardy turns the 'Dog on the Master's Grave' myth on its head. The spirit of a dead woman is wondering who is digging on her grave:

> 'Ah, are you digging on my grave
>   My loved one? – planting rue?'
> – No, yesterday he went to wed
> One of the brightest wealth has bred.
> 'It cannot hurt her now,' he said,
>   'That I should not be true.'

Nor is it her nearest dearest kin, since they do not think planting flowers would do the dead any good; nor her enemy 'prodding sly', since she thought the dead no longer worth her hate.

> 'Then, who is digging on my grave?
> Say -- since I have not guessed!'
> – 'O it is I, my mistress dear,
> Your little dog, who still lives near,
> And much I hope my movements here
> Have not disturbed your rest?'

> 'Ah yes! You dig upon my grave …
> Why flashed it not on me
> That one true heart was left behind!
> What feeling do we ever find
> To equal among human kind
> A dog's fidelity!'

But the crass canine turns out not to be a mourning cemetery dog, not by any means:

'Mistress, I dug upon your grave
To bury a bone, in case
I should be hungry near this spot
When passing on my daily trot.
I am sorry, but I quite forgot
It was your resting-place.'

'Greyfriars Bobby with a difference!' exclaimed a perceptive Hardy critic, but perhaps the poet came closer to the truth than has been presumed.[32]

As we have seen, the first incarnation of the cemetery dog is actually a suicidal dog, supposed to lose its will to live after its master's death, like Augeas the dog of Eupolis. But at least since the seventeenth century, the perception of the cemetery dog changed: these gloomy animals instead preferred to keep vigil on the tomb, waiting faithfully for the master to return, or so at least it was believed. Many of these dogs were well taken care of and lived for many years, becoming local celebrities in the process. People pointed them out as models of virtue, and travelled long distances to see and admire them. Showing no intention whatsoever to pine to death, many of these dogs appear to have led quite jolly, independent lives. Dogs are by nature territorial animals, and it would make nothing but sense for the cemetery dog to remain within the enclosed space where it had been so very kindly treated and well fed by its benefactors. If we are to believe M. Cheval and his colleagues, there were also some part-time cemetery dogs in France and Belgium. These dogs visited their master's graves to mourn each day, but otherwise led a normal existence. In addition, there was a variety of cemetery dog wannabes, supposed to be keeping vigil elsewhere after the loss of their masters: hospital dogs, jetty dogs, hotel dogs and railway station dogs.

I have found a total of forty-six cemetery dogs: fourteen hailing from the United Kingdom and Ireland, seventeen from France, eleven from the United States, and a couple from each of Sweden and Belgium. The cemetery dogs had their heyday between 1820 and 1880. The *Bulletin* of the Société Protectrice des Animaux featured not less than fourteen cemetery dog stories from 1858 until 1876, but not a single one from 1877 until 1903. This is indicative of a shift in the purpose of this valuable society: after initially being run by sentimentalists, who sighed over the yarns of dogs mourning their dead masters, it was usurped by people of a more realistic bent, who concentrated on fighting the real abuse of animals that was going on at the time, and left the idle newspaper stories of cemetery dogs alone.[33] Similarly, *Animal World* and other British animal protection magazines featured several cemetery dog stories, with pathetic illustrations, in the 1870s and 1880s; after that time, they forgot all but one of the cemetery dogs: their old favourite, Greyfriars Bobby.

15

The Truth

> He came as one who uninvited comes,
> Secure of welcome, to a kinsman's hearth;
> And rather as an inmate than a guest
> he went, unbidden. Whither? No one knew,
> Nor whence he came. An unsolved problem he,
> Like Gaspar Hauser, or the Iron Mask.
>
> E. R. Lytton Bulwer, *King Poppy*

As we have seen, cemetery dogs were far from uncommon in Victorian times, particularly in France and the British Isles. So why is Greyfriars Bobby today a world-famous cultural icon, whereas the others have been forgotten; why has Edinburgh's canine saint not been demoted to become just one of about thirty Victorian cemetery dogs? It is a contributing factor that Bobby kept a high profile in the media already during his lifetime, but this has not saved the even more widely publicised Médor, the Dog of the Louvre, from obscurity. Importantly, Greyfriars Bobby's career as a celebrity, and his beatification after death, coincided with a time when the awareness of animal rights was increasing. For the RSPCA and others, Bobby became a symbol of canine fidelity, and he helped the lot of countless other dogs through the legend that had been founded about his faithful mourning. Many a Victorian youngster must have had their view of the emotional lives of dogs permanently changed after hearing some unctuous RSPCA lecturer retell the pathetic story of Bobby's long vigil, shivering on the grave of his master in sleet and snow.

The role of Bobby's monument in perpetuating his memory cannot be underestimated. Because of the quaint Candlemaker Row drinking fountain, Bobby's story was remembered in Edinburgh and elsewhere, and told and retold in newspapers all over the world. This led to Eleanor Atkinson writing her novel about Edinburgh's famous dog, and the later exploitation of the story by Walt Disney and others, making Bobby a cultural icon. It may also be speculated that the influence of Greyfriars itself, as a historical monument to Scottish Protestant loyalty and forbearance, played a role, incorporating Bobby's story into pre-existing historical and religious traditions. It is notable that the two railway station dogs Old Shep and Hachikō also have their monuments to thank for their relative prominence in

Above left: 107. The monument to Boatswain at Newstead Abbey, from an old postcard.

Above right: 108. The Eling monument to a sagacious Newfoundland dog, from *Animal World*, April 1908.

popular culture; in contrast, the once-celebrated but statueless French cemetery dogs remain well-nigh forgotten.

Monuments to dogs existed in Britain long before Greyfriars Bobby's time.[1] The monumental tomb of Serpent, a favourite dog of Lady Stepney, had an epitaph dated 1750, and the Earl of Carlisle wrote a poem for the monument to a favourite spaniel. After the untimely death of his Newfoundland dog Boatswain in 1808, Lord Byron had a fine monument and vault constructed at Newstead Abbey, inscribed with Boatswain's epitaph; it still stands today. Since Newfoundland dogs were expensive and highly sought after in Byron's time, he was not the only person to immortalise his deceased favourite. In 1810, the Revd Thomas Phillips erected a monument to his Newfoundland dog 'Friend' in the vicarage gardens at Eling. Many wealthy owners of fine Newfoundlands and St Bernards commissioned paintings of their favourites. One of them was the dog-loving Earl of Dudley. After receiving Landseer's painting of his fine Newfoundland 'Bashaw', the Earl was not done yet, however. He commissioned the artist Matthew Cotes Wyatt to make a statue of Bashaw, and agreed to pay 5,000 guineas for it. But after Lord Dudley had died, his heirs did not appreciate the logic of spending such a prodigious sum on the statue of a dog. The disgruntled Wyatt had to keep the statue, and the marble Bashaw can today be met with at the Victoria & Albert Museum.[2]

109. The monument to Barry at the Cimetière des Chiens in Paris, a postcard from 1915.

There are fundamental differences between the monument to Boatswain and that to Greyfriars Bobby, however. The early monuments to Newfoundlands were just as much for the wealthy owners of these expensive and coveted dogs, as for the deceased animals themselves. In contrast, the humble little Bobby was honoured not because he was 'somebody's dog', but for his own perceived merits: he was the most faithful dog in the world, and a potent argument for the RSPCA and other animal protectionists to argue that dogs were sentient and emotional beings. Moreover, Bobby's monument was not erected in the private grounds of some nobleman, but in a public place, for everyone to see and admire. The Greyfriars Bobby monument has been claimed to be the first modern public statue to depict a dog on its own, and I have found no evidence to the contrary.[3]

The animal rights movement in Britain and France made sure that the Candlemaker Row dog monument would not be the last public statue to celebrate the memory of a faithful or heroic dog. In 1900, a monument to celebrate the life-saving St Bernard dog Barry (1800–1814) was erected at the famous Cimetière des Chiens at Asnières near Paris; it is still there to be admired today. A shaggy-haired Barry is seen carrying a child nearly his own size, with the epitaph: 'He saved forty people – He was killed by the forty-first!' Although Barry undoubtedly was a very clever and heroic mountain rescue dog, the traditions that he once saved a child by allowing it to ride on his back, and that later his life was ended when he was shot by a hunter mistaking him for a wolf, have both been proven to be devoid of factual foundation. Since Barry actually spent his declining years in comfortable retirement in Berne, where his body was stuffed after death and exhibited for many

110. The statue of the Brown Dog, from
Animal World, November 1906.

years, the Paris monument celebrates his heroic qualities rather than marking the
site of his remains.[4]

After the loss of a much-publicised 1903 lawsuit against University College
London, concerning the vivisection of a brown mongrel dog, the London anti-
vivisectionists were determined that the Brown Dog should not be forgotten. They
commissioned the sculptor Joseph Whitehead to make a bronze statue of the Dog,
which was mounted on a granite drinking fountain with troughs for both humans
and animals, just like the monument to Greyfriars Bobby. On top of the column,
the handsome, dignified-looking Brown Dog sat upright with his head held high,
looking almost defiantly at his human tormentors. Far from extolling the faithful
devotion of a dog, and implying that humans were worthy of such extraordinary
canine loyalty, the Brown Dog's message was a disturbing and controversial one at
the time, however: the vivisection of dogs was not just cruel, but morally corrupt.
When the Brown Dog drinking fountain was erected in Latchmere Park, Battersea,
in 1906, with a very inflammatory inscription condemning the Dog's tormentors,
there was outrage in London's medical world, and the medical students started
full-scale riots. Since the students tried to steal the statue more than once, it had to
be guarded by the police. After the cost of protecting the Brown Dog around the
clock had become prohibitive, the craven Battersea politicians ordered the Brown
Dog drinking fountain to be destroyed in 1910. London had lost its equivalent to
Greyfriars Bobby, because the defiant Brown Dog's controversial inscription was
unacceptable to the powerful medical establishment of the time.[5]

Modern research on dog behaviour would suggest that dogs are perfectly capable of grieving a dead or departed human or nonhuman animal with whom the dog has bonded. There are also several verified instances of dogs remaining with their dead masters for some considerable period of time, after the master has met with some lethal accident or disease when travelling in a desolate area. The most famous of them concerns the young artist Charles Gough, who perished high up on Helvellyn during a tour of the Lake District in 1805. When his body was found three months later, his little dog still remained nearby. There was widespread admiration for the faithful dog, and a monument was erected in its honour, although some sources claimed that the dog had been feeding from the body, nearly reducing it to a skeleton. Another, more recent monument, at the Derwent Dam in Derbyshire, celebrates the heroic sheepdog Tip, who had kept vigil by the body of her dead master for fifteen weeks.[6]

In contrast, it is not logical behaviour for a dog to linger round, or rest upon, its dead master's grave. Firstly, a dog has no clear concept of death, nor the ability to connect the once-living master with the lifeless flesh being buried in the coffin. Secondly, one of the primary instincts of a healthy dog is that of self-preservation; it would make no sense for the dog to pine to death lying on the master's grave, instead of getting on with life.[7]

As we have seen, the old legends of excessive canine fidelity had widespread sentimental appeal; in particular, the legend of the 'Dog on the Master's Grave' can be found all over the world, in many different versions. It seems to have been a very appealing thought to the Victorians that dogs were capable of such intense affection, with the smug extension that the humans themselves were the deserving recipients of such sterling loyalty. It would appear as if this sentimental reasoning was taken advantage of by some canine adventurers: stray dogs who took up residence in a suitable cemetery, where the dismal, half-starved animals were surprised to find themselves well looked after by kind, dog-loving people, who presumed they were keeping vigil on the graves of their masters. In Paris, the Dog of the Innocents and the Dog of the Louvre were seen and fed by many people, as were the cemetery dogs of London, Liverpool and Newcastle. It is telling that in a more critical age, the cemetery dogs were often exposed as unconscious impostors: they had nothing whatsoever to do with the person on whose grave they were supposed to be keeping vigil, and their perceived 'faithful mourning' had just been sentimental misinterpretation.

Greyfriars Bobby's story is the most prominent variant of this ancient and widespread myth of canine loyalty. But there is no reliable evidence that Bobby was ever mourning his dead master, or keeping vigil on his grave. The assertion on the fountain inscription that he 'lingered near the spot' is certainly false: Bobby roamed all over the district as it pleased him. Albeit conveniently ignored by the historians of Greyfriars Bobby, there is much to be said for the hypothesis that Bobby was an unconscious impostor, who made use of the 'Dog on the Master's Grave' legend to improve his lot in life.

111. The Dog of Helwellyn, from George R. Jesse's *Researches into the History of the British Dog*.

112. A French dog keeps vigil over a deceased traveller, from Emile Richebourg's *Histoire des Chiens Célèbres*.

113. Two dogs keep vigil over the corpse of their fallen master, from Emile Richebourg's *Histoire des Chiens Célèbres*.

114. The faithful greyhound of the officer Saint-Léger comes to visit him outside his prison tower, from A.-F.-J. de Fréville's *Histoire des Chiens Célèbres*.

A FAITHFUL DOG.

115. When the Welsh shepherd Daniel Thorp perished while trying to cross the Mardy Mountain in a snowstorm, his sheepdog kept vigil by his body. From the *Illustrated Police News*, 28 December 1895.

So, where did Greyfriars Bobby come from, and who was his master? My own suggestion would be that Bobby I, the stray terrier mongrel, came into Greyfriars in or around 1860. It is very likely that Peter Brown, the Heriot's gardener, lifted Bobby over the wicket gate to Greyfriars, after the little dog had annoyed him by trespassing into the hospital grounds from the Vennel. At Greyfriars, Bobby was so very well treated by James Brown and his other friends that he decided to stay on as a resident cemetery dog. This version of events was attested to by Peter Brown himself in 1889, by another person who had heard Brown explain Bobby's origins in exactly the same way, and by the quaint *Reminiscences of Heriot's Hospital*.[8]

Once upon the time, before becoming a stray, Greyfriars Bobby I is likely to have had a master, but the identity of this individual will never be known. The 1889 suggestion that Bobby must once have been a gentleman's dog, because he disliked people in shabby working attire, is contradicted by numerous other sources saying that Bobby had friends from all walks of life. Bobby might have come to Edinburgh with the cattle herders driving their herds to the market, becoming lost as they went along Lauriston Place; or he might have strayed from some humble abode in the Grassmarket or West Port area, trotting up the Vennel to George Heriot's Hospital to make a new and better life for himself.

Greyfriars Bobby I led a quiet existence in the kirkyard for a number of years, before the great newspaper hubbub about the Burgh Court business erupted in 1867. There is much to suggest that Bobby I died in or around May 1867, and that a clandestine substitution of dogs took place at that time. Greyfriars Bobby II, the

Skye terrier, whose origins are as obscure as those of his predecessor, held court at Greyfriars for many years. Younger and more vigorous than the gloomy-looking Bobby I, he was an independent dog who made a good life for himself in the Greyfriars burial grounds. Bobby II was affectionate to his various human friends, and grateful for being well fed and kept warm. It does not appear as though he considered that he needed a master, until during the last year of his life, when the old dog was adopted by the Traills and allowed to end his days in comfort. He was a clever little dog, a good ratter, and an enemy to be reckoned with for the cemetery cats; see here a better obituary for him.

The biographer of a dog really tells the story of the human attitudes to that particular dog, before and after the animal's death. The monument to Greyfriars Bobby, Edinburgh's Dog in the Iron Mask, was surreptitiously assaulted by various people 'in the know', who claimed that the story of his 'faithful mourning' was only a myth. Each time, Bobby was defended by his loyal friends, and in the end the scoffers were defeated; with time, two more monuments were erected to Edinburgh's dog saint. Eleanor Atkinson conjured up a history for Greyfriars Bobby, featuring the pathetic shepherd Auld Jock; it was perpetuated by Walt Disney, and still has followers today. In a 1981 manuscript, the erudite Forbes Macgregor marvelled at the obduracy of 'the phantom Auld Jock, whose 'habitation is in the air, being the best condition'd creature imaginable' (Pope). In a 1990 letter, Macgregor still deplored that 'the myth of Auld Jock, the Pentland shepherd, is still going strong in song and story, like Santa Claus'.[9] The monster Forbes Macgregor himself created, John Gray the dog-owning policeman, is likely to be equally difficult to exorcise. In this book, I have finally allowed Greyfriars Bobby to rise up from his pedestal, and free himself from the fetters of the sentimental Victorian notions about how a dog was supposed to behave. Thus Greyfriars Bobby, a dog enough for two, suitably has three different histories.

Not long after his death, Greyfriars Bobby usurped the mantle of Saint Guinefort, becoming a canine saint, revered for his devotion and fidelity. The books and films about him are still popular, and he has launched a thousand school projects from Inverness to Chittagong. His value for the Edinburgh tourist industry must be very considerable indeed. Like some bizarre four-legged anchorite, he still sits motionless on top of his monument, to receive homage from the wide-eyed tourists and their flashing cameras. We are all but mere mortals, dogs and humans alike, but the legend of Greyfriars Bobby, the most faithful dog in the world, will live forever.

Notes

1 Introduction

1. The various fictional accounts of Greyfriars Bobby are worthless for the serious historian, but the non-fiction books by Forbes Macgregor, *Authenticated Facts relating to Greyfriars Bobby* (Edinburgh 1981) and *Greyfriars Bobby: The Real Story at Last* (London 2002) are valuable sources, as are J. Mackay, *The Illustrated True Story of Greyfriars Bobby* (Glasgow 1986) and G. Robinson, *The Greyfriars Bobby A–Z* (Edinburgh 2008). See also the articles by S. Stevenson (*Book of the Old Edinburgh Club* NS 4 [1997], 85–8) and H. Kean (*Society & Animals* 11 [2003], 353–73 and K. Kete (Ed.), *Cultural History of Animals* 5 [2007], 25–46), and the useful *Bobby's Bothy* and *Greyfriars Bobby* magazines.

2. There have been features on the world's most faithful dog in many publications: by A. Bryant (*Illustrated London News* 229 [1956], 286–7), F. A. J. Couldery (*Singapore Free Press* 25 February 1956), A. Alpin Macgregor (*Country Life* 8 September 1960, 484–5), E. Wallace (*New York Sunday News* 19 May 1968, 6–7), M. Jägerbrand in a journal for the Swedish police (*Svensk Polis* 2002(9), 18–9) and E. Spanjer in a Dutch dog journal (*Hondenleven* 2009(1), 33–40). *Look and Learn* magazine featured Bobby in No. 277, 6 May 1967.

3. Research for this book has been performed at the National Library of Scotland, Edinburgh Central Library, the British Library, the Bibliothèque Nationale of Paris, and the Royal Library of Stockholm. Archival material has been consulted at the City of Edinburgh Archives, Edinburgh Room of the Central Library, and the City of Edinburgh Museum, Huntly House. Mr George Robinson, Secretary of the One o'Clock Gun & Time Ball Association, is thanked for sharing much important original material about Greyfriars Bobby, accumulated during more than a decade of research, and also for providing valuable advice throughout the process of researching and writing this book.

2 Greyfriars Bobby Finds Himself Famous

1. *Scotsman* 13 April 1867.

2. Namely in the following papers: *Caledonian Mercury*, *Dundee Courier & Argus* and *Daily News* of 15 April; *Standard* and *Sheffield & Rotherham Independent* of 16 April; *Hull Packet* of 19 April; *Penny Illustrated Paper*, *Illustrated Police News*, *Manchester Times* and *Leicester Chronicle* of 20 April; *Era* of 21 April; *Royal Cornwall Gazette* of 25 April; *Jackson's Oxford Journal* of 27 April 1867.

3. In Australia, the story of Greyfriars Bobby was reproduced by *Melbourne Argus* 4 July 1867, *Queenslander* 3 August 1867, and *Sydney Morning Herald* 9 September 1867; in New Zealand, by *North Otago Times* 23 December 1870 and *Otago Daily Times* 14 September 1872.

4. On Mr Traill's biography, see the articles by B. J. Beacock (*Greyfriars Bobby Magazine* December 2003 – February 2004, 5–6 and June–August 2006, 6–7) and P. Player (*Greyfriars Bobby Magazine* June–August 2006, 4–5); also *Edinburgh Evening News* 6 March 2006.

5. The Burgh Court records of 1867 have been destroyed, but they were quoted in *Edinburgh Evening Dispatch* 7 February 1889 and *Animal World* 20 [1889], 34–6.

6. W. Moir Bryce, *History of Old Greyfriars Church, Edinburgh* (Edinburgh 1912); A. Steele, *The Kirk of the Greyfriars* (Edinburgh 1993). The wall between the two churches was pulled down in 1929, when the two factions of the Church of Scotland reunited.

7. A. Turnbull, *William and Robert Chambers* (Edinburgh 1952); S. Scott, *William Chambers of Glenormiston* (Biggar 1997); *Greyfriars Bobby Magazine* September–November 2004, 16–17.

8. *Edinburgh Evening Dispatch* 8 February 1889; *Animal World* 20 [1889], 34–6.

9. W. Chambers, *Kindness to Animals* (London & Edinburgh 1877), 54–6.

10. On Caspar Hauser, Germany's Boy of Mystery, who appeared in Nuremberg in 1828 and was believed by some to be the kidnapped Crown Prince of Baden, see J. Bondeson, *The Great Pretenders* (New York 2004), 72–126.

11. *Inverness Advertiser* 10 May 1864.

12. *Ayrshire Express* of 1865, reprinted in a book entitled *Dogs* as 'Greyfriars Bobby. The First Report.' and copied by George Robinson.

13. On Sergeant Scott, see B. J. Beacock (*Greyfriars Bobby Magazine* December 2004 – February 2005, 4–5); *Edinburgh Evening News* 23 December 2003 and 12 June and 10 August 2006; also an article by J. Thomson entitled 'Colour Sergeant Scott and Greyfriars Bobby' from an unknown magazine, kept in the Greyfriars Bobby dossier at the City of Edinburgh Museum.

3 Greyfriars Bobby as an Edinburgh Celebrity

1. *Scotsman* 18 April 1867.

2. *Scotsman* 24 April 1867, 3.

3. *Scotsman* 16 August 1934, 11.

4. On Gourlay Steell, see the *Oxford DNB* and J. Halsby & P. Harris, *The Dictionary of Scottish Painters* (Edinburgh 1998).

5. *Scotsman* 18 April 1867.

6. *Caledonian Mercury* 18 April 1867; *Edinburgh Evening News* 14 February 1889.

7. *Scotsman* 18 April 1867.

8. See *Animal World* 1 [1869–70], 129 and 5 [1874], 37, and the City of Edinburgh Museum's Greyfriars Bobby collection (HH 2201 (g) 1962). The Catalogue of the City of Edinburgh Art Collection correctly describes it as a pencil on paper sketch, inscribed 'Gourlay Steel RSA 1867' and presented by Joan Leitch in 1962, but Macgregor, *Greyfriars Bobby*, wrongly describes it as an etching. There is also an obscure reference to a privately owned 'engraving' of a Gourlay Steell painting in *Edinburgh Evening News* 21 July 1961.

9. *Dundee Courier & Argus* 24 February 1868; *Aberdeen Journal* 11 March 1868.

10. *Animal World* 20 [1889], 34–6; Mr Dudgeon's obituary was in *Dumfries Courier* 13 February 1895.

11. *Dundee Courier & Argus* 29 April 1867. Little is known about Cormack Brown except that a portrait by him is kept at the Tweeddale Museum, Peebles.

12. On Robert Walker Macbeth, see the *Oxford DNB* and J. Halsby & P. Harris, *The Dictionary of Scottish Painters* (Edinburgh 1998). Macgregor, *Greyfriars Bobby*, mixes up the Macbeth etching with the Patterson cabinet card. According to Macgregor, *Authenticated Facts*, paragraph 42, the original Macbeth painting was owned by a lady in New Zealand in 1934, but although George Robinson has made inquiries in those parts, he has been unable to track it down.

13. *Greyfriars Bobby Magazine* September–November 2002, 6–7.

14. *Chatterbox* 22 June 1867; H. Weber, *Friedrich Wilhelm Keyl* (Heidelberg 1989), 86. The whereabouts of Keyl's original drawing remain elusive.

15. *Glasgow Herald* 22 February 1872; H. T. Hutton, *The True Story of Greyfriars Bobby* (Edinburgh 1931), 20–1.

16. S. Dunlop, *A Short Guide to the Greyfriars Churches and Churchyard* (Edinburgh 1927), 4.

17. Macgregor, *Authenticated Facts*, paragraph 42; Robinson, *Greyfriars Bobby A–Z*, 25.

18. B. R. W. Lockhart, *Jinglin' Geordie's Legacy* (East Linton 2003); Hutton, *The True Story of Greyfriars Bobby*, 14–5.

19. *Aberdeen Journal* 24 July 1867. In addition to Brown, two gravediggers were employed at Greyfriars.

20. *British Workman* 1 January 1868, 148; *Harper's Weekly* 1 April 1871.

21. S. Smiles, *Duty* (London 1880), 36.

22. *Aberdeen Journal* 15 May 1867. Neither George Robinson nor myself have been able to track down the original anti-Bobby article in the relevant issues of the Edinburgh *Daily Review*, however. Might there have been another short-lived anti-Bobby paper at the time?

4 Greyfriars Bobby's Fairy Godmother

1. Baroness Burdett-Coutts' biographers are E. Healey, *Lady Unknown* (London 1978) and D. Orton, *Made of Gold* (London 1980); also A. Sakula (*Medical History* 26 [1982], 83–90. For her alarming experiences with the stalker Dunn, see J. Bondeson, *Queen Victoria's Stalker* (Stroud 2010), 139–44.

2. Edinburgh City Archives, Town Council Record vol. 300, 30 November 1869, ff. 451–2.

3. *Dundee Courier & Argus* 17 November 1869; *Edinburgh Evening Courant* 17 November 1869; *Aberdeen Journal* 24 November 1869.

4. *Edinburgh Evening Courant* 1 December 1869.

5. *Animal World* 2 [1870–71], 177.

6. These poems are in *Animal World* 3 [1871–72], 39 and 7 [1876], 135, respectively.

7. *Animal World* 1 [1869–70], 36 and 129–30.

8. *Animal World* 18 [1887], 92–3. On collecting dogs and draught dogs, see J. Bondeson, *Amazing Dogs* (Stroud 2011), 104–28 and 158–61 respectively.

9. H. Kean, *Animal Rights* (London 1998), 54–8.

10. Namely in *Animal World* 5 [1874], 36–9. There is a file on the Greyfriars Bobby drinking fountain in the Edinburgh City Archives, Monuments Catalogue A–G.

11. Edinburgh City Archives, Town Council Record vol. 305, 31 October 1871, ff. 293–6.

12. *Scotsman* 1 November 1871, 2.

13. *Glasgow Herald* 1 November 1871; *Pall Mall Gazette* 4 November 1871; *Aberdeen Journal* 8 November 1871; *Graphic* 11 November 1871; *Star* 11 November 1871.

14. *Scotsman* 13 November 1871, 2.

15. *Animal World* 3 [1871–72], 49–50.

16. R. L. C. Lorimer, *Edinburgh, Scotland's Capital* (Edinburgh 1967), 82.

17. R. Brassey, *Greyfriars Bobby* (London 2000).

18. Email to George Robinson from Mrs L. Beech, Royal Archives, Windsor, dated 18 January 2011.

19. *Glasgow Herald* 23 November 1871; *Leeds Mercury* 25 November 1871; the same article was in the *Sheffield and Rotherham Independent* 28 November 1871.

20. *Animal World* 3 [1871–72], 68.

21. *Dundee Courier & Argus* 19 January 1872.

22. Reprinted in *North Otago Times* 14 September 1872, 3. Even the New Zealanders had a healthy interest in Greyfriars Bobby.

5 Greyfriars Bobby's Monument

1. *Scotsman* 2 August 1934.

2. *Weekly Scotsman* 26 December 1931, 2 January 1932.

3. *Scotsman* 31 July 1934.

4. *Scotsman* 5 March 1953.

5. *Scotsman* 11 August, and J. Wilson McLaren, *Edinburgh Memories and Some Worthies* (Edinburgh 1926), 121–2.

6. Both these photographs are held by the City of Edinburgh Museum's Greyfriars Bobby collection.

7. *Weekly Scotsman* 9 February 1932.

8. *Weekly Scotsman* 9 February 1889, 4. The Baroness Burdett-Coutts may well have paid for the consultation.

9. Macgregor, *Authenticated Facts*, paragraph 53; B. J. Beacock (*Greyfriars Bobby Magazine* December 2003 – February 2004, 5–6). Traill and his family lived at the tenement building at No. 14 Keir Street until May 1870, when they secured more salubrious housing at Greyfriars Place when Mr Currie's lease expired. The statement by John Traill Leitch (*Weekly Scotsman* 9 January 1932) that Greyfriars Bobby died in the Keir Street flat must be wrong, since the Traills had nothing to do with that flat in early 1872.

10. *Scotsman* 17 January 1872. It was quite widely reproduced in other papers, including *Morning Post* 18 January 1872.

11. *Scotsman* 13 August 1934, 11.

12. Quoted by W. G. Stables, *Aileen Aroon* (London 1884), 237–43.

13. *Lancet* i [1874], 78.

14. *Scotsman* 15 November 1873, 6.

15. *Animal World* 5 [1874], 36–9.

16. E. S. Turner, *All Heaven in a Rage* (London 1964), 141–60, 219–37; Kean, *Animal Rights*, 70–95.

17. *Bulletin de la Société Protectrice des Animaux* 19 [1874], 10, 13; *Musée Universel* 1873, 32.

18. *Scotsman* 10 April 1874, 7.

19. William Gordon Stables is in the *Oxford DNB*; see also S. Graham, *An Introduction to William Gordon Stables 1837–1910* (Twyford and Ruscombe Local History Society 2006).

20. Stables, *Aileen Aroon*, 237–43. The review of this book in *Liverpool Mercury* 24 December 1883 particularly admired the section about Greyfriars Bobby.

21. Healy, *Lady Unknown*, 179–80.

22. These letters are held by the City of Edinburgh Museum's Greyfriars Bobby collection.

23. Bondeson, *Queen Victoria's Stalker*.

24. C. Hibbert, *Queen Victoria: A Personal History* (London 2000), 347.

25. Healy, *Lady Unknown*, 197–205.

26. *Newcastle Courant* 18 February 1881.

6 Attack on Greyfriars Bobby

1. *Little Folks* issue 202 [1874], 404; *The Children's Treasury* 18 November 1876; *The Child's Companion* 1 June 1880.

2. *Sporting Times* 30 April 1881, 3.

3. *Kilmarnock Standard* 18 March 1944.

4. *Leeds Mercury* 5 December 1872; *Dundee Courier & Argus* 20 June 1874.

5. T. Wilson Reid, *Gabrielle Stuart; or, The Flower of Greenan* (Edinburgh 1882), vol. 1, 227–8, vol. 2, 5–11. On Reid's campaign against Greyfriars Bobby, see *Kilmarnock Standard* 18 March 1944 and *Edinburgh Evening News* 15 January 1971; also F. Macgregor in J. and M. Lindsay, *The Scottish Dog* (Aberdeen 1989), 102–5.

6. *Kilmarnock Standard* 18 March 1944.

7. J. Colquhoun, *The Moor and the Loch* (Edinburgh 1884), vol. 1, 352–3.

8. *Animal World* 16 [1885], 174.

9. *Animal World* 20 [1889], 34–6. See also the article by B. J. Beacock (*Greyfriars Bobby Magazine* September–November 2010, 3–5).

10. Edinburgh City Archives, Town Council Record, 5 February 1889, f. 111.

11. *Scotsman* 6 February 1889; *Pall Mall Gazette* 7 February 1889.

12. *Scotsman* 7 February 1889.

13. *Scotsman* 8 February 1889. This article was reproduced in part in the equally pro-Bobby *Pall Mall Gazette* 9 February 1889.

14. *Scotsman* 8 February 1889.

15. *Scotsman* 11 August 1934.

16. *Edinburgh Evening Dispatch* 7 February 1889.

17. *Weekly Scotsman* 9 February 1889, 4.

18. *Animal World* 20 [1889], 34–6.

19. *Edinburgh Evening News* 14 February 1889.

20. *Ayrshire Post* 8 February 1889.

21. *Scotsman* 12 February 1889.

22. J. Baillie, *Walter Crighton, or Reminiscences of George Heriot's Hospital* (Edinburgh 1898), 151–2, 157.

23. B. Douglas in *The Animal's Guardian* 1 [1890–91], 137–9.

7 Eleanor Atkinson's Novel about Greyfriars Bobby

1. *Animal World* 1 [1869–70], 129–30.

2. *New York Times* 25 February 1900, 27.

3. *Elmira Daily Gazette and Free Press* 16 March 1900 and *Brookfield Courier* 25 April 1900.

4. *Camperdown Chronicle* 12 March 1912 and *West Australian* 16 July 1913; *Otago Witness* 25 August 1883 and *Nelson Evening Mail* 13 April 1907.

5. H. Hutton, *Greyfriars Bobby* (Edinburgh 1902). On the Greyfriars Bobby postcards, see *Bobby's Bothy* 1(2) [2001], 13, *Canadian Museum of Animal Art Letter* No. 4, 1999, and some of the illustrations in this book.

6. *Scotsman* 31 December 1906 and 5 January 1907.

7. P. Preston (*T.P.'s Magazine* 2(8) [1911], 209–15); *Clyde Times* 5 October 1911, 5.

8. On Eleanor Atkinson's biography, see F. L. Lederer (*Journal of the Illinois State Historical Society* 68 [1975], 308–18); I. Visser (*Greyfriars Bobby Magazine* March–May 2007, 10–1); homepage www. eleanoratkinson.org. When George Robinson wrote to Susan M. Smith, Mayor of Rensselaer, with regard to erecting a memorial plaque to Eleanor Atkinson, the reply (letter, dated 1 May 1997) reveals that the Mayor was no close student of 'Greenfriars Bobby', as she referred to the famous book.

9. *New York Times* 10 March 1912.

10. *Boston Globe* 2 March 1912.

11. *New York Sun* 17 February and 5 April 1912.

12. *Lewiston Evening Journal* 20 July 1912.

13. *Brooklyn Daily Eagle* 9 August 1913.

14. B. J. Beacock (*Greyfriars Bobby Magazine* June–August 2006, 10–1).

15. I. Visser (*Bobby's Bothy* 2(3) [2002], 17 and *Greyfriars Bobby Magazine* March–May 2007, 10–1); *Edinburgh Evening News* 7 March 2006.

16. *New York Sun* 1 June 1912, 11.

17. *Brooklyn Daily Eagle* 1 May 1915.

18. *New York Times* 9 November 1924.

8 Rebecca West v. Greyfriars Bobby

1. *Scotsman* 16 May 1912.

2. *Scotsman* 24 April 1915, 8.

3. *Scotsman* 13 February and 4 December 1926, and 26 January 1927.

4. *Scotsman* 9 May 1930.

5. Mildred Adams in the *New York Times* 5 January 1930. Bobby was also featured in the *Melbourne Argus* 14 January 1928.

6. R. West (*Nash's Pall Mall Magazine* 88 (11) [1931], 25).

7. *Weekly Scotsman* 12 December 1931.

8. *Weekly Scotsman* 26 December 1931 and 16 January 1932.

9. *Weekly Scotsman* 2 January 1932.

10. *Weekly Scotsman* 9 January 1932.

11. *Weekly Scotsman* 16 January 1932.

12. *Scotsman* 11 August 1934, 13.

13. *Scotsman* 13 August 1934, 13.

14. *Scotsman* 25 March 1936.

9 Two Films about Greyfriars Bobby

1. T. Milne (*Monthly Film Bulletin* 46 [1979], 237); B. J. Beacock (*Greyfriars Bobby Magazine* June–August 2010, 19–20).

2. On Lassie and other acting dogs, see P. Haining, *Lassie* (London 2006) and Bondeson, *Amazing Dogs*, 69–86.

3. *New York Times* 7 January 1949.

4. Anon., *Challenge to Lassie* (London n.d.).

5. Robinson, *Greyfriars Bobby A–Z*, 7.

6. Anon., *Souvenir Brochure: World Premiere of Walt Disney's Greyfriars Bobby* (Edinburgh 1961).

7. There were features in *Scotsman* 28 June 28 1960, *Illustrated London News* 24 September 1960, 536–7, *Country Life* 8 September 1960, 484–485 and *Weekly Scotsman* 13 July 1961, 10–1. For some reviews, see *New York Times* 12 October 1961 and *Irish Times* 30 October 1961.

8. *Scotsman* 26 March 1955 and 29 May 1959; *Edinburgh Evening Dispatch* 11 June 1955; *Edinburgh Evening News* 31 December 1954, 11 and 16 June 1955.

9. *Scotsman* 27 July 1960.

10. *Edinburgh Evening Dispatch* 18 January 1963.

11. *Edinburgh Evening News* 10 and 27 May 1971.

12. *Guardian* 8 June 1972.

13. *Scotsman* 30 April 1979.

14. *Los Angeles Times* 24 August 1986.

10 Forbes Macgregor's Investigation

1. National Library of Scotland MSS Acc. 7354 (ii): F. Macgregor, 'How the true account of Greyfriars Bobby came to be written'.

2. National Library of Scotland MSS Acc. 10549/2: F. Macgregor, 'Minutes Book'.

3. *Scotsman* 11 and 16 August 1934.

4. Macgregor, *Authenticated Facts*, paragraphs 53 and 3, respectively. Forbes Macgregor is not the only person to have demonstrated that Eleanor Atkinson's novels are a mixture of fact and fiction. When Dr Robert Price, an expert on Johnny Appleseed, approached the elderly Eleanor Atkinson to query some of her sources for the novel, she merely replied, 'I made it up!' (*Pittsburgh Press* 6 November 1955).

5. In a long letter from Forbes Macgregor to Mr Cruikshanks, in the Greyfriars Bobby dossier at the City of Edinburgh Museum, Huntly House.

6. F. Macgregor (*Scots Magazine* 130 [1989], 357–63).

7. For more information about Gray the policeman, see Robinson, *Greyfriars Bobby A–Z*, 23, B. J. Beacock (*Greyfriars Bobby Magazine* September–November 2003, 6–8) and Anon. (*Greyfriars Bobby Magazine* March–May 2009, 2–4). A copy of Gray's death certificate, donated by Forbes Macgregor, is in the Greyfriars Bobby collection of the Edinburgh Room.

8. Macgregor, *Authenticated Facts*, paragraph 25.

9. *Kilmarnock Standard* 18 March 1944. See also B. J. Beacock, *Greyfriars Bobby Magazine* June–August 2003, 6–7.

10. *Kind Words* 15 August 1867.

11. Macgregor, *Authenticated Facts*, paragraph 21.

12. Macgregor, *Authenticated Facts*, paragraph 57. A copy of the original letter, donated by Forbes Macgregor, is in the Greyfriars Bobby collection of the Edinburgh Room.

13. Macgregor, *Authenticated Facts*, paragraph 56; letter from Forbes Macgregor to Mr Cruikshanks, in the Greyfriars Bobby dossier at the City of Edinburgh Museum, Huntly House.

14. Macgregor, *Authenticated Facts*, paragraph 48.

15. Forbes Macgregor's letter to John Thomson, dated 14 December 1990, in the Greyfriars Bobby dossier at the City of Edinburgh Museum, Huntly House.

16. *Sunday Herald* 26 March 2000; *Daily Mail* 24 May 1999 and *Edinburgh Evening News* 2 March 2000. Gilhooley never actually published anything about Greyfriars Bobby, and present-day Edinburgh local historians tend to have a low opinion of his researches.

17. Forbes Macgregor's letters to John Thomson, dated 14 December 1990, 22 December 1990 and 1 March 1991, are in the Greyfriars Bobby dossier at the City of Edinburgh Museum, Huntly House.

18. Letter to George Robinson from Mr Tom Barclay, Librarian at South Ayrshire Council, dated 22 May 2006.

11 Greyfriars Bobby as a Cultural Icon

1. In contrast, the Abebooks database has 793 copies of Atkinson, 76 copies of Brassey and 44 copies of Brown advertised for sale.

2. *Animal World* 1 [1869–70], 129–30 and 5 [1874], 36–9.

3. Alex Bruce, *Rhymes and Notions* (Edinburgh n.d.); W. A. Cribbes, *Greyfriars Bobby* (Edinburgh 1950); B. Boyd & M. Elder (Eds), *A Hantle o Verse* (Edinburgh 2003), 61–2.

4. *Edinburgh Evening News* 29 November 2003.

5. *Bobby's Bothy* 2(1) [2002], 2–3 and *Greyfriars Bobby Magazine* September–November 2008, 4–5. According to Macgregor, *Authenticated Facts*, paragraph 42, another plaster cast of the Greyfriars Bobby statue was owned by a lady in Portobello.

6. *Edinburgh Evening News* 20 July 1956.

7. Macgregor, *Greyfriars Bobby*, 59.

8. On Bum, see *Greyfriars Bobby Magazine* March–May 2008, 2–6; also *Edinburgh Evening News* 23 November 2007 and 8 April and 19 July 2008, and *San Diego Union-Tribune* 31 July 1997.

9. On travelling dogs, see Bondeson, *Amazing Dogs*, 87–103. The chapters on Greyfriars Bobby and Owney in R. Gordon, *It Takes a Dog to Raise a Village* (Minocqua, Wisconsin 2000), contain nothing new or interesting, but this book introduces some other eccentric 'community dogs' adopted by small American towns.

10. On this film, see Mackay, *Illustrated True Story*, 44–7; B. J. Beacock (*Greyfriars Bobby Magazine* March–May 2006, 6–8); M. Hubbard (*Media Education Journal* 41 [2007], 34–7). The quote is from *Daily Express* 28 November 2002.

11. Coconut Tam really existed: he was an Edinburgh street trader who made his living selling coconuts from a barrow, see Robinson, *Greyfriars Bobby A–Z*, 13. In real life, he had nothing to do with Greyfriars Bobby, however.

12. *Edinburgh Evening News* 6 November 2002; *Scotsman* 13 October and 8 November 2002; *Daily Telegraph* 7 November 2002.

13. *Daily Telegraph* 7 November 2002. Other authorities on small terriers may well disagree with this adventurous conclusion.

14. *Sun* 14 November 2002.

15. *Glasgow Daily Record* 10 February 2006; *Guardian* 10 February 2006; *Irish Times* 10 February 2006; *Daily Express* 21 May 2005; in addition, there were some lukewarm reviews in the *Independent* 4 February 2006, *Birmingham Evening Mail* 10 February 2006 and *Birmingham Sunday Mercury* 12 February 2006.

16. *Sunday Times* 23 May 1999; *Daily Mail* 24 May 1999.

17. *Sun* 1 April 2000.

18. *Edinburgh Evening News* 26 August 2003; *Daily Mirror* 22 June 2005; *Daily Star* 13 February 2007; *Daily Mirror* 27 March 2009 and *Edinburgh Evening News* 25 September 2009, 29 October 2009 and 12 June 2010.

19. *Edinburgh Evening News* 29 April and 3 May 2008; *Edinburgh Evening News* 12 January 2009 and *Sun* 15 January 2009; *Scotsman* 9 January 2010; *News of the World* 6 February 2011.

12 What Do We Really Know about Greyfriars Bobby?

1. *Weekly Scotsman* 9 January 1932.

2. Reid, *Gabrielle Stuart*, vol. 2, 6.

3. *Inverness Advertiser* 10 May 1864; Chambers, *Kindness to Animals*, 54–6.

4. *Scotsman* 13 April 1867.

5. *Scotsman* 11 August 1934.

6. Edinburgh City Archives, Town Council Record vol. 300, 30 November 1869, ff. 451–2.

7. Stables, *Aileen Aroon*, 237–43; *Animal World* 16 [1885], 174.

8. Letters to George Robinson from Julie Hutton, Lothian Health Services Archivist, University of Edinburgh, 2 April 1997, and from Anne M. Grannum, Crematorium Superintendent, City of Edinburgh Council, 18 March 1997.

9. On this photograph, see also the article by S. Stevenson (*Book of the Old Edinburgh Club* NS 4 [1997], 85–8).

10. M. P. Lee, *Skye Terriers* (Dorking 2002), 121.

11. *Weekly Scotsman* 9 February 1889, 4; Stables, *Aileen Aroon*, 237–43.

12. Reid, *Gabrielle Stuart*, vol. 1, 228 and vol. 2, 9.

13. Dunlop, *Short Guide*, 4.

14. These include William Chambers, Wilson McLaren, the *Animal World* journalist, Robert Scott Riddell the Greyfriars organist, William Brodie and the 1889 *Scotsman* witnesses.

15. Doug Mann, writing to the *Scotsman*, 12 and 23 July 1997.

16. *Edinburgh Evening News* 14 February 1889.

17. In the *Scotsman* 16 August 1934, 11, the portrait is stated to have been painted in 1868, but no source is provided for this statement.

18. Macgregor, *Authenticated Facts*, paragraph 13.

13 Legends of Canine Fidelity

1. On old dog lore in general, see A.-F.-J. de Fréville, *Histoire des Chiens Célèbres* (Paris 1796) and E. Richebourg, *Histoire des Chiens Célèbres* (Paris 1867); also P.-A. Bernheim, *La vie des Chiens Célèbres* (Paris 1998), 211–28 and the article by W. F. Bucke (*Pedagogical Seminary* 10 [1903], 459–513).

2. J. S. Watson, *The Reasoning Power in Animals* (London 1867), 150–4.

3. J. Viscardi, *Le Chien de Montargis* (Paris 1932); G. Leloup (*Bulletin de la Société d'Emulation de Montargis* No. 44, 1978).

4. On this dog drama, see Bondeson, *Amazing Dogs*, 74–5.

5. On the Gelert legend, see S. Baring-Gould, *Curious Myths of the Middle Ages*, 1st series (London 1877); D. E. Jenkins, *Bedd Gelert* (Bedd Gelert 1899), 56–74; J.-C. Schmitt, *The Holy Greyhound* (Cambridge 1983); S. Blackburn (*Bulletin of the School of Oriental and African Studies* 59 [1996], 494–507). A complete list of sources is provided by Bondeson, *Amazing Dogs*, 119–29.

6. J. Robert, *Le Chien d'Appartement et d'Utilité* (Paris 1888), 122–3.

7. *Illustrated London News* 1 February 1845, 10.

8. *Animal World* 2 [1870–71], 29, 3 [1871–72], 91 and 6 [1875], 2.

9. *Bulletin de la Société Protectrice des Animaux* 21 [1876], 53–4 and 127–8. On the history of this association, see G. Fleury, *La Belle Histoire de la S.P.A. de 1845 à nos Jours* (Paris 1995).

10. W. L. Lindsay (*Journal of Mental Science* 17 [1871], 25–82 and *Mind in the Lower Animals* (London 1879), vol. 2, 130–48).

11. H. Maudsley (*Mind* 4 [1879], 410–3).

12. There have been occasional yarns about suicidal dogs in the 'from our foreign correspondent' columns of modern tabloid newspapers: see *Daily Mirror* 18 February 1930, 3, and 19 October 1989, 3. See also *Fortean Times* 198 [2005], 4.

13. E. Ramsden & D. Wilson (*Endeavour* 34 [2010], 21–4).

14. I. C. Storey, *Eupolis* (Oxford 2003), 56–7, 378–81.

15. S. Bochart, *Hierozoicon* (Leipzig 1793), vol. 1, 785; *Times* 27 September 1817 3a; *Leisure Hour* 12 February 1870, 107.

16. F. C. Woodward, *Stories about Animals* (Boston 1851), 5.

14 Cemetery Dogs

1. On Lydia Sigourney, see N. Baym (*American Literature* 62 [1990], 385–404.

2. A.-F.-J. de Fréville, *Histoire des Chiens Célèbres* (Paris 1796), vol. 2, 53–7.

3. C. Juranville, *Voyage au Pays de Caniches* (Paris n.d.), 160–2. 'The Dog of the Tombs' is briefly discussed in the anonymous *Canine Biography* (Bath 1804), vol. 2, 27.

4. Juranville, *Voyage au Pays de Caniches*, 162–3.

5. H. Coupin, *Les Animaux Excentriques*, 4th edn (Paris n.d.), 384–5.

6. F. O. Morris, *Dogs and their Doings* (London 1870), 98–100; G. Jungmarker (*Samfundet Sankt Eriks Årsbok* 1983, 165–76).

7. E. Simpson (*Art Journal* 1888: 33–6). A similar yarn, ending with the death of both the master (guillotined) and his faithful spaniel (from a broken heart) is recorded by C. Williams, *Dogs and their Ways* (London 1893), 74–5; see also K. McDonogh (*History Today* 46 (8) [1996], 36–42).

8. Casimir Delavigne's poem is translated in *Fraser's Magazine* 10 [1834], 677–8.

9. Anon., *Tombeaux du Louvre. Histoire Véritable de Médor, ou le Chien Fidèle* (Paris 1830) v. Anon., *Médor, ou Le Chien du Louvre* (Paris 1830) and Anon., *Les Tombeaux des Innocens et du Louvre, et l'Histoire du Chien Fidèle* (Paris 1831).

10. L. Börne, *Lettres écrites de Paris* (Paris 1830), 142–7.

11. R. Lestrange, *Les Animaux dans la Littérature* (Paris 1937), 126–7; R. Trouilleux, *Histoires Insolites des Animaux de Paris* (Paris 2003), 108.

12. As observed by K. Kete, *The Beast in the Boudoir* (Berkeley CA 1994), 22–35.

13. These five articles are in the *Bulletin de la Société Protectrice des Animaux* 5 [1858], 433–4, 8 [1862], 329–30; 19 [1874], 396–7, 20 [1875], 13–4, 435–6. Another example of the tendency of the nineteenth-century French press to invent spicy stories on certain pet subjects is provided by J. Bondeson, *Buried Alive* (New York 2001), 172–6.

14. Reprinted from the *Petit Journal* in the *Animals Guardian* 3 [1892–93], 133.

15. Contemporary sources on Fidèle are *Nyaste Freja* 30 March 1841 and *Magasin för Konst, Nyheter och Moder* 18 [1841], 40–3.

16. O. Sandholm, *För vem är Du Hund?* (Stockholm 1970), 62.

17. G. Jungmarker (*Samfundet Sankt Eriks Årsbok* 1983, 165–76); see also H. Öjmyr (*Blick – Stockholm då och nu* 3 [2006–2007], 24–7).

18. J. Taylor, *The General Character of the Dog* (London 1804), 132–4. What may well be a garbled version of this cemetery dog tale is in Benedict-Henry Revoil's *Histoire Physiologique et Anecdotique des Chiens de Toutes de Races* (Paris 1867), 295.

19. *Cottager's Monthly Visitor* 10 [1830], 79–83.

20. *The Children's Friend* 1 May 1824.

21. *Caledonian Mercury* 7 April 1834.

22. E. Jesse, *Gleanings in Natural History*, 3rd series (London 1835), 34; *John Bull* 31 December 1837; *Trewman's Exeter Flying Post* 10 July 1856; C. St John, *A Tour in Sutherlandshire*, vol. 2 (Edinburgh 1884), 208–9; Morris, *Dogs and their Doings*, 106–8; F. Power Cobbe, *The Friend of Man* (London 1889), 89–110; *Animal's Guardian* 3 [1892–93], 203.

23. Rollo is featured on the Freerepublic online discussion forum.

24. The story of Old Shep is given on the Roadsideamerica website, and in the *Fort Benton River Press* 6 July 2005.

25. J. Michell and R. J. M. Rickard, *Living Wonders* (London 1982), 127–8; *Washington Post* 3 June 1994, A28.

26. M. Burton, *Just like an Animal* (London 1978), 78.

27. *Daily Mirror* 11 December 1908, 4, and 14 December 1908, 4.

28. From the Swedish internet forum Flashback.

29. *Buffalo Evening News* 13 February 1930; *Milwaukee Sentinel* 14 June 1931.

30. *Toledo Blade* 11 November 1909; *New York Times* 18 August 1918; *Milwaukee Journal* 7 April 1922; *Pueblo Indicator* 19 March 1932; *Palm Beach Post* 11 July 1954; *Hartford Courant* 26 May 1954.

31. *Daily Mirror* 15 December 1977, 7; *Bath and West Evening Chronicle* 18 and 23 October 1978; Burton, *Just like an Animal*, 78–87; Michell & Rickard, *Living Wonders*, 127–30.

32. T. Johnson (*Victorian Poetry* 17 [1979], 9–29).

33. Some 'funny' French newspapers still published the occasional cemetery dog story, and a few British and American evening newspapers featured 'faithful mourners' well into the 1950s, but no person of intelligence believed them.

15 THE TRUTH

1. On epitaphs and monuments to dogs, see *Chambers's Journal* 3 May 1884, 285–7; N. B. Penny (*Connoisseur* 192 [1976], 298–303); C. Kenyon-Jones, *Kindred Brutes* (Aldershot 2001), 23–50; T. Mangum in D. Denenholz Morse and M. A. Danahay (Eds), *Victorian Animal Dreams* (Aldershot 2007), 15–34; and I. H. Tague (*Eighteenth-Century Studies* 41 [2008], 289–306).

2. On these monuments to Newfoundland dogs, see Bondeson, *Amazing Dogs*, 166–75, and its references.

3. The leading present-day expert on dog monuments and statuary is Dr Hilda Kean, who has published extensively on this subject: *Society & Animals* 11 [2003], 353–73, *Journal of the History of Culture in Australia* 24 [2006], 135–62, K. Kete (Ed.), *Cultural History of Animals* 5 [2007], 25–46, *International Journal of Heritage Studies* 15 [2009], 413–30, and *London Journal* 36 (2011), 54-71.

4. M. Nussbaumer, *Barry vom Grossen St. Bernhard* (Bern 2000), 47–56; Bondeson, *Amazing Dogs*, 191–5.

5. On the Brown Dog riots, see P. Mason, *The Brown Dog Affair* (London 1997); Kean, *Animal Rights*, 136–55; Bondeson, *Amazing Dogs*, 228–47, and its references. A replacement monument was erected much later, but nobody bothered much about it.

6. F. Haley (*North West Monthly* 1(10) [1950], 7–11); J. Michell and R. J. M. Rickard, *Living Wonders* (London 1982), 127; R. Woof (Ed.), *The Unfortunate Tourist of Helvellyn* (Wordsworth Trust 2003); *Guardian* 15 March 2003.

7. E. Ramsden & D. Wilson (*Endeavour* 34 [2010], 21–4).

8. *Edinburgh Evening News* 14 February 1889; J. Baillie, *Walter Crighton, or Reminiscences of George Heriot's Hospital* (Edinburgh 1898), 151–2, 157.

9. National Library of Scotland MSS Acc. 7354 (ii): F. Macgregor, 'How the true account of Greyfriars Bobby came to be written'; Forbes Macgregor's letter to John Thomson, dated 14 December 1990, in the Greyfriars Bobby dossier at the City of Edinburgh Museum, Huntly House.

Index